SpringerBriefs in Religious Studies

For further volumes:
http://www.springer.com/series/13200

Trudy D. Conway

Cross-cultural Dialogue on the Virtues

The Contribution of Fethullah Gülen

 Springer

Trudy D. Conway
Department of Philosophy
Mount Saint Mary's University
Emmitsburg, MD
USA

ISBN 978-3-319-07832-8   ISBN 978-3-319-07833-5   (eBook)
DOI 10.1007/978-3-319-07833-5
Springer Cham Heidelberg New York Dordrecht London

Library of Congress Control Number: 2014942049

Printed on acid-free paper

Springer is part of Springer Science+Business Media (www.springer.com)

To my children, Sedira and
Daniel Kouchek, from whom
I have learned so much about the virtues
and who bring endless joy into my life

Preface

I welcomed the encouragement by the Rumi Forum of Washington, D.C. to write this book on the virtues in relation to the Gülen movement for its reflection is tied closely to my personal journey over the past 35 years. In marrying a devout Muslim from Iran, I began a journey of understanding and dialogue with people of the Islamic faith and culture. The journey has enriched my life in countless ways and has brought me to value the virtue of hospitality deeply and a range of related virtues central to such understanding and dialogue. I am grateful for the rich opportunities I have had to interact with people of the Islamic faith from Iran, Afghanistan, Pakistan, Egypt, the Arab Emirates, Azerbaijan, and Turkey. They have taught me much about our common humanity and the rich diversity of cultural and religious traditions. Numerous books approach the Gülen movement through a political or sociological lens with the critical aim of identifying both strengths and weaknesses of this movement. The critical analyses of these studies are undeniably important. In contrast, this work pursues another type of inquiry. It seeks to explore the movement through a different lens by offering a descriptive account of the fundamental virtue orientation of this influential, peaceful, Islam-inspired international movement. It argues that this virtue orientation enables one to understand best both the origin and the telos of this movement. All subsequent critical analyses, focused on assessing the movement's principles, practices, projects, and institutions, must begin with understanding this foundation and orientation.

My initial interest in the virtue of hospitality developed in response to the very positive experiences I had of Middle Eastern hospitality while living in Iran from 1977 to 1979, after accepting an appointment to teach Philosophy at Pahlavi University (currently Shiraz University). During this turbulent period of the Iranian Revolution, I was welcomed graciously by family members, students and colleagues of Shiraz University, neighbors in our Shiraz community, and Iranians I met in travels throughout Iran. I was fortunate enough to have additional positive experiences in the Arab Emirates, where I interacted with students from a range of Middle Eastern societies studying at the American University of Sharjah. Given these experiences, I welcomed the opportunity to attend philosophical conferences in Turkey and to participate in a Council on International Education Exchange seminar in Turkey focusing on religion and politics. Interactions with all these peoples of the Islamic faith were characterized by the hospitality I came to associate with Islamic culture. But the experience that engaged my strong personal and philosophical interest in exploring this virtue was my participation in the 2007 intercultural dialogue trip through Turkey sponsored by the Rumi Forum of Washington, D.C. This trip introduced me to members of the Gülen movement and the movement's key emphasis on the virtue of tolerance. The Turkish term *hoşgörü* is commonly translated into English as "tolerance," but as this study will argue, the term has a far deeper spiritual meaning closer to the meaning of the virtue of hospitality. While tolerance means to refrain from harming, to put up with in a way characterized by forbearance, *hoşgörü* fosters welcoming interactions among diverse people. Gatherings of members of the Gülen movement in their universities, schools, hospitals, media centers, homes, and dialogue centers clearly manifested this virtue which I had come to value as most characteristic of these people. These gracious and welcoming encounters sparked my interest in reading the works of Fethullah Gülen and the seminal works that inspired him. I hoped to discover both the role the virtue of hospitality played in shaping this movement, and what people of all cultures, but most importantly contemporary Western culture, might learn from reflection on this important virtue and its related virtues and practices.

During these years of interaction with people of the Islamic faith abroad and in the United States, another story came to influence my reflections. Upon my return from Iran, William Collinge, a colleague in my university's Theology department, introduced me to the story of the people of Le Chambon-sur-Lignon, France—a community who lived the virtue of hospitality in ways that evoke deep admiration within students of ethics.[1] My reflections on and interest in hospitality were deepened by the story of the lives of these rural peasants in southern France during World War II. Moved by accounts of these French Huguenots who welcomed Jewish refugees into their homes at grave personal risk during the Holocaust, I brought to campus members of this community, both Chambonnais who did the welcoming and refugees who survived because of such welcoming. I remain convinced that the efficacious moral goodness of these people embodied the kind of human community Fethullah Gülen sought to encourage and model. Their story supports his conviction that there are universal moral virtues found within different religious and cultural communities. The Le Chambon story confirms that if persons could be encouraged to practice the virtue of hospitality in their everyday lives, then such a virtuous response would come naturally even in times requiring great moral courage.

The Chambonnais respected the refugees who came to their doorsteps as human persons who shared a common humanity while at the same time had robust cultural and religious identities. They revealed what the philosopher Elaine Scarry calls "generous imaginings" which enabled them to place themselves in the life experiences of foreigners different from themselves. They welcomed foreigners

---

[1] There are a number of accounts of the community of Le Chambon, but the most extensive philosophical study is Philip Hallie's *Lest Innocent Blood Be Shed* (New York: Harper Perennial, 1994). Pierre Sauvage's *Weapons of the Spirit* (1989) offers a cinematic account of his being a refugee saved by the Chambonnais.

into their midst and did so without requiring that either of them abandon their own deep moral and religious commitments. Rather than simply tolerating their guests' differences, they respectfully affirmed them, encouraging and helping the refugees to live as practicing Jews. They actively sought out opportunities for interactions that advanced their mutual understanding of their respective beliefs and practices. Similar to the convictions of Fethullah Gülen, they believed the people of the Abrahamic tradition are called by God to welcome and respect all human persons as persons. The Jewish philosopher Levinas captures well the spirit of hospitality embodied in the Le Chambon community when he writes,

> That a people should accept those who come and settle among them—even though they are foreigners with their own customs and clothes, their own way of speaking, their own smell—that a people should give them an *Akhsaniah*, such a place at the inn, and the wherewithal to breathe and live—is a song to the glory of God ... (98)

The Chambonnais could offer hospitality to refugees in such dangerous times because the practicing of the virtues was at the very core of their communal identity. The texts they read, the hymns they sang, the sermons they heard, the actions they witnessed, the lessons they passed on to their children—all focused on the living of the virtues. In a similar way, the virtues one immediately notices in encounters with members of the Gülen movement are rooted in the ways lived by the Prophet Mohammad and members of the first Islamic community, ritualized in prayers and practices, and explored in the writings of Fethullah Gülen. As with the Chambonnais, central among the virtues of the Gülen community is the virtue of hospitality. Their hospitable welcoming enables others to learn of the insights of their founder and thriving worldwide community. In turn, reflection on what is encountered in these texts and interactions enables others to extend and deepen their own exploration of the virtues and the role they play in a well-lived life.

I have appreciated the opportunity to engage in this exploration. It has extended philosophical reflections developed in my book *Wittgenstein on Foundations* and articles exploring the writings of contemporary Western philosophers as they bear on the conditions and possibilities for cross-cultural dialogue and the virtues central to it. It has also extended the discussion of the virtues developed in my recently published work *Where Justice and Mercy Meet*. My interactions with members of the Gülen movement enabled me to move from abstract philosophical conceptualizations and theorizing on these issues to reflections on the lives of people living them.

The completion of a work always evokes feelings of relief followed by a sense of gratitude for those who played a role in its creation. My work has always centered on the activity of teaching and learning from students. I appreciate the conversations I have had with students in courses exploring the virtues in general and hospitality in particular, especially in my courses on Moral Philosophy, Intercultural Dialogue, Virtues and Vices, Tolerance/Intolerance, Forgiveness and Mercy, and Compassion: East and West. I also appreciate my good fortune in teaching at a university with a strong Core curriculum that provides ample opportunity to explore the virtues with colleagues in faculty development programs and informal interdisciplinary conversations. These conversations with students and colleagues led to scholarly presentations and publications strengthened by discussions with philosophers at conferences and with my brother, Jeremiah Conway, with whom I share common philosophical interests and have enjoyed philosophical conversation for decades. I am grateful to Andy Fiala, the journal editor of the Society for Philosophy in the Contemporary World for granting permission to draw on segments of my works published in their journal.

Philosophical readings and exchanges have deepened my reflection on the virtues. But in the end, most of what I have learned about the virtues in general and hospitality in particular has been through witnessing the practicing of the virtues by others. In early childhood, I was impressed by my parents' interest in and respect for people of other faiths and cultures, attitudes I failed to see in many others in our local community. In our local Catholic school, my mother was the only teacher in the 1950s to bring students to visit the local synagogue and other houses of worship and to invite persons of other religious faiths and cultural backgrounds to speak in her classes. As my parents aged and the religious-ethnic makeup of our New York City neighborhood dramatically changed, I was impressed to see them begin Spanish language studies at a nearby university and volunteer to tutor Chinese immigrant children in our home. Their interest in other religions and cultures likely brought me to be open to my good fortune in meeting my husband, Abdolreza Banan, who first introduced me to the Islamic faith and culture. Our own journeying between cultures and traditions has deeply enriched our lives and marriage and helped us raise two wonderful children, Sedira and Daniel, who move with ease amidst diversities of race, religion, class, and culture. We are grateful for our very good fortune in meeting members of the Rumi Forum of Washington who introduced us to the beliefs and activities of the Gülen movement. We are especially grateful for the very gracious hospitality of Dr. Ali Yurtsever, former Director of the Rumi Forum of Washington, and Ms. Jena Luedtke, Director of Interfaith and Intercultural Dialogue, during and after our intercultural dialogue trip to Turkey, and Emre Celik, current Director, in subsequent years. Through them we have had opportunities for ongoing encounters with worldwide members of this movement at symposia, Iftar and friendship dinners, lectures, and conferences. For all of these gatherings which so embody the hospitable spirit of the poet Rumi, we are most grateful. Over time, members of the Gülen movement have begun to characterize their international movement as the "Hizmet movement." This characterization avoids misrepresentation of the movement as a cult focused on a religious leader. Hizmet translated as "service to humanity" captures well the fundamental ethos of the movement, which originated under the inspiration of Fethullah Gülen but went on to develop rich and highly varied ways of developing and embodying this service-to-others ethic throughout the world. Given the aptness of this more recent description focused on a religiously inspired ethic of peace and dialogue, it is fitting to use it throughout this work.

The hospitality and support of the Rumi Forum of Washington made possible this study. Raising children in a bicultural family brings one to recognize the importance of actively promoting understanding and dialogue across cultures and religions. Raising our children during three decades of heightened tensions between our countries (Iran and the United States) made us deeply value the good work of the Hizmet movement. The size and impact of this movement has grown at an amazing rate over the last three decades. Scholarly accounts face the challenge of keeping abreast of the numbers of schools, charitable organizations, and dialogue centers associated with this expansive movement. It is evident that Fethullah Gülen has developed an efficacious spiritual movement that speaks to the needs of our age, rooted in the conviction that peaceful relations among persons and communities must be rooted in commitment to mutual understanding and dialogue. Gülen's writings and, even more importantly, the living witness of those he has inspired bring us to see how central the practicing of virtues is to the furthering of such understanding and dialogue. It is my hope that this book may introduce readers to the Hizmet movement's understanding and practicing of the virtues and thereby deepen their own cross-cultural exploration of the virtues. I am convinced understanding of this Gülen-inspired movement is best understood through the lens of the virtues they foster and live. I remain convinced that we have much to learn from these steadfast supporters of peaceful relations and dialogue. Through them we can begin to understand better what is most needed within our families, local communities, and global interactions.

Trudy D. Conway

Contents

Biography

Trudy D. Conway received her Ph.D. in Philosophy from Fordham University in 1981. After teaching at Shiraz University (formerly Pahlavi University) in Iran, she began teaching at Mount Saint Mary's University in Maryland where she is currently a Professor of Philosophy. In addition to two other books, Wittgenstein on Foundations (1989) and Where Justice and Mercy Meet (2013), she has published a range of scholarly articles on contemporary philosophy, the virtues, and crosscultural understanding and dialogue. She has served as president of the Society for Philosophy in the Contemporary World and Delta Epsilon Sigma, held two endowed professorships, one sponsored by the National Endowment for the Humanities, and received numerous teaching, social justice, and service awards. She is active in a number of organizations promoting crosscultural understanding and social justice initiatives. She teaches undergraduate courses in the history of philosophy, contemporary philosophy, ethics, and specialized courses on the virtues.

Chapter 1
Introductory Overview of the Hizmet Movement

The twentieth century ended with the emergence of a world of ever increasing global interaction and awareness. The technological advances of that century produced a world defined by global outreach that rendered possible cross-cultural encounters which had the potential to enhance mutual understanding and enrichment. Ironically, while offering such promise, the twentieth century was at the same time marred by international and internecine strife and conflict. Seared into memory was the striking image of the new millennium event of September 11, 2001, interpreted by some as both a symbol and harbinger of a clash of civilizations. Central to this image was the perception of an unavoidable conflict between the contemporary Islamic and Western worlds. Popular media solidified and fueled such an oppositional dynamic, increasingly taken as an assumption and starting point of inquiry and analysis. Regrettably such oppositional conceptualization diminished possibilities, even hope, for interactions resulting in mutual understanding and enrichment. Ironically, technological advances, rendering possible communication and face-to-face encounters, at the same time articulated and repeatedly reinforced negative preconceptions and assumptions undermining such possibilities.

All too often, current media coverage of the Islamic world is rooted in limited understanding and even grave misunderstanding and distortion. Framed by the presumption of a clash of civilizations, the Islamic world is often viewed as both threatened by and threatening Western culture. Reductively viewed as a one-dimensional, radically alien haven of anti-Western fundamentalism, the Islamic world is perceived as a threatening source of violence and hatred, rather than a geographically vast, culturally diverse, internally multifaceted, dynamic world of 1.4 billion Muslims living in over fifty societies. Presumed to hold an alien and hostile worldview, the commonality and historically interactive religious, philosophical, artistic and cultural aspects of the Islamic world remain deemphasized and all too often unrecognized. With good reason, numerous scholars challenge the assumption that there exists "an Islamic world" pitted against "a Western world" and draw attention to the fact of Muslims living peacefully in a broad diversity of cultures and societies, some of which are and some of which are not predominantly made up of Muslim populations.

T. D. Conway, *Cross-cultural Dialogue on the Virtues*,
SpringerBriefs in Religious Studies, DOI: 10.1007/978-3-319-07833-5_1,
© The Author(s) 2014

Within this age of globalization can be found individual persons who move with ease, grace and hope amidst the cultural and religious diversity defining our contemporary landscape. Such persons recognize and work to actualize the possibilities of encounter and understanding offered in this age. Aware of how their own lives have been enriched by such interactions, they seek out the commonalities rendering possible such encounters and welcome the diversity making them both challenging and enriching. Such attitudes may be rooted in personal character and temperament, pivotal personal experiences, transformative relationships or philosophical and religious viewpoints. Even more strikingly, at times one comes across extraordinary persons who dedicate themselves to the articulation of a range of attitudes, understandings and behaviors that enable and sustain such positive encounters. Fethullah Gülen has distinguished himself as one such person, steadfastly committed to a dialogue, rather than a clash, of civilizations.

Following the terrorist attacks of 9/11/2001, Gülen issued a press release and published in the *New York Times* a statement emphatically denouncing the attacks, emphasizing that "terror can never be used in the name of Islam or for the sake of any Islamic ends. A terrorist cannot be a Muslim and a Muslim cannot be a terrorist. A Muslim can only be the representative and symbol of peace, welfare, and prosperity" (*Pearls of Wisdom* xvii). In response to terrorist defenses of violence perpetrated in the name of Islam, Gülen argues on Islamic principles that,

> Islam never approves of any kind of terrorism. Terrorism cannot be a means for any Islamic goal, and a terrorist cannot be a Muslim nor can a true Muslim be a terrorist. Islam orders peace and a true Muslim can only be a symbol of peace and the maintenance of basic human rights... The Qur'an...declares that one who takes a life unjustly is as if he/she took the lives of all humankind, and that one who saves a life is as if he/she saves the lives of all. In the words of our Prophet, a Muslim is one from whom comes no harm, neither from his/her tongue nor hand (http://en.fgulen.content/view/968/2/).

Gülen called on Americans not to forcefully retaliate against such terrorists in a way that would in turn unleash escalating violence against innocent persons. The only enduring and effective way of combating terrorism is to use non-violent methods furthering education and human development and to work to address injustices that produce human suffering. Only these efforts can address effectively the conditions of ignorance, deprivation and despair in which extremism and terrorism fester.

Gülen's influential writings and witness have inspired Muslims globally to commit themselves to the goals of peace, dialogue and human flourishing across all civilizations and have provided a powerful counterpoint to many assumptions about Muslims uncritically accepted and promulgated in our contemporary world. The ever-widening influence of persons who live the beliefs and virtues affirmed by Fethullah Gülen has come to be identified as the Turkey originating, faith-based *Hizmet* ("service to humanity") movement focused on the good works of people in local communities. The activities and initiatives of this movement, which consistently focus on direct personal encounters, provide a powerful counterweight to the all-too-common image of Islam as a brutal, violent and oppressive religion.

The Hizmet Movement: Its Beginnings and Development

What has come to be called the Hizmet Movement is singularly traceable to the charismatic spiritual leader, scholar, writer and poet M. Fethullah Gülen. The character, way of living, addresses and writings of Gülen have drawn a wide following within and beyond Turkey. In particular Turkish Muslims, but also persons of a range of religious beliefs and cultural origins, have been drawn to and influenced by his core commitment to the practice of dialogue, tolerance and compassion. Though deeply rooted in Islamic belief and philosophy, Gülen's teachings have a breadth of scope and application that speaks to persons from a range of traditions, perspectives and life experiences. His teachings have inspired members of what can best be described as a growing international social movement of moderate Muslims committed to fostering peaceful interactions, humanitarian social responsibility and human development of all persons.

Born in 1941 in Erzurum in eastern Turkey, Gülen was educated under the guidance of a number of renowned Islamic scholars and spiritual leaders. His father, a revered scholar and Imam, gathered guests, especially scholars, to discuss spiritual issues. His mother taught the Qur'an to local girls since formal Qur'anic schools had been banned at that time in secularist Turkey. His religious education was complemented by intense work in the modern social and physical sciences and Western philosophical writings (Rousseau, Balzac, Dostoyevski, Tolstoy, Camus, Sartre and Marcuse among others). Gülen's early spiritual formation was shaped under the significant Sufi influence of Sheikh Muhammed Lüfti Efendi, a renowned Sufi master and poet. Gülen was deeply inspired by the extensive writings and persona of Bediüzzaman Said Nursi, author of *Risale Nur*, who emphasized the engagement of Islam with modernity, especially modern science.[1] Having been impressed by the lives of students of Nursi, he was drawn to a study of the writings which evoked their following. The Nur movement, inspired by the literary works and behavior of Nursi, emphasized the living of a moral life shaped by Islam, the pursuing of knowledge and wisdom, the building of relations based on mutual trust and solicitude, and the seeking of peace through social justice and spiritual-intellectual enlightenment. Nursi also emphasized Islam's compatibility with democratic civil society and scientific development. Influenced deeply both by his thought and personal character, Gülen became a follower of Nursi. This emphasis on the integrated development of both intellect and moral character and thought and action would become central and enduring components of Gülen's thought. Distinctive practices of Nursi played a formative role in the development of Gülen and shaped definitive characteristics and practices of the international Gülen Movement, later termed the Hizmet Movement. Gülen participated in Nursi *cemaats* and *dershanes*, locally formed organizations responding to the abolishing

---

[1] The collected writings of Said Nursi can be found in *Risale-I Nur Külliyati* (*The Epistles or Treatise of the Light*), volumes 1 and 2 (Istanbul: Nesil 1996). Nursi's books were once banned in Turkey, testifying to estimations of their power and influence.

of Sufi orders and Islamic schools (*madrasas*) in the secularized Turkish republic. Informally organized *cemaats* gathered persons interested in exploring the challenges and responsibilities of Muslims engaged in the modern world. *Dershanes* were reading circles gathering Muslims in private homes to read the Qur'an and other spiritual writings, especially those of Nursi. These informal organizations tapped a deep desire for fellowship and intellectual inquiry among Muslims in a highly secularized society.

Gülen was also deeply impressed by Nursi's establishing of hospitable houses of study for small groups of students attending local high schools and universities. Hospitable programming, geared toward encouraging the mutual development of persons, proved to be the enduring legacy of Nursi's influence on Gülen, and this virtue of hospitality, in turn, proved to be the defining hallmark of the followers of Gülen. During the period of the 1950s and 1960s, the influence of the Nur movement grew in Turkey even to the point of generating government criticism, resulting eventually in Nursi's persecution and imprisonment, primarily due to his strong emphasis on the influential role of religion in society.[2] Even after Nursi's death in 1961, his beliefs and commitments continued to inspire followers like Gülen.

Gülen's personal development and legacy never veered from this initial influence of Sufis and Nursi, all of whom drew spiritual inspiration from the Persian poet and spiritual leader, Mawlana Jalaluddin Rumi who established his Mawlawi Sufi brotherhood in Konya, Anatolia (now Turkey). In 1958 upon being awarded a state preacher's license, Gülen commenced his own vocation as a preacher in a way which revealed his commitment to lifelong learning, moral development and humanitarian service. Noted for their strong emotive content, his sermons focused on stories about Mohammad and the earliest Islamic community as providing exemplars of the virtuous Islamic life lived in community. Due to his character and erudition, Gülen soon became a charismatic leader of Friday prayers and organizer of evening lectures focusing on personal and civic morality through an Islamic lens. Just as Nursi had inspired Gülen, so too his sermons and talks, noted for their strong emotional power, called Muslims to live the Islamic way of life as modeled

---

[2] Although Nursi played no role in the fomenting of the March Rebellion in Istanbul (1909), he was arrested due to his involvement with the Society for Muslim Unity, judged to be influencing the rebellion. Nursi was eventually acquitted of the charges. Many interpreted the charges as rooted in the government's radical secular intent to exclude religion from involvement in the political and public spheres. Nursi was again arrested and imprisoned for eleven months on the charge of creating an illegal Sufi order due to his developing of a following (*Nurcu*, literally "followers of Nursi") who read his banned works. Gülen would be subjected similarly to political accusations of undermining the Turkish secular system of government a number of times. After the 1971 military coup he was arrested, but the charges were subsequently dropped. He was subjected again to accusations following the 1980 military coup; Prime Minister Turgut Özal intervened on his behalf, valuing his moderate Islamic influence in contrast with that of extreme secularists. Governmental concern consistently focused on limiting the role of religion in the modern secular state. After years of court investigations and hearings, the case against Gülen was finally dropped, exonerating him of any wrongdoing against the government, in 2006.

by the Prophet Muhammad. Gülen deeply emphasized the steadfast commitment of the Prophets' companions to the living of the virtues ideally embodied by the Prophet. Muslims were called to cultivate both the intellectual and moral virtues, so that they could aspire to goodness of both mind and character. In addition they were called to live active lives, in which these virtues produced good actions and works serving both God and humanity.

In 1966, Gülen began to teach courses on the Islamic sciences at Izmir's Kestanepazan Qur'anic School. 1967 proved to be a distinctive turning point in Gülen's life with his appointment as a preacher in Izmir, a secularist city of Turkey. Gülen's fame grew as he poignantly faced the challenge of preaching in such a context. Soon *cemaats* began to be formed to discuss his teachings. His sermons soon drew thousands of devotees, seeding a community of followers drawn by his beliefs consistently exemplified in his own personal behavior. Followers were deeply impressed by the consistency of Gulen's words and deeds, recognizing that such unity of belief, word and action revealed a virtuous integrity. His public addresses and sermons deepened his charismatic presence, and their message called persons to a vibrant intellectual enlightenment, coupled with strong moral formation, and directed to the active using of talents to improve both the local and universal human community. Within a short period of time, the ever-widening circle of his influence became evident. Welcoming opportunities to speak, be it in mosques, local gatherings or town meetings, his developing message of tolerance, dialogue and compassion gripped intellectuals, students, and local community members—all persons yearning for a spiritual orientation that encouraged personal engagement with existing social circumstances and needs of the current world. Read by a wide range of audiences, Gülen's speeches drew on the natural and social sciences, Islamic theology, Sufi poetry, philosophy and economics, but always with an emphasis on the call to communal service directed toward human well-being. His formal teaching attracted a generation of young students, and his philosophy of educational reform began to influence educational theory and pedagogical practices developing in the 1960s. By the time of his formal teaching retirement in 1981, he had developed a voice of significant influence in Turkey and had inspired a generation of followers; soon such influence would grow to have strong international impact. Gülen began to be referred to as *Hodjaefendi* (esteemed teacher), a respected form of address for those possessing a depth of religious knowledge and moral character, rather than a term indicating leadership in an institutionalized structure. Gülen repeatedly emphasizes that he serves, not as a founding head of an organization, but rather as a scholar whose life and work continues to influence the reflections, commitments and lives of others. Continuing to deliver influential sermons in major mosques and to write prolifically, Gülen became a strong public figure within Turkey and of increasing international influence. Since his retirement, Gülen has focused his attention on the active promoting of hospitable dialogue, especially among groups of persons of differing ideologies, religions, philosophical perspectives and cultural traditions in communities across the globe.

Under Nursi's initial influence, Gülen's enduring commitment to an understanding of Islam centered on the virtue of hospitality naturally overflowed into his initial establishment of philanthropically funded "Light Houses"—residential homes for university students of diverse studies who subsequently went on to successful careers in a range of professions. The establishment of these hospitality houses increased rapidly across Turkey. Always faithful to this initial pivotal commitment to the virtue of hospitality, the Hizmet movement gradually grew from an emphasis on houses of hospitality to encompass five fundamental initiatives, namely: education, public media, business networks, dialogue centers and charitable works. All five initiatives promoted the virtues of Islamic living, but always as understood through the lens of the virtue of hospitality.

Growth Beyond Houses of Hospitality: Educational Initiatives

Soon after the establishment of Gülen's hospitality houses, it became apparent that further student support was needed. The building of communal residences, eventually numbering over two hundred, enabled students to reside communally in close proximity to the schools they were attending. The dormitories attracted students deeply committed to living their Islamic faith. Gülen himself resided in one of these residences for 4 years until the 1980 military coup which resulted in the banning and restricting of religious practices within educational residences. Due to the positive reputation of such houses, especially as tied to their promotion of a strong commitment to learning and moral living, numerous Turkish cities sought to have them established close to local educational institutions. Successful professionals and their families, inspired by Gülen's beliefs and initiatives, welcomed the opportunity to participate in these evolving networks of fellowship and to fund the expansion of these initiatives. The success of these residences led naturally to the founding of the first Gülen schools in 1982 when the Izmir communal residence was expanded into a self-standing school and another school opened in Istanbul. Enthusiasm and financial support for these Gülen inspired schools continued to gain momentum, especially when it became evident that students of these school were succeeding academically and passing university entrance examinations at high rates.

Attracting widening interest, such Gülen schools rapidly increased in number and demand in the 1980s. As required in secular Turkey, these schools did not mandate the teaching of religion, but had a broad primary ethical emphasis and orientation, judged to lie deeper than specific religious and ethnic identities and political viewpoints.[3] Central to the mission of these schools was an emphasis on

---

[3] Gülen schools in Turkey teach religion for 1 h per week as part of their comparative religion curriculum; Gülen schools in some countries do not require the study of religion, although most teach comparative religion. But all schools place great emphasis on ethical living, scientific proficiency and multi-linguistic fluency.

faculty serving as positive role models for students and encouraging commitment to lifelong learning and ethical living. Within a few years, two hundred schools had developed throughout Turkey, due to their strong academic reputation. With the collapse of the Soviet Union in 1991, Gülen recognized the need to open schools in Central Asia to strengthen and support local communities, especially those with strong Turkish speaking Muslim populations. Within a few years, over two hundred and fifty schools were opened in Central Asia. Recognizing the positive influence of these institutions, the then current President of Turkey, Turgut Özal encouraged the expansion of such educational outreach. Expanding to include Georgia and Moscow, these schools came to be associated with peace facilitation and the building of bridges of dialogue between varying faith and ethnic communities. Their faculties were not restricted to followers of Gülen, but drew persons committed to core educational values and goals of the schools. Given the strong emphasis on character formation, faculty were expected to both model and encourage the development of virtuous character traits seen as encouraging peaceful relations and non-violent solutions to tensions and conflict. Clearly identified with the image of facilitators of peace and dialogue, these schools gradually expanded to include regions of the Middle East and Africa where they came to be described as "Islands of Peace" in regions rife with the risk of conflict. Central to their mission was the active encouraging of character traits and behaviors that furthered peaceful interactions grounded in mutual understanding, respect and the protection of human rights. By the end of the first decade of 2000, it is estimated (although figures vary) that there were over eight hundred Gülen schools in 120 countries, including Turkey, Azerbaijan, Kyrgyzstan, Afghanistan, Turkmenistan, Uzbekistan, Kazakhstan, Georgia, Moldova, Ukraine, Pakistan, the Philippines, Cambodia, Vietnam, Mongolia, Brazil, Russia, Rumania, Bulgaria, Bosnia-Herzegovina, Albania, Australia, Indonesia, Thailand, Malaysia, South Korea, Japan, South Africa and the United States. Although religiously inspired, these schools do not provide religious instruction, and their curricula are designed in terms of the national standards of the local ministries of education.

Consistent with the central emphasis on cross-cultural dialogue, all Gülen schools have a multi-linguistic emphasis. The curriculum is taught in English and regional languages, with the Turkish language offered as an elective. Consistent with the view that Islam can and must engage modernity and be a positive force for enlightened social development and civic responsibility in the modern world, all Gülen schools emphasize modern sciences and technology, but always in ways that complement the spiritual and ethical inquiry distinctive of the human spirit. To emphasize the global outreach of such an educational commitment, Gülen schools sponsor periodic Academic Olympiads that gather distinguished students from schools across the world for academic competition and recognition. Such educational commitment was eventually taken to a higher level through the establishment of six universities in Central Asia, Fatih University in Istanbul (1996), and a university in Northern Iraq (2009). The Hizmet's movement's strong emphasis on rational inquiry, dialogue, and respectful engagement of differences has enabled these schools to function as islands of peaceful exchange, especially within regions, such as Bosnia, Serbia and Iraq, where the specter of clashing religious and ethnic differences risked undermining the possibility of dialogue so needed to foster and sustain peace and strengthen civic society. Gaining a strong reputation for offering high quality education and being a stepping stone for professional advancement and peaceful communal relations, the Gülen schools continue to be sought out by families and community leaders in a wide range of countries.

Broadening the Scope of Public Discourse: Media Initiatives

Recognizing the link between learning through formal education and the educating of citizens through media outlets committed to the furthering of inquiry and truth, the Hizmet movement subsequently focused on media development. In the late 1970s, teachers influenced by Gülen's educational ideas founded the Teachers' Foundation and published a best-selling monthly journal entitled *Sizinti* which broadened exposure to their educational philosophy and the prolific, newly published writings of Gülen. Such media exposure was taken to another level, with the 1986 founding of the *Zaman* newspaper headquartered in Istanbul. Now in circulation to over eight hundred thousand readers in fifteen countries, the independent *Zaman* publication is currently ranked first among media publications in Turkey and is translated into 10 global languages. Media outreach continued to develop with the addition of television programming through Samanyolu Televizyonu (STV), Ebru TV (the U.S. based English language network) and a range of publishing houses. The Hizmet movement's publications and television programming maintain its commitment to ideals and beliefs central to its identity and mission. All of its media outlets emphasize moderate Islamic beliefs, core moral virtues and the importance of education and service in civic life. In addition, the ongoing encouragement of learning is fostered through weekly "reading circles" in many local communities. Said Nursi had fostered such gatherings or *dershanes* to promote rational reflection, discussion, informative socialization, solidarity and community.[4] Such gatherings manifest on a grass-roots level the core commitment to hospitality. The circles are designed to deepen and refresh participants' inquiry while at the same time sustaining and strengthening community among persons committed to Gülen ideals and beliefs.

The Journalists and Writers Foundation which was inspired by Gülen in 1994 concentrates its efforts on promoting dialogue among persons of differing

---

[4] The idea of these *dershanes* was combined with the idea of hospitality houses. Residences and apartments were established to house these discussions, primarily focused on Nursi's writings, and to provide places of temporary residence for university students. Yavuz and Esposito (2003, p. 13) notes that by 2001 there were over 5,000 *dershanes* in Turkey, fifty-three in the Central Asian republics and over seventy in Europe.

ideologies, religions, cultures, and social strata and honoring persons who encourage peaceful interchange and reconciliation. Its initial gatherings were successful in bringing together intellectuals, politicians, artists, academics and scientists for vibrant, civil discussion of wide ranging topics such as the challenges facing Turkish democracy, pluralism, freedom of expression and belief, and the authority of the modern nation state. All such media endeavors have a singular goal, namely the promotion of dialogue which sustains civil discourse over time. The foundation seeks to model, inspire and facilitate such dialogue. It gathers a wide range of groups of people for discussions, often over shared meals, with the aim of promoting the call expressed by the Turkish poet and Sufi mystic Yunus Emre seven centuries earlier: "Come, let us be together, let us make things easier; let us love and be loved." The success of these gatherings sustain the belief that people of varying points of view can find common ground and recognize shared concerns and interests. All such endeavors emphasize the positive role Muslims can play in contributing to and shaping the public sphere in a way that allows for and engages a diverse range of viewpoints. Herein Islam is not seen as rigidly tied to a reified, pre-modern tradition, but as dynamically engaging contemporary issues, facing modern societal challenges, and strengthening the tolerant civic interactions vital to democratic life.

Marshalling Philanthropic Resources: Professional Network Development

Early on, Gülen recognized such influential initiatives could only be sustained through the commitment of a vast network of generous supporters. Philanthropic outreach was a natural outcome of this developing communitarian movement centered on the virtue of hospitality. Currently there exists a very well developed network of supporters of Gülen initiatives in Turkey and worldwide, mainly within the middle-class business sectors. Since no government funding supports such initiatives, the generosity of individuals is required to sustain all initiatives. Gülen's educational beliefs and initiatives motivated highly successful community, industrial and business leaders to dedicate themselves to the promotion of quality education, based on the belief that the enlightenment offered through education renders possible the furthering of a more just and humane society. Such emphasis is seen as a necessary condition for building and sustaining truly democratic societies since education is what provides equal opportunity to develop the talents and capabilities of citizens. Especially emphasized in such philanthropic generosity is the use of funding to support students at pivotal stages of their development. Such support evokes gratitude and dedication which in turn deepen reciprocal civic solicitude. Support by others, especially anonymous benefactors not seeking recognition, encourages an ethos of service to others. Such generosity builds civic ties and loyalties within local and regional communities. And such generosity transcends nationally boundaries, with persons from one society interacting supportively through trade and good works with members of other societies.

The Hizmet Movement has amassed an amazingly vast, locally situated network of financial support, including *İş Hayati Dayanişma Derneği*, a supportive associative network of thousands of business leaders and merchants. This network of capital support is largely directed to the funding of the movement's educational initiatives. Such philanthropic networking is fundamentally rooted in the Islamic belief that material prosperity is a blessing when directed to virtuous activity serving human well-being and development as intended by God.

Facilitating Respectful Interacting and Understanding: Dialogue Centers

Prior to Gülen's rise to public influence, no major contemporary figure in Turkey was actively promoting interfaith and intercultural dialogue. Gülen came to be identified with creating opportunities for such dialogue on local levels and in meetings with distinguished religious leaders, especially within the Abrahamic tradition. In all such gatherings he emphasizes, that "All of us believe in the same God. We might understand things differently but why should that keep us from working together to uplift humanity and turn it toward God? Why should we let our differences divide us… ?" (Ünal vi). Gülen has met with leading figures of the major world religions, including among others Pope John Paul II, the Greek Orthodox Patriarch, the Patriarch of the Turkish Orthodox Church, the Patriarch of the Turkish Armenian community, the Chief Rabbi of the Turkish Jewish community, and Israel's Sephardic Head Rabbi. He continues to take steps to support the ending of conflict in the Middle East through fostering open dialogue among the religious leaders of the region. In a meeting with Pope John Paul II at the Vatican in 1998, Gülen proposed concrete measures that could be taken to further peace in this region where all three Abrahamic religions originated and peoples reside. Besides such high level interactions, the Hizmet movement is most noted for its frequent and extensive local gatherings of persons, be they in discussion groups, seminars or dinners, all of which are hospitably designed to welcome others, facilitate face-to-face interactions and seed further opportunities for ongoing dialogue.

Under Gülen's influence, Turkish secular community leaders were encouraged to join such conversations aimed at promoting mutual understanding and respectful exchange, even between groups perceived to be at odds. Attendees at reconciliation dinners in Turkey express amazement that even those who critique Gülen initiatives are invited to these gatherings which embody Gülen's call to "show tolerance to those with different ideas and beliefs, love each other, work for unity, and serve others by educating them" (Ünal vi). Recognizing the importance of institutionalizing such ongoing commitment to building bridges of dialogue, the Hizmet Movement opened "Centers of Dialogue" outside Turkey, providing opportunities for persons of different religious sects and faiths to interact, especially in societies in which Islam was not the predominant religion. In the United States there currently exist a number of such centers, i.e. the Niagara Foundation in Chicago, the Istanbul Center in Atlanta, Pacifica Center in Los Angeles, Interfaith Dialogue Center in New Jersey, and Institute of Interfaith Dialogue in Texas. Such centers are also found in Europe, South America, and the Far East. Committed to building bridges between persons of different faiths and cultures, these centers host luncheons, conferences, seminars, trips to Turkey, Iftar dinners, and joint church-synagogue-mosque activities. The common aim of all such activities is to create hospitable gatherings bringing together people of differing beliefs and practices so that they may find common ground, combat bigotry, prejudice and ignorance, and build mutual trust and understanding. For many persons, their first and lasting impression of the Hizmet Movement is the hospitality of such gatherings. Through these gatherings they begin to envision, hope for and seek out opportunities for other hospitable encounters with persons of varying races, religions, ethnicities and traditions.

Promoting Human Well-Being: Charitable Initiatives

From its inception, the Hizmet movement has placed strong emphasis on caring service to fellow persons in imitation of the virtuous behavior of the Prophet Muhammad. In *Pearls of Wisdom* Gülen develops his view that the Prophet Muhammad affirmed the equality of all persons and "established that superiority lies in virtue, piety and morality" rather than wealth, power and prestige (7). The movement's emphasis on educating both the mind and spirit in schools was complemented by the establishing of six highly rated hospitals committed to holistic health and medical service. Gülen spearheaded the formal establishment of a wide range of charitable organizations committed to recognizing the needs and promoting the well-being of other persons, especially those of local communities. Fittingly its service outreach *Kimse Yok Mu* (translated from the Turkish as, "Isn't there anyone who cares?" or "Is anybody there?") established in 2004 is fundamentally grounded in pro-active, local responses to those in need. Such solicitous outreach began with service initiatives in the poorer Eastern parts of Turkey. Gülen was convinced much of the Kurdish unrest stemmed from conditions of entrenched poverty. Believing peaceful relations are tied to the meeting of human needs and promoting of social justice, Hizmet projects stress the providing of services and goods needed to promote human well-being and flourishing, especially in emergency situations. The vast network of local Gülen supporters can be tapped to meet specific, often urgent, human needs as they arise in particular local circumstances, with emphasis always being placed on local, face-to-face, grass-roots communal projects. Given the international reach of the movement, emergency relief can be quickly mobilized to respond to crises and with ample resources, based on estimates that its relief efforts raise over sixteen million dollars annually. For example, in the late summer of 2009 *Kimse Yok Mu* organized a team of medical and search-and-rescue crews in response to severe flooding in the province of Khatlon in Tajikistan which resulted in the destruction of a local hospital and school and the displacement of 2,500 Uyali residents of the local 6,000 population. Tajikistani Gülen school personnel and local entrepreneurs were able to mobilize this effort quickly and efficiently. The Gülen networks also allow for sustained projects committed to the ongoing improvement of conditions in local communities. For example, it is not uncommon for doctors serving in Gülen hospitals to dedicate their vacation time in service to needy communities in Africa. Members of the Hizmet movement pro-actively seek to deepen and creatively express their commitment to such outreach, seeing it as a welcome means of concretely putting their beliefs into practice.

This extensive network of philanthropic participants strengthens the movement, ensures its legacy, builds social capital and generates influence in the public sphere. Over time the Hizmet movement has established what are called *Işik Evler*, translated as "lighthouses," residences gathering followers for prayer, discussion and communal living. Students residing in these houses commit themselves to the study of Nursi and Gülen writings, the development of inner moral discipline and piety, and supportive concern for others through the development of compassion and related virtues. Persons exposed to such initiatives are deeply impressed by the extent to which Fethullah Gülen successfully developed a grassroots following and networking, aptly characterized as "a movement" that institutionalized his beliefs and practices in over fifty countries with the aim of promoting human understanding, peace and well-being in service to God and humankind. As such an organic Islamic movement, it has the power to transform Muslim communities throughout the world and provide powerful witness to the possibility of hospitable interactions engaging persons of varying faiths, cultures, races and ethnicities. As a multi-faceted and wide-ranging religiously based network, the Hizmet movement embodies a moderate and progressive Islam that stands in contrast to the radical, fundamentalist image of Islam that so captivates the media. From these initial "lighthouses" a path was shaped for reinforcing and informing others about the beliefs and virtues identified with the Prophet Muhammad and the first emerging Islamic community. Members of the Hizmet movement, rooted in Turkey, seek to witness what is seen as the true spirit of Islam—one committed to peaceful relations, human development and ethical living. Central to its understanding of Islam is an emphasis on the virtues identified as essential to Islamic life and revered on a fundamental level in all religious and cultural traditions.

References

Gülen, M. F. (2006). *Pearls of wisdom.* Somerset, NJ: The Light.
Nursi, S. (1996). *Risale-I Nur Külliyati (the epistles or treatise of the light).* Istanbul: Nesil.
Ünal, A., & Williams, A. (2000). *Advocate of dialogue.* Fairfax, VA: The Fountain.
Yavuz, M. H., & Esposito, J. L. (2003). *Turkish Islam and the secular state.* Syracuse: Syracuse University Press.

Chapter 2
The Importance of the Virtues in General and Hospitality in Particular

In his book, *Islam the Straight Path*, John Esposito describes Islam as a religion that focuses on orthopraxy (correct action) rather than orthodoxy (correct doctrine) (85). He explains how in Christianity theology is the queen of all sciences, while in Islam (as in Judaism) conformity to God's law in practice has pride of place. *Shariah*, the Divine Law, is conceived as a road on which all Muslims journey. Such journeying consists of the performance of good actions and submission to the will of God that bring joy and peace. Of course Islamic right action is interwoven with religious belief. Islam has a rich and sophisticated tradition of theological and philosophical reflection which develops in great detail fine points of Islamic metaphysics, epistemology and jurisprudence. The writings of the contemporary Islamic scholar Seyyed Hossein Nasr provide a rich overview of the philosophical and theological writings of the Islamic tradition in dialogue with those of the Western tradition. But, as Esposito emphasizes, the vital core of Islam is most fundamentally a way of living—an *ethos*—tied to the five pillars of Islam. Muslims *proclaim* belief in one God and affirm Mohammad as the Messenger of God (*shahada*); Muslims *pray* five times daily a ritualized prayer (*salat*); Muslims *share* annually a set percentage of their assets to promote the social welfare of their community (*zakat*); Muslims *fast* during Ramadan, and if financially and physically able, Muslims *make the pilgrimage* to Mecca (*Hajj*). These central practices define Muslims and from them flow other practices which shape their daily lives. And central to this way of living are the virtues. Often identified unofficially as the sixth pillar of Islam, *jihad*—the inner and communal struggle to live a good Islamic life—calls Muslims to aspire to live virtuously. Staying on the straight path of Islam is synonymous with living a virtuous life. Living this life is the source of both personal and communal peace.

Interactions with members of the Hizmet movement reveal this aspiration. Key virtues define the movement, the lives of its members and the practices of its institutions. Accounts of encounters with members strikingly focus on the virtues they live rather than fine points of doctrinal belief. And of all the virtues they embody, the most prominent and most frequently mentioned in these accounts is the virtue of hospitality. (An example of written accounts can be found in *When I Was in Turkey* published by the Rumi Forum of Washington, D.C.) For this reason

T. D. Conway, *Cross-cultural Dialogue on the Virtues*,
SpringerBriefs in Religious Studies, DOI: 10.1007/978-3-319-07833-5_2,
© The Author(s) 2014

a study of the virtues, but most especially the virtue of hospitality, within the movement and in relation to other traditions may provide a key to understanding the Hizmet movement.

The virtue of hospitality has played a predominant role in the Hizmet movement since its inception. This is not surprising given the role this virtue plays in the Middle Eastern world which was the originating locus of the message of Islam. This virtue holds prominence in a number of religious and cultural traditions, but not to the extent to which it is revered in Islamic societies. Since the Gülen movement seeks out what is common in varying traditions, and hospitality is directed toward welcoming the other in a way which both emphasizes commonality and appreciates difference, it is not surprising that this virtue is so esteemed and practiced by followers of Gülen. Hospitality is a pivotal virtue, for it enables persons to open themselves to others so that they may both discover what is common and begin to explore what is richly diverse. Through hospitality we learn of each other. Hospitality allows the commencement of a journey which deepens our understanding of the human condition and sustains hope for dialogue and understanding among persons.

The virtues provide a lens through which Gülen's beliefs, practices and legacy can be understood. The Sufi tradition which deeply influenced Gülen places strong emphasis on the formation of inner character manifest in words, actions and even gestures. One's way of living in the world is shaped by one's inward character. The Sufi conception is in agreement with Aristotle's understanding that one's character (*ethos*) fundamentally shapes one's way of living and interacting with others (one's *ethic*). The personal and communal living of a virtuous life remains central to the Hizmet movement, and the emphasis on virtues in general and on particular virtues shapes all of its education, media, service and peace-building initiatives. In *Cihad veya l'la-yi Kelimetullah* (*Jihad for Raising the Word of* God), Gülen describes "the greater jihad" as a person's inner striving to develop and practice moral virtues. Living a virtuous life is seen as the fundamental calling of all Muslims (Ünal 70-1). The excellence of the virtues is seen as bringing to fulfillment the possibilities of human nature, allowing persons to flourish and live in a way attuned to their nature as created by God. As Gülen states in *Key Concepts in the Practice of Sufism*, "There is a mutually supportive and perfective relation between an individual's actions and his inner life. We may call it a 'virtuous circle'…[d]etermination, perseverance, and resolve illuminate one's inner conscience and the brightness of his inner conscience strengthen his will-power and resolve, stimulating him to higher horizons" (v). The devout Muslim is called to wage the greater jihad, understood as an inner struggle to cultivate virtues and avoid vices, as supported by the lesser jihad, the communal struggle to develop local institutions that promote the formation of virtues and practice of good works. While distinguishing the greater and lesser jihad, Gülen more importantly recognizes their interdependence. He writes that, "Reaching spiritual perfection and helping others to do so are points of consideration. Attaining internal perfection is the jihad; helping others attain it is the lesser jihad. When you separate one from the other, jihad is no longer jihad" (Ünal 74). Many of the Hizmet educational and service initiatives can be understood as stemming from the interdependence of these two conceptions. Gülen strongly argues against the misunderstanding of jihad rooted in political ideology that emphasizes the waging of violent war against non-Muslims. Islamic jihad is fundamentally a matter of striving to attain and promote Islamic virtuous living which enhances the well-being of both self and others and resisting what undermines them. Muslims are called to a lifetime pursuit of deepening understanding of the virtues and lifetime struggle to live virtuously.

The virtues are found in all cultural traditions and shape related cultural conceptions and practices, and yet often persons fail to attend explicitly and thoughtfully to the extent to which understanding of the virtues shapes their attitudes and actions. In addition many persons are exposed only to the understandings of the virtues passed down within their own religious and cultural traditions. They rarely encounter people outside their own tradition, and when they do, even more rarely do they begin a journey affording deepening understanding of other traditions. Through his emphasis on the central virtue of hospitality, Gülen opens a shared space in which persons can deepen and enrich their understanding of their own and others' conceptions and practices regarding virtues. Because of his valuing of hospitality in word and deed, Gülen was able to open himself to the riches found in varied cultural, religious and philosophical understandings of the virtues. This encounter brought him to recognize the human commonality found across all cultural and religious traditions and to value the richness of varied cultural traditions.

Gülen's virtue-based approach to moral living resonates well with contemporary discussions of Aristotelian ethics, continuing an ethical legacy historically preserved and appropriated by medieval Islamic philosophers. Aristotle is the most noteworthy thinker within the tradition of Western virtue-based ethics, and his moral reflections were valued by Islamic scholars for centuries. It is not surprising that a Turkish thinker influentially situated at the nexus of the Western and Islamic traditions reveals this influence of Aristotle's ethical reflections.

Understanding the Virtues

In an important scholarly article, Martha Nussbaum, a prominent contemporary American philosopher, explores the centrality of discussion of the virtues to contemporary philosophical debate (Nussbaum 1988). Recognizing the limitations of both Utilitarian and Kantian ethical frameworks and the importance of tying ethical theory to the concrete experience of persons in particular life circumstances, Nussbaum explores Aristotle's virtue-based ethics and the rich conception of the virtues it offers. She values such an account for it directly engages particular contexts, historical traditions and life experiences. While emphasizing the concrete circumstances of human lives in their multiplicity and mutability, this approach does not succumb to the negative implications of a moral relativism that denies the existence of any criteria of moral living beyond those articulated in local traditions. Aristotle's conception focuses on a broad universal account of human flourishing that is always instantiated and played out within the cultural diversity of humankind. At the same time it builds on a conception of humanity that lies deeper than local traditions and thereby enables critical assessment of traditions and grounds the hope for understanding persons of differing traditions.[1] This account which affirms both commonality and diversity sets up an understanding of the virtues which opens the possibility of cross-cultural dialogue, so central to the Hizmet movement. Gülen's reflections on the virtues draw on the moral writings of the Islamic philosopher Ibn Miskawayh (c. 930–1030), specifically his work *Tahdhib al-Akhlaq* which builds on the Aristotelian conception of virtue as a mean situated between two vices, characterized by extremes of excess and deficiency. Gülen envisions virtue as the center of a circle and vice as entailing movement away from the center. As one moves further from the virtuous center, the vice becomes stronger and more powerful. Rather than a median (virtue) point on a line between extreme end points (vices), the circle imagery illustrates how there is a nuanced range of variations on the vices surrounding the central virtue (*Essays-Perspectives-Opinions* 70).

Both Gülen and Aristotle emphasize a conception of the virtues affirming both human commonality and diversity. On the basis of this understanding of the virtues and the role they play in human flourishing, Aristotle articulates an account of the virtues that is both universal, as tied to our human condition, and culturally specific, as tied to the ways of people as lived within particular cultural-historical traditions. Each of the virtues focuses on a sphere of human experience that plays a role in all human living and flourishing. Each sphere displays a particular human circumstance in which persons face choices and may choose wisely or unwisely. As Nussbaum notes, each virtue "names a sphere of life with which all human beings regularly or more or less necessarily have dealings" (35). Aristotle is famous for his conception of virtue as a mean situated between two extremes (vices) of excess and deficiency which influenced Islamic philosophers' moral theories. For example, courage is the mean between rashness and cowardice; moderation is the mean between intemperate overindulgence and insensibility; generosity is the mean between wasteful prodigality and miserliness. The virtues, which consist of hitting the mean at the right time, in the right way, and for the right end, are difficult to develop and depend on habituation over time. Given their importance to living well,

---

[1] Nussbaum emphasizes that this account provides a basis for critiquing the practices of local traditions which neglect or hinder the development of important virtues (33). In another essay entitled "Internal Criticism and Indian Rationalist Traditions", Nussbaum stresses the importance of internal criticism of local practices, recognizing the resources within traditions for critical self-examination and reform. As a modernist, Gülen emphasizes the importance of such examination and reform within dynamic, vital traditions which can engage contemporary circumstances and challenges.

they are worthy of concern and care. For this reason Aristotle stresses, "It is not unimportant, then, to acquire one sort of habit or another, right from youth. On the contrary, it is very important, indeed all-important" (Aristotle 1999, 1103b, p. 19). Consistent with this understanding, later chapters will explore how character formation in youth is central to the design of all Gülen schools.

In observing various cultures, one can recognize these virtues at play, even if one has not been involved in serious and extensive reflection on the virtues. In one's travels, one recognizes other persons performing courageous, compassionate, or generous actions. Scholars seek to define broadly the virtues, offering a thin account of what is entailed in choosing wisely in such particular spheres of human living. For example, courage has to do with choosing wisely in relation to risks of harm, temperance with choosing wisely in relation to bodily appetites and their pleasures, and generosity with choosing wisely in relation to the sharing of one's material goods. Within varying cultural traditions, there develop thick accounts of these universal virtues, that is, concrete, fleshed out specifications of these universal virtues. In travelling to other cultures, we can identify shared conditions of human existence. We can discern types of situations all persons face and in response to which they must choose and can begin to explore and reflectively examine specific cultural accounts of wise choosing. Such encounters deepen our moral reflection, broaden our moral imagination and enable us to explore insightfully what is involved in human persons choosing and acting well in response to circumstances we all face as human. To offer one illustration, in all societies there is a notion of "good temper", a wise moral response to perceived slights or wrongs. In ancient Greek society, "justifiable anger" or good temper was considered to be a virtue. Whereas in traditional Buddhist society, the virtuous mean would be more closely identified with a mildness rather than temper, for the Buddhist attends deeply to the suffering temper inflicts on both self and other. But interestingly, in some translations of Aristotle's discussion of "justifiable anger" the mean is translated as "mildness" in recognition of the wise person's always veering away from the excesses of anger and the harm they cause. Consistent with this understanding, later chapters will discuss Gülen's emphasis on forgiveness and reconciliation in response to harms done to persons. Courage, in all societies, is associated with the response to anticipated risks or harms. Nussbaum stresses that the ancient Greeks initially conceived of courage as a matter of sword-waving in response to life-threatening situations but over time refined their sense to a more inward and civic understanding of wise behavior in such threatening circumstances (Nussbaum 1988, p. 38). In this sense, someone like Socrates was esteemed for his courage in facing an unwarranted death sentence in a way that maintained his fundamental convictions. Rather than escaping and thereby risking the undermining of respect for civic institutions and the rule of law, Socrates faced his trial and execution with courage and equanimity. Gülen's own personal life story models well the virtuous response to situations in which one risks or is subjected to wrongful judgments and harmful actions. Like Nursi, Gülen honorably endured court charges and investigations before being finally exonerated or acquitted. And both men did so in peaceful ways that remained faithful to their fundamental convictions.

Ongoing critical inquiry enables persons to grow wiser in their understanding and practicing of the virtues. Encounters with others from different traditions help us to articulate, refine and examine critically our local conceptions of the virtues. Thus Aristotle's approach as developed in the *Nicomachean Ethics* and *Politics* views "the beliefs of the many different societies... not as unrelated norms, but as competing answers to questions of justice and courage (and so on) with which all the societies (being human) are concerned, and in response to which they are all trying to find what is good... [They are] the ways in which different societies have solved common human problems" (Nussbaum 1988, p. 39). With this account, persons seek a wiser understanding of human flourishing rather than a passive, uncritical perpetuation of established norms and practices.

This Aristotelian approach resonates with the approach that Gülen takes in his own ethical reasoning. Gülen attends closely to the virtues, emphasizing the universal importance of understanding, cultivating and practicing them. He states that, "Such moral standards as truthfulness, chastity, honesty, respect for elders (especially parents), compassion, love, and helpfulness are always universally accepted values" (Ünal 59). He conceives of the virtues as grounded in common dimensions of human living, recognized and addressed by all human communities. For this reason humans can identify and respond to shared needs, conditions, concerns and aspirations. On this basis we can take an interest in and develop concern about the well-being of others. But at the same time, Gülen values highly the rich diversity of cultures which present variously nuanced conceptions of and practices regarding the virtues. Through exchanges with persons from other traditions, we are better able to articulate, refine and improve our understanding of what is good and true, thereby enabling us to live better human lives. Growing in wisdom requires such commitment to ongoing inquiry and refinement. It appears that both Aristotle and Gülen believe that growing in wisdom requires the recognition of both the worth of tradition, as the home of one's inquiry and formation, and the need for ongoing critical reflection on one's tradition. For, as stressed by Aristotle, human persons are always searching for the good, rather than just preserving the way of our ancestors. And if our traditions are to remain vital and dynamic, they must have the capacity to address and respond to contemporary conditions and challenges.

Interaction with persons of other cultural traditions helps us refine our understanding of the virtues. Such exposure brings us into contact with cultures that have deeply attended to specific virtues, enabling insightful articulation and highly refined practicing of specific virtues. For this reason some cultures are noted for very fine attentiveness to particular virtues, enabling them to be "finely aware and richly responsible".[2] Thus encountering persons of these cultures can deepen and refine our own ethical sensibilities.

---

[2] In "Finely Aware and Richly Responsible': Moral Attention and the Moral Task of Literature", Nussbaum provides a detailed analysis of the novelist, Henry James' understanding of the moral life as bringing persons to be "finely aware and richly responsible".

For example, cultures deeply influenced by Buddhism reveal heightened attentiveness and sensitivity to the virtue of compassion. Buddhism offers a rich legacy of exegetical writings on compassion and a panoply of practices tied to this virtue. Not without good reason is compassion seen as the hallmark of a Buddhist way of living. Contemporary Western societies are distinguished by their heightened preoccupation with the distinctly modern, liberal virtue of tolerance. Western legal systems have produced extensive theoretical analyses and systematic articulations of legal protections stemming from this definitive concern with the virtue of tolerance judged to be essential to the civic life of pluralistic democratic societies. Middle Eastern culture, deeply influenced by Islam, is perhaps best known for its longstanding and central emphasis on the virtue of hospitality. In many local contexts this virtue is seen as trumping all other virtues in pressing circumstances. Muslims' daily prayers bring them to reflect repeatedly on both compassion and mercy as Divine attributes they are called to emulate. One can turn to such varied cultural traditions to deepen one's own reflection on the virtues for a variety of reasons. It may be that one's own culture insufficiently attends to particular virtues, neglecting what was once of concern within one's tradition or what has rarely been the focus of attention. The other culture may push one to critically examine the assumptions underlying one's own culture's understanding, pushing one to raise questions that have not been explored within one's own tradition. The other culture may also bring one to recognize what is well worth preserving and cherishing within one's own tradition.

The fruitfulness of such cross-cultural dialogue on the virtues becomes more evident through an exploration of two virtues strongly associated with Western liberal society and Islamic societies. Though related, the different understandings of these virtues may prove highly illuminating. Both societal traditions are associated with virtues tied to choosing wisely in response to the human fact of diversity. Western liberal societies are noted for the central emphasis they place on the virtue of tolerance, while Islamic societies are noted for the central emphasis they place on the virtue of hospitality. Interestingly, the Hizmet movement, originating in Turkey which lies at the nexus of the interaction between Western European societies and Middle Eastern societies, places great emphasis on the virtues of both tolerance and hospitality. Within this movement tolerance is seen as a minimum virtue, undeniably valued and encouraged, but appreciated primarily as opening the path to the more esteemed virtue of hospitality. Turkish scholars emphasize that the Turkish word *hosgörü* is difficult to translate into English. Often translated as tolerance in English, it is understood to be a richer, more robust virtue than "tolerance". It seems that a major commitment of the Hizmet movement is to lessen intolerance and call people to tolerance with the hope that they will begin a journey enabling them to move beyond tolerance to hospitality as richly understood within Islamic and other religious traditions. In so doing, the Hizmet movement reveals concretely the value of cross-cultural dialogue, whether focused on the virtues in general, specific virtues or a wide range of related topics. Central to this movement is the call to reflect on and live the virtues.

It is hoped that the following consideration of the virtues of tolerance and hospitality from two different traditions will exemplify the rich insights that can be gained through a cross-cultural exploration of the virtues. Such consideration also brings us to explore the richness of Gülen's reflections on both these virtues and the constellation of related virtues which have played such an influential role in shaping distinctive practices of the Hizmet movement.

References

Aristotle. (1999). *Nicomachean ethics* (2nd ed.) (T. Irwin, Trans). Indianapolis: Hackett.

Esposito, J. (2011). *Islam, the straight path* (4th ed.). New York: Oxford University Press.

Gülen, M. F. (2004a). *Essays-perspectives-opinions*. Somerset, NJ: The Light.

Gülen, M. F. (2004b). *Key concepts in the practice of sufism, Emerald hills of the heart*. Rutherford, NJ: The Light.

Nussbaum, M. (1985). Finely aware and richly responsible: Moral attention and the moral task ofliterature. *Journal of Philosophy, 82*(10), 516–529

Nussbaum, M. (1988). Non-relative virtues: An Aristotelian approach. *Midwest studies in philosophy, XIII*, 32–52.

Nussbaum, M. (1992). Internal criticism and indian rationalist rraditions. In Michael Krauz (Ed.), *Relativism: Interpretation and confrontation*. Notre Dame, IN: University of Notre Dame.

Ünal, A., & Williams, A. (2000). *Advocate of dialogue*. Fairfax, VA: The Fountain.

Yurtsever, A. (Ed.). (2009). *When I was in Turkey*. Washington, DC: Rumi Forum.

Chapter 3
From Tolerance to Hospitality

Tolerance: The Definitive Virtue of Western Modernity

Tolerance is seen as the quintessential modern Western virtue, distinctly tied to the emergence of the Western liberal tradition. Aristotle conceives of the virtues and vices as settled dispositions to choose wisely or unwisely in relation to a specific type of human situation. Broadly conceived, tolerance involves choosing wisely in relation to the fact of diversity. Michael Ignatieff ties intolerance to experiences of difference that evoke a response of being ill-at-ease, suspicious, and distrustful which can lead to reactions of alienation, resentment and hostility. Intolerance thus sets up a "primal opposition between 'them' and 'us'" (83). Intolerance fundamentally entails refusals to let the other be, ranging from minimal interference to the inflicting of suffering, even death. Tolerance identified as a distinct virtue emerged in the modern European period in response to exhaustion from suffering caused by intolerance among Christians.

Tolerance never surfaces in pre-modern accounts of the virtues. Specific texts in Plato and Aristotle promote practices tied to tolerance and reveal interest in alien beliefs and practices, but there is no explicit affirming of such a virtue itself. Emphasis is placed on the discerning of singular, objective truths and the ascent from the multiplicities of conjecture, opinion and belief to enduring knowledge of what is singularly true and good. In such accounts one tolerates diversity based on the recognition that persons and cultures stand at different stages of the ascent to enlightenment. Based on such hierarchical ascent, critiques of what deviates from the true and good are justified in light of risks of harm-doing to soul and society. Plato refers directly in a negative way to the tolerance associated with democracy as promoting the free flourishing of diversity rather than the developing of the "right transcendent natural gifts" which recognize the risks involved in the tolerance of "multi-colored" pluralism (*Republic*, VIII, 557-8). While Plato manifests a spirit of tolerance through dialectical inquiry emphasizing respectful engagement of a variety of views, he clearly denies tolerance as a political, civic virtue. Similarly in Aristotle's catalog of the virtues, no explicit discussion of tolerance surfaces. And yet Aristotle hints at an unnamed virtue evoking goodwill

T. D. Conway, *Cross-cultural Dialogue on the Virtues*,
SpringerBriefs in Religious Studies, DOI: 10.1007/978-3-319-07833-5_3,

towards others, even alien strangers. Situated between extremes of obsequious behavior which extols every view and churlish behavior which opposes all variant views in ways which cause pain, the laudable state is the virtue in accord with which "one accepts or objects to things when it is right and in the right way" with civility (*Nicomachean Ethics*, 1126b). But the aim remains the promotion of concord among decent persons, their coming to be "in concord with themselves and with each other, since they are practically of the same mind, for their wishes are stable, not flowing back and forth like a tidal strait. They wish for what is just and [good], and also seek it in common" (1167b).

With such accounts, emphasis is placed on striving unrelentingly toward discernable truth and refusing toleration of the variant. What is deviant and erroneous should be shunned rather than tolerated, but always in the right way and at the right time. While not tolerating a diversity of views and practices out of a commitment to what is singularly good and true, wise persons tolerate others so long as they stand committed to growing in awareness of truth through dialogical inquiry. A similar approach can be found in Christian medievalists who explore ways of responding to the misguided other.[1] While Thomas Aquinas' prime concern is bringing persons to submission to truth through inquiry, guidance or rule, he emphasizes a tolerance of diversity only insofar as it brings some good or prevents some serious harm. Justifiable refusal to tolerate diversity that threatens the well-being of persons condones the taking of severe measures to prevent such risks. Pluralistic diversity is seen as a falling away from truth which risks the insidious influence of the misguided and erroneous who should only be tolerated when their influence can be contained or minimized. Due to the ancient Greek and Christian medievalist strong attachment to notions of fixed, universal truth discerned through rational inquiry or revelation, strong advocacy of tolerance stands without strong warrant. And yet the dialectical method of Plato's dialogues, Aristotle's inquiry and medieval disputations exemplify a spirit of tolerance through their respectful engagement of contrary claims.

With Locke, tolerance emerges as the distinctly modern virtue in the Western tradition. Locke's concern is narrowly focused on the construction of a conceptual framework through which the specific problem of religious conflict among Christians can be both understood and resolved. Seeking a "thorough Cure" for intolerance, Locke presents a broad philosophical argument supporting religious tolerance, but only among Christians (Locke 11). Identifying tolerance as the chief characteristic of authentic religion, Locke calls for the cessation of religious suppression and persecution. Arguing for the necessity and advantage of tolerance, he extols the virtue as a matter of prudential judgment, rationality, and a necessary condition of the public good. The case for tolerance is based on the fact of pluralism, the autonomy of the willing subject, the unintelligibility of coercion of

---

[1] Namely infidels, apostates and heretics standing in varying degrees from revealed truth (see Thomas Aquinas, *Summa Theologiae*, II-II, Q. 10, articles 8, 10, 11; Q. 11, article 3 as found in Baumgarth and Regan).

belief, the recognition of the fallibility of human inquiry, and the role that tolerance plays in the ongoing disclosure of truths. Locke states the negative effects of intolerance and the positive effects of tolerance, setting up a political solution to the problem of tolerance. Religious institutions and individuals must be tolerant of diversity, for "peace, equity, and friendship are always mutually to be observed ... without pretense of superiority or jurisdiction over one another" (28). Toleration must be extended to all (Christian) persons and groups except those preaching intolerance, having allegiance to external princes wielding absolute authority (Catholic Papists), and atheists incapable of taking oaths, the foundation of civil society. "Mutual toleration of private persons differing from one another" (28) will ensure non-interference in the lives of others not sharing the same convictions and commitments. Locke states that in such a society, "all good subjects ... without any distinction upon account of religion, [will enjoy] the same favor of the prince, and the same benefits of the laws ...[and] none will have any occasion to fear the severity of the laws, but those that do injuries to their neighbors, and offend against the civil peace!" (68-9). Locke was convinced such a tolerant society would secure a peaceful polity.

With Locke's seminal account the understanding of tolerance as a virtue is established in the Western tradition and subsequently extended beyond application to Christians. To tolerate is to refuse suppression or interference, to let others be in their diversity. One may live according to one's beliefs and practices so long as one does not violate the right of others to live similarly or undermine the "moral rules necessary for the preservation of civil society" thereby "undermining the foundations of society" (61). Locke's account establishes the long-enduring understanding of tolerance as the act of refraining from interfering with others when one has the power to interfere. One agrees to put up with the other who is different. Thus tolerance is a minimalist virtue; one minimally and indifferently allows others to be in their difference. Such a minimalist account construes tolerance negatively as drawing a limit to acts of intolerance and does not foreclose the possibility of looking condescendingly, even with loathing and disdain, upon the other whom one tolerates. Besides such initial exhaustion from the suffering brought on by intolerance, tolerance is justified as a matter of the principles of consistency and respect for autonomy. By opposing meddling by each in the other's affairs, one maintains a principled distance, refraining from interference in the lives of others, so long as their behaviors do not undermine the peaceful functioning of a pluralistic, tolerant society. A spirit of resigned acceptance of lamentable difference for the sake of peace pervades this understanding of tolerance. With such an account one tolerates with regretful resignation that which one looks down upon, creating a relation of inequality that casts the tolerated in a position of disdainful non-approval and presumed inferiority. Our everyday speech discloses such negative orientation. As Michael Walzer states, "In ordinary speech, it is often said that toleration is a relationship of inequality where the tolerated groups or individuals are cast in an inferior position. To tolerate someone else is an act of power, to be tolerated is an acceptance of weakness" (52). For this reason, no one wishes to be merely tolerated.

Beyond Tolerance: The Virtue of Hospitality

In *On Toleration* Walzer recognizes that "toleration [of pluralism] brings an end to persecution and fearfulness" (99) and may promote on a minimal level "peaceful coexistence of groups with different histories, cultures and identities" (2), but does not promote true social harmony. Walzer calls for the creation of a "shared space" allowing social arrangements through which we can truly coexist with difference (12). But this requires far more than resigned acceptance of lamentable difference or benign indifference toward difference. Given this, human persons in their diversity are called to move beyond the virtue of tolerance to the more robust virtue of hospitality. Michael Walzer calls for "something better ... beyond toleration" that entails mutual respect (52). Walzer never develops an account of this requisite virtue. As the subsequent analysis will explore, Fethullah Gülen envisions an understanding of tolerance that calls us to open ourselves to developing a more robust virtue than this minimal tolerance. Gülen clearly attends closely to the important virtue of hospitality which has been comparatively neglected in the writings of Western philosophers.

Gülen often stresses the commonality found across various religious traditions. The virtue of hospitality is revered within various religious traditions from ancient through contemporary times. The following four quotations from the ancient Greek, Catholic, Islamic and Sufi traditions capture well dimensions of this virtue of hospitality.

> Every stranger ... comes from Zeus, and whatever ... we
> give him he'll be glad to get. So, quick ... give our newfound
> friend some food and drink and bathe the man in the river,
> wherever you find some shelter from the wind.
> The virtuous Nausicaa in
>
> Homer's *Odyssey* VI 226–232

> Respect for the person proceeds by way of respect for
> the principle that everyone should look upon his neighbor (without
> any exception) as 'another self' above all bearing in mind
> his life and the means necessary for living it with dignity.
> Pope Paul VI, *Gaudium et Spes* 27:1

> Humans, we have created you from male and female and
> have divided you into nations and tribes that you might
> come to know one another.
>
> *Quran* 49:13

> If any person enters this house, give them food and shelter
> without asking of their religion or origin.
> Portal Sign, Entrance to Sufi Community, Shiraz, Iran

Buddhist ethics speak of the virtues as shaping a distinctive *ethos* or way of living in the world. The Buddhist may be right in calling us to move beyond this minimal practice of tolerance to a different *ethos*, an abode of dwelling that describes a fundamental way of being in the world with others. Buddhists speak of four heavenly abodes (*Brahma Viharas*) or dwelling places of happiness (compassion, joy, loving-kindness, and equanimity). In *Tolerance, A Study from Buddhist Sources,* Phra Khantipalo emphasizes how central a true, robust tolerance, as understood by Buddhists, is to the Buddhist way of dwelling. Interestingly this central virtue remains unnamed within the Buddhist tradition. *Ahisma* (non-harming) and a host of related virtues clearly negate intolerance, as shown in the details of the following description,

> Intact is the strength of one who keeps his heart in obedience to reason and strays not to ways of ill-will, aversion and hate. He hurts not himself, he hurts not others. He is a blessing to himself and to all else. He becomes beloved of all. His paths are made smooth. None envy him. No one is against him. Nobody grows jealous of him. He wings through life like a swan through the blue sky unhindered, an object of delight to all eyes. Where such a loving one dwells, there all is at peace; for the loving one never interferes with other's rights, with other's freedom, with other's lives, in any way. He helps others in pleasant, kindly acts, endearing, encouraging, energizing and vitalizing all with his benign nature. (*Dhramapradipika of Gurulugomi, IV* as quoted in Khantipalo 26)

Perhaps the closest understanding of this ethos is the virtue of hospitality. Philosophers in the Western tradition have failed to attend to this virtue as shown in its absence in their listing of virtues. The only notable exceptions are the contemporary philosophers Derrida and Levinas, and the latter's considerations are not surprisingly deeply immersed in Judaic religious thought. In contrast to philosophical accounts, religious traditions offer rich accounts of hospitality as a key virtue to be cultivated in communities. When Job sought to evidence his human goodness, he spoke of his hospitable response to strangers (Job 29:16). As described by Matthew's Gospel, the way of Jesus requires the welcoming of strangers into their midst (Matthew 25:34-5). In Chap. 53 of his Rule, St. Benedict discusses the reception of guests, stating, "Let all guests who arrive be received like Christ, for He is going to say, 'I came as a guest, and you received Me'" (Matthew 25:35). And let all due honor be shown. ... As soon as a guest is announced, therefore let ... the brethren meet him with all charitable service ... In the salutation of all guests, whether arriving or departing, let all humility be shown. ... let all kindness be shown him." As far as Christian failures of hospitality, in his *Divine Comedy* Dante reserves a place in the lower levels of hell for those who violate hospitality. In Circle 9, Ring 3 of Hell, he describes those who betray the virtue of hospitality as frozen in hell, with their eyes sealed by icy, frosted tears. In Purgatory VIII, Dante expresses his gratitude for the hospitality of Verona's Scaligeri during his own homeless, impoverished exile.

Historically, hospitality was a virtue revered by the people of India, but its application was extended in important ways by Buddha following his enlightenment. In India the practice of hospitality (*sakkāra*) entailed welcoming and caring for the needs of guests, travelers and strangers. But the range of hospitality was severely limited by the caste system which restricted its practice to members of one's own caste. Buddha transformed the practice, encouraging his followers to be hospitable to all persons, no matter their caste, economic status or religion. In *Old*

Path White Clouds, his beautifully written account of the life of Buddha, Thich Nhat Hanh writes of the befuddlement of a young Untouchable boy when Buddha greeted, touched him, enjoyed his company and found him to be beautiful. Buddha revered the practice of reciprocal hospitality—all persons welcoming each other, offering comfort, food and lodging and valuing each other's presence. Refusals of hospitality were judged as base and shameful. Similar to the Middle East caravanserai, members of Buddhist communities built rest lodges (*āvasatha*) at the edges of towns or in areas located on remote byways between villages so as to respond to the needs of wayfarers. Individuals also anticipated the situation of travelers in specific settings, as shown in their building bridges, digging wells, planting trees and placing water pots at intervals to ease the wayfarers' journeys and refresh their bodies and spirits. Practicing hospitality was seen as mutually beneficial to those who offered and those who received it. Individuals and communities were revered for their practicing of this virtue.

Contemporary Westerners tend to think of hospitality as merely a private act tied to demands of social etiquette, the welcoming of friends as reflecting a code of private social obligation. In contrast, in Middle Eastern society, formed in the virtues of local cultures and Islam, hospitality—the welcoming and honoring of strangers not of one's tribe—is revered as the most esteemed of the virtues, disclosing the true moral character of an honorable, virtuous person. Expectations of hospitality, not limited to family or friend, extend to non-members of communities crossing tribal borders and private households. Wayfarers in societies where travelers often lacked access to food and rest between caravanserais could always count on the hospitable response to strangers. Such esteemed hospitality is neither decreed and enforceable by law, nor formally codified in detailed rules of etiquette. The gracious welcoming of the stranger into one's community and home is seen simply as the humane response to other persons. Such response is understood to be what makes civil society possible and what renders diverse communities more livable.

The foreigner, as shown in its etymological root *foras,* is defined as the one who comes from outside the shared civic life of a community. In speaking a foreign tongue, foreigners audibly announce their coming from a differing community. And yet the foreigner is not tolerated as an uncivilized barbarian who babbles incoherent nonsense. It is presumed that he or she comes from some homeland, some community with manners, meanings and mores whose members speak another mother tongue. The foreigner is recognized to be another human person from another land and people. And yet even, and particularly, as foreigner the other is allowed to enter households and is welcomed hospitably, even being given refuge when needed. The hospitable expectation is that foreigners will be respectfully welcomed even before their origin, identity, language or name is announced. Correspondingly, the guest is reciprocally expected to recognize and honor the ways of the local household and community.

At times of crisis, the hospitable response to other persons may be placed over and above all other demands and expectations. Jacques Derrida offers one of the very rare discussions of hospitality in Western philosophy. He provides a very interesting discussion of the ultimate demands of hospitality in his analysis of Kant's "On a Supposed Right to Lie Because of Philanthropic Concerns", exploring the moral challenge faced by people when persecutors seek to find out the whereabouts of those to whom one has given refuge and protection (2000, p. 71). In his writings on hospitality, Derrida refers to this humane response of offering refuge as absolute, unconditional hospitality. Striking examples of such unconditional hospitality are found within various communities. Marcus Luttrell, an American Navy Seal, describes in *Lone Survivor* his experience of such unconditional hospitality after being seriously wounded by Taliban crossfire which resulted in the death of his four fellow Seals.[2] In grave danger of being captured by the Taliban in the Hindu Kush Mountains of Afghanistan, Luttrell was taken in by the local Pashtun community despite the likelihood of retaliatory violence by the Taliban. In ensuring his care and protection even in circumstances of grave risk to their village, members of this Pashtun community practiced what their ethical code, termed the *Pashtunwali,* expected of them. Such a code required their "sharing of the pot" (*lokhay warkawal*), the opening of their community to any and all persons at risk or suffering. Pashtuns viewed their Islamic faith and cultural tradition as requiring such magnanimous hospitality. In a similar way the Chambonnais community of southern France practiced a supererogatory level of hospitality when they hid thousands of Jewish refugees in their homes in circumstances of both grave risk and scarce material resources under the Nazi occupation (Hallie 1994). Having themselves suffered religious intolerance and persecution, the Chambonnais were sensitive to the suffering of others and viewed welcoming at-risk strangers into their homes both as the natural human response and the obvious Christian expectation. Both Muslims and Christians view themselves as *called* to hospitality since they conceive of all persons as fellow creatures equally originating in the creative love of God. Such accounts provide powerful examples of cultural expectations of the hospitable response that allows for the extending of gracious and respectful relations beyond the intimate bonds of blood and heart. Through such a response, hospitality makes possible and widely extends the sharing of the goods of a civic life.

It may be the case that our postmodern world, so defined by its attentiveness to pluralism, needs to attend to a virtue esteemed by more traditional societies, many religious communities and the members of the Hizmet movement. Possibly this virtue identifies what is most needed for understanding how we might maintain the commitments that define our identity and community while opening ourselves respectfully to those who do not necessarily share those same commitments. The Western philosophical tradition offers meager discussions of hospitality. Given this, it is not surprising that the postmodern philosopher Jacques Derrida turns to religious sources identified by the Jewish philosopher Emmanuel Levinas to gain insight into this virtue. Drawing on the *Torah* that emphasizes fraternity, humanity

---

[2] I appreciate my student Brenna McDonnell's introducing me to this narrative centered on the *Pashtunwali.*

and hospitality, Derrida declares that *hospitality is ethics itself* and not simply one ethic among others (2000, p. 151). Like the Buddhists, Derrida speaks of hospitality as an *ethos*, a fundamental way of dwelling in the world. Ethics begins in the fundamental capacity to recognize, receive and welcome the other (1999, p. 27). Far from a minor or insignificant virtue, hospitality is central to human flourishing and truly harmonious social relations within and across cultures. If Derrida and Gülen are right, then what may be most needed in our contemporary world is a move first from intolerance to tolerance and then from tolerance to hospitality.

Hospitality defines a way of dwelling with others which is far different from benign indifference, forbearance or principled non-interference. The hospitable response begins with the simple, but powerful, act of perceptual recognition that the other is present saying "I am here; recognize and acknowledge me". Grievous harm-doing may be rooted in this fundamental failure to recognize and acknowledge persons, that each of us is "a human bring among other human beings" (Gülen 2006, p. 76). Hospitality demands that we perceive that the other person has a face, a voice, and a point of view to be heard. Such a simple act of recognition is at times glaringly lacking and is often a significant source of grave intolerance that may even go unnoticed. Intolerance often sets up a subordination that fosters silence, marginalization and invisibility. Intolerance closes off the self from others and thereby opens the door to the infliction of suffering. In contrast, tolerance allows the other to be, but puts up with the other in a way that keeps the other at a manageable distance. Such distance may protect persons from varying degrees of interference that cause suffering. But such distance itself contributes to misinformation and limiting, disabling prejudgments which can in turn confirm initial disdainful responses. We tolerate the other, but always at a distance. But having never moved toward the understanding interaction may render possible, we keep ourselves open to the possibility of intolerance and the harmdoing it risks.

In contrast, hospitality recognizes the presence of the other and draws the other into interaction, creating a dialogical space that previously did not exist. With both intolerance and tolerance, we remain focused on the self and have no reason to welcome the other. Ignatieff emphasizes that "the systematic over-evaluation of the self results in a systematic devaluation of strangers and outsiders. In this way narcissistic self regard depends on and exacerbates intolerance" (83). Such narcissism fuels the viewing of the other in purely negative terms, often rendering the other "an instance of everything one does not want to be" (80). Such narcissistic response fuels an atomistic individualism focused on the self or my own kind and disables the possibility of encountering and interacting with others. Both intolerance and tolerance end up leaving the other fundamentally unknown. In contrast, hospitality opens interaction with others, based on the hope of learning from them and their understanding of us, mutually helping us to face our deluded or inflated self-images and our misunderstandings. With hospitality, we do more than merely restrain ourselves from interference, we restrain ourselves from facile judgments, recognizing our limited understanding and how much needs to be learned. When we see the suffering caused by intolerance, we are right in valuing tolerance as a virtue well worth praising and cultivating in our communities. Such forbearance restrains the impulse to harm. But perhaps the religious traditions are right in calling us to practice the far more demanding but humanly more enriching virtue of hospitality.

One is hard pressed to identify philosophers within the Western tradition who have written on the virtue of hospitality. Besides the writings of Derrida, there is little philosophical commentary on this virtue. But the twentieth century German philosopher, Hans-Georg Gadamer offers a rich analysis of dialogue that offers resources for exploring a philosophical account of this virtue and an explanation of its significance. His inquiry originates in an awareness of the embeddedness of human persons in a communal tradition among other diverse traditions. Like Gülen, he begins with the basic recognition of the plurality of human communities. All human understanding takes off from inherited ways of making sense of the world. We are born as secular Germans, Turkish Muslims, Tibetan Buddhists, American Catholics, etc. These inherited worldviews which form the scaffolding of our thought, shape our understanding of ourselves and the world. Without them there could be no reflection and understanding. One's confidence in and commitment to such a worldview need not be a condescending arrogance that unreasonably presumes the exclusive superiority of one's own point of view. Rather, one may stand confidently committed to the truths of the home tradition into which one has been raised and enculturated, but in recognizing the centrality of beliefs, claims and practices to the shared life of one's own community and tradition, one reasonably must extend such recognition to other communities. One must acknowledge that other persons also come to this encounter from a locally situated shared social world shaped by a complex array of commitments and practices that form an intelligible view of and way of being in the world. Recognizing this, one attends to other persons as dwelling within a cultural form of human life that can be meaningfully articulated and understood. At the same time such recognition acknowledges the complexity of both such articulation and understanding. In learning of aspects of such a world, one may find oneself far from initially agreeing with or appreciating others' beliefs and practices, and yet acknowledging their centrality and reasonableness within another tradition.

The possibility of a hospitable dialogue is rooted fundamentally then in due respect for persons and the intelligibility of human traditions in their diversity. Rather than resting with passive acknowledgment of such diversity, such hospitable recognition of pluralism draws one toward engagement rather than indifference. One seeks to understand others in both their commonality and difference; one seeks to engage in dialogue defined by a distinctive spirit of hospitality. But such dialogue can be taken seriously only on the basis of respect for persons and the assumption that such dialogue may disclose something of worth.

Such hospitable dialogue places far more demands on persons than tolerance. While tolerance may entail benign indifference, hospitality requires mutual recognition, respect and response. It calls us to the great challenge of seeing the other as neighbor and guest. Literally all other persons are "neighbors" (from the Middle English root *neih* translated "near"), that is, beings close to us on the basis of our shared humanity. Encountering persons from different cultural traditions, religions, ethnicities, or races, we welcome them hospitably as "guests" (from the Middle English root *gest* translated "stranger") to our homes and tables. Hospitality calls us to be aware of the possibility of not welcoming—our tendency to silence, misunderstand, distort and be threatened by that which is different. Often intolerance is rooted in prejudice, fear, distortion and ignorance which bring persons to distrust, despise and traduce others, even before they are encountered and known. Both intolerance and indifferent tolerance risk fixating on differences, blind to any commonalities, keeping others at a safe distance. As Ignatieff recognizes, intolerant (and I would add minimally tolerant) people are fundamentally incurious, uninterested except in so far as the others' behavior confirms their assumptions and prejudgments. Both maintain distance, while hospitality overcomes the distance, bridging the divide. The hospitable person welcomes and engages the other as neighbor and guest, and thereby opens the possibility that the other's world and experience can be understood and might be edifying.

Hospitality also brings us to encounter the other face-to-face in his or her irreducible uniqueness as an individual who should never be reduced to mere group membership. As the philosopher Martin Buber so emphasizes, in such encounters I meet a *thou* who is a singular person, not merely one of a kind (Buber 2000). In encountering another person, we move beyond facile and often inaccurate characterizations passively received from the media and uninformed chatter about groups of persons. We also refuse to reduce this uniquely existing, mysteriously complex individual to one of "them"—a mere one of their kind, representative of an easily and permanently classifiable people.

Opening oneself to the other entails a true wondering about the other, based on the assumption that there is someone present worth encountering and understanding. Such opening demands the practicing of a cluster of hermeneutic virtues: an open-mindedness which requires that we attend to the claims of the other as *truth* claims held with conviction and commitment. It requires a charitable hearing that attempts to do justice to these claims, which in turn requires an imaginative empathy which allows us to begin to conceive the other's experiences in their alterity and complexity. Such responses encourage us persistently to avoid hasty, facile interpretations often passed on unknowingly about the other. Rather than trying to dismiss or discredit the other to ensure the triumph of the self, this response seeks to understand the other's standpoint, so such ideas might "become intelligible without our having to agree with them" (Gadamer 1989, p. 303).

Hospitality recognizes our situatedness in a home that roots, binds and defines us. For example, frequently on Gülen inspired, crosscultural trips to Turkey, Turkish Muslims encounter American Christians, recognizing each has an identity made up of heartfelt and truth-binding commitments and convictions. Resisting facile stereotypes of each other, both welcome the other as a member of a people and tradition, but also as a unique individual person who can never, and therefore should never, be reduced to a mere group member. Hospitality recognizes the human person's origin, his or her ties to a home that roots, shapes, and binds. It is this mutual recognition and respect of such a home that define hospitable encounters. As the philosopher Charles Taylor emphasizes, failures of such recognition and respect "show not just a lack of respect. [They] can inflict a grievous wound, saddling its victims with a crippling self-hatred. Due recognition is not just a courtesy we owe people. It is a vital human need" (26). Hospitality requires that we begin with Taylor's "presumption that all human cultures that have animated whole societies over some considerable stretch of time have something important to say to all human beings" (66). Gülen's Sufism brings him to be open and highly attentive to the riches and resources of other traditions. In his poem "The Guest House", Rumi speaks of the differing ways that "guests" enter our lives, whether these "guests" are feelings, thoughts, or persons. He writes that,

> This being human is a guest house. Every morning is a new arrival … of an unexpected visitor… Welcome and entertain them all. Treat each guest honorably… meet them at the door laughing, and invite them in. Be grateful for whoever comes, because each has been sent as a guide from beyond.

As Klas Grinell explains in his essay, "Border Thinking: Fethullah Gülen and the East–West Divide", Sufis emphasize that,

> Since we are parts of the same whole, we belong to the same creation. Civilizations in the meaning of cultural entities are just different ways of expressing life in this creation. Every civilization has developed some knowledge and understanding, but often failed to see that it was only a partial understanding. From the mystical perspective, however, they are not dichotomous but complementary (81).

Anticipating something important to be learned draws us into respectful interactions with each other. Each encounters the other as he or she wishes to be encountered—with respectful welcome.

Taylor stresses that this view that all cultures have something worth hearing is a presumption in the sense of a "starting hypothesis with which we ought to approach the study of any other culture. The validity of the claim has to be demonstrated concretely in the actual study of the culture" (66-7). He goes on to explore whether we owe all cultures such presumption and whether "withholding the presumption might be seen as the fruit merely of prejudice or ill-will … [or] even tantamount to a denial of equal status". Taylor argues that the presumption of worth must shape our initial interactions with all persons, if they are to be fruitful encounters. He grounds this in the reasonableness of the supposition "that cultures that have provided the horizon of meaning for large numbers of human being, of diverse characters and temperaments, over a long period of time—that have, in other words, articulated their sense of the good, the holy, the admirable—are almost certain to have something that deserves our admiration and respect, even if it is accompanied by much that we have to abhor or reject (72-3). Taylor concludes that "only arrogance, or some other moral failing … can deprive us of this [presumption]". Arrogance and condescension close off access to the other, while humility and respect open access. One begins to see here what both Aristotle and Gülen stress, that is, the unity of the virtues. The practicing of hospitality requires, evokes, and further refines the practicing of a cluster of related virtues. As will be developed in subsequent chapters, this is clearly shown in encounters with persons inspired by the beliefs of Gülen. Their hospitality quickly discloses their patience, humility, kindness, generosity and hopefulness among other virtues.

While the hospitable response is fundamentally oriented toward the other, it also promotes a self-encountering. Ironically in seeking to understand the other, we come to better self-understanding. Often by welcoming encounters with others, we unexpectedly come to understand ourselves and our own home. As Derrida states, "The master of the house is at home, but nonetheless he comes to enter his home through the guest—who comes from outside. The master thus enters from inside *as if* he came from the outside. He enters the home thanks to the visitor, by grace of the visitor" (2000, p. 125). This is experienced in a poignant way on the Turkish cultural trips sponsored by the Washington, D.C. Rumi Forum. In bringing Americans of a range of religious and philosophical viewpoints to encounter the Turkish culture and Islamic faith in travels throughout Turkey, the Turkish hosts grow in deeper understanding and appreciation of their own identities and commitments. Formal programming, but even more importantly, informal conversations bring persons to disclose themselves to others in a way that fosters both mutual and self-understanding. A pride and enthusiasm for who they are as Muslim Turks is manifested by hosts and comes to be deeply respected by guests. So too participants frequently comment upon their return home about how their journey has been equally one of self-discovery as of other-discovery. It is likely that this double-leveled discovery accounts to a great extent for the joy of these journeys (Yurtsever).

Encountering others brings us to articulate and reflect on our own beliefs and commitments, preventing us from lapsing into thoughtless conformity and passive acquiescence. Dialogue with others also encourages critical reflection on one's judgments and convictions, allowing thoughtful consideration of what otherwise may be passively inherited judgments and claims. The philosopher Buber describes the sphere of the "between" in which dialogue takes place, wherein each of us moves beyond our taken-for-granted, largely unexamined familiar world, broadening our horizon to include that of the other. The philosopher Gadamer stresses that in the context of dialogue a "fusion of horizons" may occur, allowing for the widening and enriching of our own limited horizon. It seems that hospitality is the precondition of such a sphere of the between or fusion of horizons. Hospitality opens the possibility of our mutual attending to each other, our articulating and explicating what we hold to be true, good and beautiful, and our discovering of insights and oversights, agreements and disagreements. Most importantly, hospitality opens the space allowing the possibility of ongoing, continuing dialogue and deepening discovery of the true, good and beautiful.

Entering dialogue in such a spirit of hospitality, we stand both committed to our own point of view and open to the equally committed point of view of the other. Such a posture is far from easy and rests on acknowledgement of our human finitude and fallibilism. Rather than affirming a vacuous relativism, it affirms the conviction that, as Karl Popper states, "truth and goodness are often [very] hard to come by" (Mendus 24). Hospitable dialogue is distinguished by an intellectual humility whereby one assumes one is not mistaken in one's convictions and commitments, but remains humbly open to ongoing understanding of and reflection on them. We take the other's truth claims seriously even as they question ours. Through such dialogue we avoid both an arrogant, close-minded, intolerant dogmatism which refuses to subject itself to reflection, revision or expansion and an empty skepticism that concedes all judgments are equally groundless and inquiries are futile. Such humility presupposes that, as finite inquirers, we are always on the way to truth. Such a posture proceeds not from an emasculating skepticism but a humble acceptance of our all-too-human finitude.

Such dialogue requires hospitable public spaces and associations that foster the articulation and engagement of differences. It is rooted in the overarching requirement that we respect persons and their beliefs and truth claims, even when they differ from our own. It brings us to respectfully consider the significance and worth of variant points of views and ways of life. The active intending of dialogue in circumstances that risk grave misinterpretation and misunderstanding renders it a hopeful, but not naively optimistic venture. We commence dialogue with the other, acknowledging that it may not lead to unanimity and may leave us facing a non-reducible plurality of claims. But by actively intending dialogue, we promote conversation and reasonable discourse, activities that foster and sustain human civility and community. Such civility is absolutely essential to democratic society and international cooperation especially in today's world of unavoidable interaction.

During Rumi Forum trips to Turkey, such civility and community developed during the time spent together. Christians, at times coming with negative assumptions about Muslims after the September 11th tragedy, saw their preconceptions vanish in conversations in the homes of Muslim families expressing the depth of their sadness about the World Trade Center death and destruction. Atheistic Marxists' suspicions of the intentions and motivations underlying generous gestures of hosts softened, and interactions brought them to open themselves to unanticipated dimensions of respect and admiration. Extended dialogues on serious topics, light-hearted humorous exchanges over delightful meals, and shared amazement at breathtaking religious and historical sites narrowed distances and built fellowship among these original strangers. These encounters modeled the possibilities that can be actualized in the context of hospitality.

Fethullah Gülen often stresses the role interpersonal dialogue and encounter play in the strengthening of democratic societies, especially those characterized by religious and ethnic pluralism. Michael Walzer states that, "there can be a better response to pluralism [than mere tolerance], it seems to me: democratic politics itself, where all members of groups are [in principle] equal citizens who have not only to argue with one another, but also, somehow, to come to agreement" (97). Democracy requires the learning of such articulating, negotiating, and dialoguing in light of the fact of our differences. This in turn requires the fostering of a range of skills and behaviors, developed in the context of associational activity that teaches person how to deliberate, discuss, make decisions and assume responsibility. True civility in our age then requires far more than a minimally tolerant response to pluralism, in which we prize our autonomy and non-interference with others. Rather such times call for open hospitable interactions, engaging both our commonalities and differences, ever sensitive to the challenge and fragility of such dialogue. We have ample evidence of the strong presence of intolerance within and between societies. Realizing how positive the virtue of tolerance is in contrast to the vice of intolerance, we can still recognize the problematic aspects of remaining minimally with a mere tolerance of each other. Given this, our times demand that on many levels and in many ways we work resolutely to eliminate conditions that thwart and undermine such dialogue as rooted in virtues, work intentionally to encourage the cultivation of a host of virtues bearing on hospitality (humility, patience, civility, courtesy, compassion, forgiveness and most importantly respect for persons) and work actively to seek out and pro-actively create ways of fostering that dialogue which lets that which may appear so alien begin to speak to us. The Hizmet movement not only affirms this understanding of dialogue but intentionally and actively works to further such dialogue through one-on-one encounters and programs, initiatives and institutions that sustain it. The movement places the cultivation of civic virtues at the very center of its initiatives.

The modern French philosopher René Descartes in his *Passions of the Soul* describes the virtue of generosity as the basis of friendship and community. He argues that the inter-religious European wars, which triggered the call for tolerance, were rooted in distinctly unchristian behavior of Christians driven by arrogance and vanity. Generosity directed toward the well-being of others focuses on developing and acting in good will toward other persons that deserve respect and freedom (384). Herein we promote not the passive, grudging, minimal construal of the virtue of tolerance, seen as acquiescence to a regrettable pluralism, but the active virtue of hospitality, which wisely and generously promotes the mutuality of respect which distinguishes persons and civil societies at their very best. Admittedly the practicing of this virtue is far from easy. But as Hans Oberdiek rightly stresses "all virtues are difficult or they would not be virtues!" (139).

Given the suffering caused by intolerance in our contemporary world, it would be misguided to decry or dismiss tolerance as a second rate virtue. Tolerance admirably prevents suffering and allows others to be. But tolerance should be promoted only as a first step toward respectful recognition and inclusion or when we simply cannot rise to what is better. Tolerance minimally allows for non-interference with groups that have been marginalized, persecuted or rendered invisible. It prevents suffering but may in some circumstances maintain the dynamic that makes suffering always possible. Our contemporary world, racked by extremes of fanatical tribalism and partisan self-absorption, pits groups against each other, making us long for tolerance. But our contemporary situation calls us to recognize that more than tolerance in the end is required if we are to *thrive* in a pluralistic world.

Hospitality calls us to move beyond tolerance to a form of recognition, grounded in principles of justice, namely, equality, respect, inclusion and recognition of our shared human capacities, potentialities and vulnerabilities. All of us who are home, thriving in our local communities, would be shaken by the thought of being dispossessed, exiled, maligned, persecuted or oppressed and therefore should generously extend this same recognition to other persons, most especially those at such risk. Hospitality requires personal and public recognition of both our commonality and differences and alone renders possible truly peaceful co-existence of persons who hold different beliefs and practice different ways of living. Such hospitality is the very core of the Hizmet movement.

The recent case of *l'affaire du Foulard* in France may be illustrative of these points. The case concerns the practice of immigrant Muslim women wearing the Islamic head garb in French public schools. Until fairly recently the French community tolerated the practice. But such tolerating in no way brought persons to understand the practices and beliefs of the local Muslim community. But the government then moved from non-interference to intolerant suppression of the practice, generating debate about whether other religious garb and display, such as Christian crosses and Jewish yarmulkes, should be similarly banned in schools. Governmental statements and citizens' comments in many cases revealed that both intolerance and tolerance of the practice were tied to erroneous judgments about the practice itself and facile assumptions that all Muslims espouse illiberal views threatening the democratic functioning of society. As Anna Galleotti expressed long before the practice rose to such controversy, the democratic "liberal principles of openness, inclusiveness, and more critically, of equal respect" (133) provide the basis for viewing the head scarf not as evidence of a challenge to democracy, but as a call for recognition, inclusion and equal treatment on the part of persons, especially minorities, in a pluralistic society. The controversy evidenced that more is needed than tolerant non-interference with practices in a pluralistic society. A mutually respectful dialogue might have both educated French citizens about Islamic beliefs and practices and brought Muslims to articulate and examine the rationale for a range of such practices within their home traditions. Such dialogue might have disclosed that horizons may not be as distant as they initially appear and can be expanded, and commitments critically examined. But such mutual learning and deepened understanding would have required the humble practicing of the virtue of hospitality. Each would have had to be open to and desirous of understanding the other. Such practicing of hospitality may prevent volatile cases from escalating, often resulting in more passionate demands for recognition and intolerant backlashes, further alienating groups of persons. The cultivation of tolerance and, even more importantly, hospitality would prevent the building of such tensions and distrust.

Perhaps in a world that still longs for tolerance, hospitality appears to be a supererogatory virtue. The virtues call us to cultivate states of character and practices that promote human well-being. Supererogatory virtues, displayed by extraordinarily virtuous persons, often identified as moral or religious saints, manifest preeminent goodness beyond what we normally require or expect of ethical persons. The supererogatory virtues displayed in the lives of such persons inspire and motivate us to our highest potential, pushing us to our highest human possibilities. We can conceive of obliging others to cease interfering with or harming others. But can we oblige others to be hospitable? Like mercy and forgiveness in response to harm done to us, hospitality takes us beyond what we can

command or oblige. But given the increasingly diverse makeup of contemporary
societies and global interactions, we may need to recognize the limitations of the
virtue of tolerance and begin to educate persons for the challenges of the far more
demanding virtue of hospitality.

Hospitality becomes an especially needed virtue in societies increasingly
comprised of immigrants by choice or circumstance. To affirm the virtue of hospitality in no way denies or minimizes the demands placed on persons in cultivating this virtue—significant demands placed on our perceptual, interpretive, and
imaginative faculties—and the cluster of other, closely related virtues. But hospitality may indeed be the needed stepping-stone toward developing more robust
dispositions essential to the development of the genuine, pluralistic communities
which increasingly characterize our contemporary world.

In Albert Camus' short story, *The Guest*, a Frenchman recognizes both the risk
and effort entailed in welcoming an Arab into his home during a time when
suspicion and distrust define the relations of their peoples. Camus' character also
clearly recognizes hospitality to be the virtue he must practice, even if others
misread or ridicule his actions. Camus' story speaks powerfully to our contemporary societal and international experience. Increasingly the problems we face
demand that we begin the movement beyond the insularity of tolerance toward
more open and cooperative interactions. Perhaps all of us need to work on cultivating in our communities and passing on to the next generation the practice of
hospitality. Perhaps, philosophers in our age need to open themselves to the
resources of both traditional cultures and religious traditions that esteem this
virtue, left so long unattended by the Western philosophical tradition. And perhaps
all of us need to reflect extensively on how, on many levels and in many ways, in
our lives and our communities, we can actively further an ethos of hospitality
toward other persons.

If it is true that hospitality is a virtue most needed in our contemporary world, it
would be wise and worthwhile to attend carefully to persons who put this virtue at
the center of their communal living. In attending carefully to such persons, we may
gain better insight into ways of living that are morally praiseworthy and humanely
enriching. The remaining chapters of this book focus on the distinctive ways in
which the beliefs and practices of the Gülen inspired movement draw on a rich and
central understanding of the virtues in general and the virtue of hospitality in
particular. Drawing inspiration from the 13th century Sufi poet Rumi, all Gülen
inspired activities, enterprises and interactions stem from and embody Rumi's
universal call of hospitality.

> Come, come again,
> whoever you are, come!
> Heathen, fire worshipper or idolatrous, come!
> Come even if you broke your
> vows a hundred times,
> Ours is the portal of hope,
> come as you are.

References

Aquinas, T. (2007). *Summa theologica*. Vol. I: Part II–II. Charleston, SC: Bibliobazaar.

Aristotle. (1999). *Nicomachean ethics*. (2nd ed.), (T. Irwin. Trans.). Indianapolis: Hackett.

Buber, M. (2000). *I and thou*. New York: Scribner.

Camus, A. (1990). The guest. In W. Fowlie (Ed.), *French stories*. New York: Dover.

Derrida, J. (2000). *Hospitality*. Stanford: Stanford University Press.

Derrida, J. (1999). *Adieu Emmanuel levinas*. Stanford: Stanford University Press.

Descartes, R. (1985). *The philosophical writings of descartes*. Vol. I. J. Cottingham, R. Stoohut & D. Murdock (Eds.). Cambridge: Cambridge University Press.

Gadamer, H.-G. 1989. *Truth and method* (revised 2nd ed.), (J. Weinsheimer & D. G. Marshall, Trans.). New York: Crossroad.

Galleotti, A. (2002). *Toleration as recognition*. Cambridge: Cambridge University Press.

Gülen, M. F. (2006). *Pearls of wisdom*. Somerset, NJ: The Light.

Grinnell, K. (2010). Border thinking: Fethullah gülen and the east-west divide. In J. Esposito & Yilmaz (Eds.), *Islam and peacebuilding, Gülen movement initiatives*. New York: Blue Dome Press.

Hallie, P. (1994). *Lest innocent blood be shed: The story of the village of Le Chambon and how goodness happened there*. New York: Harper.

Hanh, T. N. (1991). *Old path white clouds*. Berkeley, CA: Parallax Press.

Ignatieff, M. (2000). Nationalism and toleration. In Susan Mendus (Ed.), *The politics of toleration in modern life*. Durham: Duke University Press.

Khantipalo, P. (1964). *Tolerance, a study from Buddhist sources*. Eugene, OR: Wipf and Stock.

Levinas, E. (1994). *In the time of nations*. (M. B. Smith. Trans.). London: Athlone Press.

Locke, J. (1990). *A letter concerning toleration*. Amherst, NY: Prometheus.

Luttrell, M. (2007). *Lone survivor*. New York: Little, Brown and Company.

Mendus, S., & Edwards, D. (Eds.). (1987). *On toleration*. Oxford: Clarendon.

Oberdiek, H. (2001). *Tolerance*. Rowman and Littlefield: Beyond Forebearance to Acceptance.

Plato. 1992. *The Republic*. (G. Grube, Trans.). Indianapolis: Hackett.

Taylor, C. (1994). The politics of identity. In Amy Gutman (Ed.), *Multiculturalism, examining the politics of recognition*. Princeton, NJ: Princeton University Press.

Walzer, M. (1997). *On toleration*. New Haven, CT: Yale.

Yurtsever, A (Ed.). (2009). *When I was in Turkey*. Washington, DC: Rumi Forum.

Chapter 4
The Virtue of Hospitality: Gülen's Understanding

This chapter offers an analysis of the emergence and importance of hospitality within the Hizmet movement. While undeniably affirming the importance of tolerance in a world filled with intolerance, its understanding of tolerance can be seen as entailing a call to persons to practice and promote the far more robust virtue of hospitality. The Turkish term *hoşgöru* is often translated in English as tolerance for the lack of a better term. But the Turkish term entails more than the minimalist understanding of tolerance understood as forbearance or indifferent putting-up-with others. The more robust understanding, associated with the term hospitality, shapes the Turkish account of this virtuous way of interacting with persons and distinctly influences the understanding and practicing of a constellation of other related virtues. Stemming from this central understanding of hospitality, a constellation of related virtues radiates out from this center and helps persons better understand the fundamental beliefs and practices of followers of Gülen. This understanding in turn prompts our own reflection on the practice of the virtues.

The Influence of Sufism on Gülen's Conception of the Virtues in General and Hospitality in Particular

Gülen frequently emphasizes human persons' striving for moral excellence and perfection. Exemplary human beings provide a vision of the actualization of human potential for greatness. Such striving for moral excellence is seen as expressing a human yearning for the divine. In the Sufi tradition God is seen as lovingly calling persons, inviting all and promising a joyous welcoming. As the Qur'an states, "To all we belong, and to Him is our return" (2:156). To strive to attain moral excellence is to strive to imitate and embody as far as is humanly possible the perfect traits of the Divine. Sufism attends to the "Beautiful Names" of God which reveal divine qualities and set the basis for human aspiration of the virtues. God is named as *el-Rahmān* (all-Good), *al-Rahīm* (infinitely Merciful), *al-Karīm* (fully Generous) and thus humans aspire to be good, merciful and generous.

T. D. Conway, *Cross-cultural Dialogue on the Virtues*,
SpringerBriefs in Religious Studies, DOI: 10.1007/978-3-319-07833-5_4,
© The Author(s) 2014

Although Gülen never joined a Sufi order, his thinking and living were deeply influenced by Sufism. His work *Key Concepts in the Practice of Sufism, Emerald Hills of the Heart* provides a detailed account of his understanding of Sufism and its influence on his beliefs and way of living. To put his account most simply and directly, Sufism is Islam's inner life. This inner life reveals a path of virtuous living. As Gülen stresses, "Sufism is the path followed by an individual who, having been able to free himself or herself from human vices and weaknesses in order to acquire angelic qualities and conduct pleasing to God, lives in accordance with the requirements of God's knowledge and love, and in the spiritual delight that ensues" (xiv). Sufis seek to penetrate deeply into the inner meaning of Islamic law, practices and rituals enabling them to follow both the inner and outer dimensions of Islam with a depth of humble submission. Both Nursi and Gülen emphasize that the path of virtuous living comes from and is oriented toward God, for "To God we belong, and to Him is our return" (*Qur'an* 2:156). Under the spiritual guidance of a Sufi master, aspiring Sufis seek to understand and progress on the path to God over a lifetime journey. This journey to God is seen as identical with the journey toward ultimate truth and goodness. Gülen emphasizes the plurality of ways to God, stating that there are as many ways as the number of breaths taken by persons ((*Key Concepts* p. 117, fn. 130). For this reason, Sufi spiritual orders (*tariqas*) use differing methods and rituals to guide initiates in their spiritual progress. Gülen details the common Sufi ways observed by all these varied orders (154ff). He sees no substantial disagreement between Islamic scholars of jurisprudence who focus on discerning specific rules of worship and daily individual and communal life and Sufis who focus on attaining higher levels of spirituality through focused spiritual training. Both focus on dimensions of the Shari'a, the Qur'anic and Sunna based Islamic law, developed historically by Islamic legal scholars with the former attending to outer aspects of the law and the latter to inner meanings of the law. Both strive to enlighten and elevate human existence, equally emphasizing true belief and virtuous conduct. Sufis seek to move through the outer to the depths of the inner, focusing on the meaning and effect of religious commandments on the individual's own heart and spirit (*Key Concepts* p. xxi). This inner depth requires a heightened degree of consciousness and awareness. As Gülen states,

> The only difference is that Sufis emphasize self-purification, deepening the meaning of good deeds and multiplying them, and attaining higher moral standards so that one's conscience can awaken to the knowledge of God and thus embark upon a path that leads to the required sincerity in living Islam and obtaining God's good pleasure. [In cultivating these virtues,] men and women can acquire another nature, "another heart" (a spiritual intellect within the heart), a deeper knowledge of God, and another "tongue" with which to mention God. All of these will help them to observe the Shari'a commandments based on a deeper awareness of, and with a disposition for, devotion to God (*Key Concepts* p. xxii).

Gülen describes Sufism as "the way of being God's friend" (Unal 359). Sufis seek to "turn to God wholeheartedly and with a profound feeling of being in His company" (*Key Concepts* p. 54). This in turn leads them to commit more steadfastly to living virtuously, which in turn leads to deepened spiritual awareness.

This spiraling characterizes the rhythm of the Sufi life. Sufis strive to attain advanced levels of both knowledge and virtue through a spiritual self-discipline, simplified ascetic lifestyle, and focused directedness on loving worship of God. The term "Sufi" has been interpreted as referring to the coarse wool (*sof*) worn by Sufis, their spiritual joy (*safa*), purity (*safwat*) or wisdom (*sophos* in the Greek). One who attains such wisdom has been purified and transformed so as to be both humbled (as shown in dress) and exalted (as shown in the attaining of a more perfected state of human being), resulting in the experience of ecstatic joy. In the end, Gülen shifts from such etymological speculations to a direct focusing on Sufis as being spiritual persons who humbly strive to follow in the footsteps of the Prophet Mohammad and his Companions by imitating their way of living (*Key Concepts* p. xxiv). This interpretation places great emphasis on emulation of the virtuous character shown by Mohammad and his Companions. Early on, Sufis were described as saintly persons who led highly moral lives, following closely the example of Mohammad.

Sufism requires intense self-discipline and purification which enable the seeker to live on a heightened spiritual level which in turn deepens and intensifies the Sufi's faith commitments. Gülen outlines many of the fundamental principles of Sufism showing how the Sufi centering on God transforms human relations:

- Attaining true belief in God's Divine Oneness and living in accordance with its demands.
- Heeding Divine Speech, discerning and obeying Divine commands.
- Acting in accord with the demands of Divine will rather than self-will.
- Being open to deepening love, spiritual yearning and delight.
- Interacting with spiritual places and persons to further striving to live virtuously in the way of God.
- Being content with virtuous pleasures and never taking steps toward nonvirtuous pleasures.
- Overflowing with Divine Love and living in harmony with others through the realization that humankind's origin in Divine Love produces human brotherhood and sisterhood.
- Giving preference or precedence to the well-being and happiness of others.
- Always recalling that salvation is possible only through true conviction and virtuous conduct guided by sincere intention and the ultimate desire to please God.

Since the Prophet Mohammad is revered as the most beloved of God and the best exemplar of the Islamic way of life, all Muslims seek to imitate him in all aspects of their lives. In addition Sufis strive to penetrate and live the inner meaning of Mohammad, as providing the key through which they can open themselves to and love humanity. Mohammad's virtuous character is seen as disclosing the virtuous way of human living, the fundamental Islamic ethic.

Gülen sees the concept of *khuluq* or character as central to Sufism. One's *khuluq* shapes one's basic identity and way of acting. The Sufi standard of a well-lived spiritual life is assessed in terms of one's developing a virtuous character as stated in the Qur'anic Sura (68:4), "You stand on an exalted standard of character" (*Key Concepts* p. 73). A'isha, Mohammad's wife, described Mohammad's conduct as setting the ultimate standard of such excellence of character. Mohammad's character is seen as the fullest human embodying of God's traits. As God is all-Compassionate, Generous, Merciful, so was Mohammad compassionate, generous and merciful, and so should all Muslims strive to be. Thus Mohammad is seen by Sufis as "most advanced and greatest representative of human virtue. Developing these potentials to the highest degree possible, he attained the highest degree of human perfection" (*Key Concepts* p. 73). As Gülen frequently emphasizes in many of his writings, persons of virtuous character are respected for doing no harm in word or deed, not returning wrong with wrong, and forgiving wrongs done. In *Key Concepts in the Practice of Sufism,* Gülen concludes, "It is by good nature that a man can be perfected; it is by good nature that the order of the world is maintained" (75).

Sufis view self-discipline as the source of moral development and transformation. While remaining present in the world, Sufis seek to develop an inner core of spiritual strength enabling them to actively shape their way of being in the world (their *ethos*), rather than being dominated passively by the world. This inner core formed in love, patience, compassion and peaceful relations with others enables persons to respond to the world in ways consistent with their beliefs and commitments as expressed in an integrated, self-cultivated unity of spirit, mind, heart and body. All positive human interactions are thus inspired by a love of humanity rooted in the ultimate love of the Divine.

Gülen's Sufism discloses the deep roots of his focusing on the cultivating of the virtues in all his writings. Sufism focuses on the elevating of each individual person in pursuit of the ideal. This elevating entails a striving to attain the goal of a perfected human state of being (*al-insan al-kamil*) literally—"a true human being" (*Key Concepts* p. xx). Such striving requires *muhasaba* or on-going self-supervision, self-examination and self-critique. Such self-focusing is far from a moral scrupulosity. This focusing is directed toward discovering one's inner spiritual depth, followed by spiritual and intellectual effort to develop and cultivate virtues understood as excellent states of character. Ongoing self-examination is seen as rendering possible self-renewal. One studies one's moral faults, failings, and weaknesses in order to understand their sources. Such study helps one to examine and "revive" oneself in a spirit of hope, gentle kindness and mercy. Gülen emphasizes that such self-examination and renewal also draws God's loving mercy, furthering one's nearness to God and acceptance of God's love. Gülen does not minimize the pulls of self-deception and the challenges of such self-examination and resolve. Consciously attempting to avoid the self-deceiving of the self by the self is part of the challenge of developing the virtue of truthfulness, the ideal of which is to strive "to see oneself with the sight of God" (*Key Concepts* p. 92). Rather than seeing this living of an examined life as wracked with anxiety and risking despair, Gülen sees it as characterized by a humility which draws one into deeper, more intimate loving relation with God. He ends his discussion of self-examination with the Qur'anic words of God's response, "Nay I swear by the self-accusing soul!"(75:2) (*Key Concepts* pp. 6–9).

Sufis envision themselves on a journey sustained by hopeful expectation. Gülen explains that a hopeful expectation differs from a wish. In his discussion of *Raja* (hope), he emphasizes that "hope or expectation is [the Sufi] initiate's active quest, through all lawful means, for the desired destination. In order that God, in His mercy, might help him or her, the initiate does everything possible, with an almost Prophetic insight and consciousness, to cause all the doors of the Divine shelter to swing open" (*Key Concepts* p. 39). Divine hospitality is seen as welcoming all. The Sufi remains hopeful, knowing that his All-Munificent and All-Loving God's "Mercy extendeth to all things" (*Qur'an* 7:156) and provides a peaceful refuge of rest. The Sufi's life is also permeated with a spirit of *shukr* or thankfulness for the goods enriching his or her life. The theological virtues of faith, hope and gratitude shape the peace of the Sufi sojourner.

For Gülen the Sufi emphasis on "seclusion" primarily means the purifying of the heart of love focused on the Beloved (God). Sufis "always feel the presence of God while living among people" and "continuously discern the Divine Unity amidst multiplicity" and thus are in all moments with God (*Key Concepts* p. 19). Thus true Sufis need not seclude themselves from other people; they are, as Rumi described, persons with one foot in the center of the compass and the other foot in the communities of the peoples of the world. Sufi "seclusion" is thus thoroughly communal.

But living within community, the Sufi is not restlessly worrying about others' judgments. The Sufi "does not worry about being praised or accused, exalted or debased, or of being rewarded. Such a person does not change, and behaves the same in public and in private" (*Key Concepts* p. 62). Not surprisingly, *Sakina* (serenity) and *Itmi'nan* (peacefulness) characterize the Sufi. Due to such inner states, the Sufi experiences a calmness which allows for a steadfastness quieting all restlessness and indecisiveness. In his *Nicomachean Ethics* Aristotle describes the "great-souled" or magnanimous person (*megalopsychia*) as one concerned with the respect of admirable persons, but not interested in flattery or displays of his own traits evoking others' praise. The great-souled person neither craves nor needs attention. Having attained such inner serenity and peacefulness, the truly great-souled person will not become miserable when faced with misfortune and will be able to regain equanimity even in response to grave misfortunes. While recognizing and cherishing human goods such as family, friendship, health, etc., the spirit of the virtuous person will not be broken. For this reason Aristotle contends that a virtuous person "could never become miserable, since he will never do hateful and base actions.... [and] will bear strokes of fortune suitably, and from his resources at any time will do the finest actions, just as a good general will make the best use of his forces in war, and a good shoemaker will make the finest shoe from the hides given to him" (*Nicomachean Ethics* 1101a).

Similarly the Sufi is not deeply shaken by fear, grief, loss or anxiety. Such peacefulness is the goal all Sufis aspire to attain, confirming the Qur'anic passage "I wish to set my heart at rest" (2:260) in a state where, "No fear shall come upon them, neither shall they grieve" (2:62). Even the fear of death is eliminated, for the Sufi knows that he or she is called to "Return to your Lord, pleased and well-pleasing. Enter among My servants, and enter My Garden" (89:29–30) (*Key*

Concepts pp. 138–142). In *Gulistan* the Persian mystical poet Saadi describes this state of being befriended by God as one in which "The Friend is nearer to me than myself." As both Lover and Beloved, Sufis find themselves naturally extending a gracious welcome to all others.

The Sufi yearning (*ishtiyaq*) for nearness to God, the "Beloved Friend," evokes a joy, commonly associated with the ecstasy of the famous Turkish Whirling Dervishes, members of the Mawlawi order organized following the death of the Sufi mystical poet Rumi who so influenced Gülen. Gülen describes how the elation of such intoxicating joy brings Sufis to spin ecstatically in dance. He writes,

> Say to him who wants to prevent a man of ecstasies from going into ecstasies:
> *You have not tasted the wine of love together with us, so leave us.*
> When souls overflow with the zeal to meet the Beloved,
> Know, O you unaware of spirituality, that bodies begin to dance.
> O guide who incites lovers, stand up and move us
> With the name of the Beloved, and breathe life into us (*Key Concepts* p. 159).

While personally striving for this elated state attained by Rumi, Sufis believe the seed of this state exists within each person, capable of germinating and ripening under favorable circumstances. Sufi communities help nurture this development and foster an ethos of hospitality among members. Gülen's Sufism is distinguished by his extending this good-will, welcoming spirit and active solicitude toward all members of the human community.

Rumi's Sufism has had an enduring influence on Turkish people in general; his emphasis on universal love of God and humanity has played a powerful role in shaping a Turkish Islam distinctively characterized by hospitality. The cultivation of this key inner virtue is the basis for all of the outwardly directed activities of the Hizmet movement—its educational, media, dialogical and service initiatives. Rather than conceiving this movement as a formally organized social movement or *tariqa* with rules of living governed by a hierarchical structure under the authority of a leader, it is a Sufi inspired movement of persons seeking to embody Sufi virtues actively lived in joyful communal action and interaction.

Islamic Grounding of the Virtue of Hospitality

Hospitality, as rooted most fundamentally in the Islamic recognition that all persons are worthy of respect, is a pivotal hinge supporting the Sufi-inspired practices of the Hizmet movement. In their daily experience Muslims draw frequently on the exemplar of the Prophet Mohammad, wishing peace upon him for his modeling the perfected Divine-human and human-human relationship. Gülen frequently draws directly on many of the sayings of the Prophet Mohammad to express this affirmation of the equality and worth of all persons, emphasizing, for example, that all persons are as the teeth of a single comb. He emphasizes that true Islam does not distinguish or discriminate among persons on the basis of race, color, age, nationality, gender or physical characteristics. The editors of Gülen's *Key Concepts in the Practice of Sufism* stress that Islam applies its teachings in all their aspects to both men and women. Thus the Hizmet movement must resist and challenge societal practices of patriarchy and gender roles rooted in debilitating hierarchical assumptions. The masculine pronoun used in English translations of Gülen's works refers generically to all of humanity, both male and female. Gülen repeatedly emphasizes that in Islam all persons *as persons* are equally worthy of respect, for the Prophet states unequivocally that all persons, as coming from God, are brothers and sisters (*Essays-Perspectives-Opinions* 15). Individual persons are deeply respected to the extent that the rights and well-being of the individual person can never be sacrificed for the good of others. In affirming both the free will and responsibility of the individual agent, the person is called to moral agency. As stated in the Quran Surah (13:11), "God will not change the state of a people unless they change themselves." Thus the imperative to establish peace and human well-being is directed to each and every human agent; "Establish, all of you, peace" (2:208).

An Islamic understanding of hospitality is also seen by Gülen as rooted in the view that all persons, knowingly or unknowingly, submit to the laws of God (thus being truly "Islamic"). God as creator of the universe designs the laws of the universe to which all beings submit, even if only on a physical level in following the laws of nature. So too, the love of God as the benevolent Creator of humanity and nature is directed to all persons regardless of their race, ethnicity, gender or culture. On this basis God calls all persons to be brothers and sisters and to treat each other accordingly in all face-to-face encounters.

Central to Islam's understanding of hospitality is its recognition and affirmation of the religions of the Abrahamic tradition pre-existing it. Islam emphasizes that it affirms the prophets of both Judaism and Christianity, thus ensuring the protection of their religious freedom and rights in Islamic societies over time. This preservation of religious freedom ensures the hospitable welcoming and securing of religious diversity and grounds the basis for critiques of religious intolerance and oppression. The ultimate love of God calls believers to the love of all humanity identified as God's creatures. But members of the Hizmet movement never rest content with a mere tolerating of such religious diversity. Distinctive of the movement is the view that persons through their intelligent capacities are called to commit themselves to striving actively to understand each other and to opening themselves to others so that mutual understanding may be promoted. Such understanding and interaction are seen as the greatest promoters of peaceful associations. They recognize what the Catholic commentator Timothy Radcliffe emphasizes drawing on Isaiah (54.2), "We need to learn other languages of faith, extend our vocabularies: 'Enlarge the place of your tent, and let the curtains of your habitations be stretched out; hold not back, lengthen your cords'" (59). Gülen models this "enlarging of the tent" in seeking out meetings with major figures in the world religions. Gülen inspired gatherings, while commonly engaging members of the Abrahamic religions, also promote interactions with Buddhists in Korea, Thailand and Cambodia (Yilmaz 236; Bruckmayr 235).

Such hospitality does not deny our differences or minimize our deepest commitments and convictions, reducing persons to the lowest denominator of commonality. It calls us to affirm our commitments and convictions, while at the same time recognizing those of others. In speaking to a Dominican community in Paris, Albert Camus noted that "Dialogue is only possible between people who remain who they are, and who speak the truth" (Camus 'L'Incroyant et les chrétiens' 372 as quoted in Radcliffe 59). Dialogical conversation brings us to understand better persons of other traditions, while at the same time bringing us to understand better ourselves. Quoting Eliot, Radcliffe points out that such conversation often refines our self-understanding, helping us to "purify the dialect of the tribe" of what is narrowly ideological, prejudiced and rooted in arrogant, contemptuous views of all that is foreign to our tradition. By resisting the temptation to remain within the parochial world of the like-minded, such dialogue develops within us the courage to encounter difference and the humility and patience to expose ourselves to persons of other traditions, convictions and commitments. In so opening our hearts and minds, we make possible the broadening of our world and expanding of our discourse and understanding.

Beginning in the mid-90s, strong emphasis came to be placed by Gülen on the virtue of tolerance as laying the foundation for an active promoting of dialogue. Drawing on the exemplary behavior of members of the early Islamic community in Medina, it is clear that Muslims are called to co-exist with non-Muslims. The need for dialogue is both rooted in and necessitated by the fact of human diversity. But its very possibility and all hope for its actuality rest on there being a fundamental commonality underlying all difference. Gülen's writings repeatedly emphasize that Muslims conceive this commonality in terms of humans both coming from and oriented toward the same Creator; this affirmation provides the basis for acknowledging universal goods and values worth promoting and cherishing by and for all persons. On the basis of this conviction, Gülen seeks to identify goods affirmed as providing the basis for a universal ethic running through all cultural and religious traditions. All human societies value in some fundamental way goods such as life, knowledge, family and friendship. So too they esteem the virtues of truthfulness, courage, generosity and temperance. Such recognitions provide the basis for hope in the possibility of mutual understanding and dialogue, while never denying the challenges they pose.

Gülen actively seeks out opportunities to meet world leaders of different religions and of atheistic or non-religious persuasions, always confident some common ground can be identified. But he and his followers always come to such encounters cognizant of their having a robust religious and cultural identity as Turkish Muslims. To describe this balance of commonality and difference, Gülen often quotes the Sufi poet Rumi who describes the human person as like, "a pair of compasses, with one end in the necessary place, the center, and with the other in the seventy-two nations (*millet*)."[1] The affirming and respecting of both

---

[1] "Nations" refers to the different millets of the Ottoman Empire and the way in which they co-existed. The Ottoman Turkish term *millet* refers to a religious belief community living within the

commonality and diversity are central to the welcoming of another into dialogue. The living of these central beliefs are manifest to all persons invited to travel programs bringing people of different nationalities, faiths and walks of life to meet members of the Hizmet movement in Turkey. Rather than focusing initially on divisive points of controversy or contention, these gatherings bring people to learn of shared aspirations, values, and hopes. Such bridges diminish distance and build trust, which transform the dynamic of subsequent discussions which later may raise points of disagreement or challenge, but can draw on the resources of trust and respect.

So often conflict between peoples in the historical past and our own contemporary age results in their embedded failure to recognize the commonalities they share. Distances become so exacerbated that scant possibilities for encounter and dialogue remain. In an National Endowment of the Humanities Delaplaine seminar I led on historical cross-cultural interactions, some faculty were surprised by the extent to which reading the Christian Crusader and Arab Muslim chronicles alongside each other powerfully showed the all-too-infrequently acknowledged mirroring of esteemed virtues, deeply felt communal aspirations, and appreciation of fundamental human goods. So too the current Palestinian-Israeli conflict shows each group identically committed to its own relation to a cherished land and history and its own people's aspirations for peaceful well-being while refusing the other's identical commitments and aspirations. Gülen is highly attentive to the risks of demonizing the other when we fail to acknowledge our human commonalities. Rancor transformed into escalating rage becomes possible when we so distance and demonize others. In his essay "Compassion" in *The Fountain* (2008) Gülen describes how such a debilitating perspective can transform persons' character and temperament. Unable to move past their rancor and rage, "they incessantly run after wickedness, one evil deed after the other, trying to make the wrong done seem right, failing to recognize both sides are caught in a never-ending escalation of violence." As discussed in his 2008 *Fountain* essay "Longing for Love," "One party carves out the eye of another or murders them; the other responds by running into the crowds as suicide bombers or driving a car filled with explosives through them." All possibilities of hospitable encounter are undermined with such hostilities. Gülen stresses that the only true antidote to such hostility is inculcation of the virtues, especially in the formation of young persons. Rather than focusing on demonizing the other and pitting caricatures of their worst traits against idealized conceptions of one's own best traits, emphasis is placed on aspiring to live up to one's own ideals and esteemed character traits showing an integrity and consistency of character. Describing persons who strive to be of

---

(Footnote 1 continued)
Ottoman Empire. The term later came to refer to religious minority groups who were given legal protection under Islamic law. Central to this term is a pre-modern protecting of religious pluralism. Gülen's referencing of this passage from Rumi as quoted by Naval Sivendi in *Fethullah Gülen ile New York Sohbeti* (Istanbul: Sabah 1997) is cited by Yavuz in *Turkish Islam and the Secular State* (65).

virtuous character, Gülen recognizes, "People of [good] heart are too busy fighting their selves and their misdemeanors to be interested in the misdeeds of others. In contrast, they set an example to others of what a good person should be, leading other to attain higher horizons" (Gülen 2001).

Such dual emphasis on commonality and diversity is central to the educational philosophy of the Gülen schools. In a *Foreign Policy* interview, Gülen reiterates his central affirmation: "We must acknowledge that we are all human beings. It is not our choice to belong to a particular race or family. We should be freed from the fear of the other and enjoy diversity. ... dialogue and education are the most effective means to surpass our differences" (www.foreignpolicy.com/story.cms. php?story_id=4408). Many Gülen inspired schools have been established in countries with highly diverse religious and ethnic populations. Initially these schools focused on providing a distinctive, high quality education for Muslims of Turkish background. But with the expansion of schools by Gülen-inspired individuals, even in countries without large Islamic populations, families of varied cultural backgrounds and religious heritages (Buddhist, Christian, Hindu) were drawn to the schools based on their academic reputation. In his "Islamic Ethic of Education," Bekim Agai cites the example of Gülen schools in Albania with populations comprised of Sunni Muslims, Bektashi Muslims, Roman Catholics, and Greek Orthodox Christians (Yavuz 66). Recognizing that the Albanian government is not interested in any form of education promoting Islamic or Turkish identity, what is taught in these schools transcends and lies deeper than any specific religious, national or ethnic identity. The school places strong emphasis on students coming to know people whose diversity includes differences in cultural or religious identity, abilities and disabilities, and economic circumstances. The schools promote an ethic described as supported by but not limited to Muslims. Teachers in the school believe that in serving humanity in all of its diversity through their work, they are furthering ideals central to core beliefs of Islam as expressed in Surah 49:13 of the Qur'an, "Humans, we have created you from male and female and have divided you into nations and tribes that you might come to know one another" (*Quran* 49:13). Consciously avoiding a narrow ethnocentrism, these schools call Muslims to, "Applaud the good for their goodness; appreciate those who have believing hearts; be kind to the believers. Approach unbelievers so gently that their envy and hatred melt away; like a Messiah, revive people with your breath" (*Key Concepts in the Practice of Sufism* p. ii).

While strongly affirming the humanity of all persons, Gülen inspired schools also attend to the local situatedness of their schools, providing an education reflective of local traditions and cultural contexts. Gülen stresses that "although education is undeniably important for a country's development, the expected results will never be achieved if the young people are not educated according to the country's traditional values" (2006, p. 54). Numerous examples can be drawn from a wide range of articles discussing Gülen schools across continents. To cite but one example, in his article "Peacebuilding in Global Action," Philipp Bruckmayr provides an overview of the Gülen based Zaman International School founded in 1997 in Phnom Penh, Cambodia, stressing its educational program offers an "inclusive, spiritually grounded cosmopolitanism combined with [local] identity preservation" (245).

This approach avoids sliding into a pernicious relativism which levels all truth claims and the commitments that stem from them. Hospitality entails recognizing that both the self and the other stand on some ground, having some home of belief and conviction. Hospitable interactions require neither the adoption of the other's beliefs or way of life nor the other's assimilation into our system of belief and practice. It requires the respectful recognition and acknowledgment of another, who like me, is defined by beliefs and convictions. What it does offer is the opportunity of encounter and through that, the possibility of understanding the other. Clearly followers of Gülen come to encounters *as* persons of faith and conviction. As Gülen stresses in "Tolerance in the Life of Individual and Society," "Accepting all people as they are, regardless of who they are, does not mean putting believers and unbelievers on the same side of the scales. According to our way of thinking, the position of believers and unbelievers has its own specific value ...even though I have such strong feelings and thoughts about [the Prophet] this does not prevent me from entering into dialogue with someone who does not think or believe the same." Gatherings of people from different religious, ethnic and cultural traditions in Iftar dinners, friendship socials, seminars and travel programs manifest the living of these ideals in practice. Even more importantly Gülen schools comprised of faculty of Turkish-Islamic backgrounds and a range of varied religious and local cultural identities witness the sustained living of these ideals. To cite but one example, the Zaman International School of Phnom Penh, Cambodia models such cooperative collaboration through the daily interactions of its Muslim-Turkish and Buddhist-Cambodia faculty (Bruckmayr 242).

Gülen recognizes that our increasingly interconnected, globalized world will lessen the possibility of our interacting solely with people who echo our own beliefs and convictions. As Carroll emphasizes in *A Dialogue of Civilizations*, we may seek to "isolate ourselves and craft the arc of our lives into familiar orbits of people who look, think, speak, believe and pray like us, but such isolation or minimizing of difference is not workable over time. In today's world of global connectedness, we must develop the capacity to dialogue and create relatedness with people vastly different from us. Part of that project involves finding ideas, beliefs, purposes, projects, and so forth, on which we can achieve resonance with each other" (6). Our world is rife with examples of glaring failures of such hospitality and the suffering that follows. Gülen recognizes that policies and political interventions may suspend temporarily the violence that stems from extremes of intolerance. But the possibility of enduring peaceful interactions among persons depends on the far more demanding and substantial task of cultivating the virtues within citizens. As he emphasizes, "Hostility is unacceptable. Relationships must be based on ...love, mutual respect, assistance, and understanding instead of conflict and realization of personal interest. Social education encourages people to pursue lofty ideals and to strive for [moral] perfection, not just to run after their own desires. Right calls for unity and virtues bring mutual support and solidarity, [securing] brotherhood and sisterhood. Encouraging the soul to attain perfection brings happiness in both worlds" (2001). Based on this fundamental recognition, the Hizmet movement has dedicated itself to world-spanning educational initiatives which place great emphasis on formation in virtues.

References

Aristotle. (1999). *Nicomachean ethics* (2nd ed.), (T. Irwin, Trans.). Indianapolis: Hackett.
Bruckmayr, P. (2010). Phnom penh's fethullah gülen schools as an alternative to prevalent forms of education for Cambodia's muslim minority. In J. Esposito, & I. Yilmaz (Eds.), *Islam and peacebuilding, Gülen movement initiatives*. New York: Blue Dome Press.
Carroll, B. J. (2007). *A dialogue of civilization, Gülen's islamic ideal and humanistic discourses*. Somerset, NJ: The Light.
Gülen, M. F. (2001). A comparative approach to islam and democracy. *SAIS Review, 21*(2), 133–138.
Gülen, M. F. (2004a). *Essays-perspectives-opinions*. Somerset, NJ: The Light.
Gülen, M. F. (2004b). *Key concepts in the practice of sufism, Emerald hills of the heart*. Rutherford, NJ: The Light.
Radcliffe, T. (2008). *Why go to church, the drama of the eucharist*. New York: Continuum.
Sivendi, N. (1997). *Futhullah Gülen in New York sohbeti*. Istanbul: Sabah.
Ünal, Ali, & Williams, Alphonse. (2000). *Advocate of dialogue*. Fairfax, VA: The Fountain.
Yavuz, M. H, & Esposito, J. L. (2003). *Turkish islam and the secular state*. Syracuse, NY: Syracuse University Press.
Yilmaz, I. (2003). *Ijtihad* and *tajdid* by conduct. In M. H. Yavuz & J. Esposito (Eds.), *Turkish islam and the secular state, the Gülen movement*. Syracuse, NY: Syracuse University Press.

Chapter 5
Hospitality and Related Virtues: Gülen's Understanding

It has been argued that Gülen draws on a far richer understanding of tolerance than the Western modern conception of passive non-interference with the other. Gülen's understanding more closely aligns with the virtue of hospitality found in a range of religious traditions. In David Capes' comparative study of the Christian theologian Conyers and Gülen, he references Conyers' recognition that this robust understanding of tolerance is "not an exclusively Christian predisposition, for the practice of tolerance is often touchingly and effectively expressed in such religious philosophies as one finds associated with Hinduism, Taoism, Confucianism, and among the Sufi mystics of Islam" (209). Interestingly both Conyers and Gülen hold that all lesser virtues, including hospitality, serve the greatest virtue which is love (208). All the virtues thus further the end of peaceful relations of good-will among persons. Such tolerance is not tied to indifferent non-interference as a bulwark against the infliction of suffering but rather to concerns of human well-being and flourishing. Conyers speaks of such tolerance as tied to questions of the good as "authentic tolerance" or "high tolerance." In this sense the deeper, more extensive virtue of hospitality affirmed in religious traditions is being reclaimed.

The practice of this more robust virtue requires the practicing of a range of other virtues, all of which are emphasized in the writings of Gülen and the practices central to the members of the Hizmet movement. While the emphasis is on the humanistic practicing of the virtues as promoting human flourishing and well-being, for Gülen, as with Christians and Jews, the natural virtues all have a theological origin and end. The virtues as states of human excellence mirror Divine attributes, the goodness of God in limitless plenitude. Islam, understood as submission to a perfectly benevolent and wise Creator of humanity, calls persons to peaceful relations with all other persons. Rather than focusing on overly scrupulous avoidance of wrongdoing, Gülen stresses cultivation of the virtues expressed in an active life of solidarity with others. Gülen often recalls that when asked what faith practices are most important, the Prophet Mohammad called persons to offer all persons they encounter *salaam* (greetings of peace) and to feed those who hunger. Such hospitable greeting opens one to recognizing the needs of others (their hunger, exile, suffering etc.) and to the furthering of peaceful relations with them through a wide range of virtues. Each of the virtues related to hospitality is seen as embodying a state of human excellence and a practice of wise choosing; they are also seen as aspiring models of Divine perfections worthy of human emulation. While Gülen emphasizes the universality of the virtues as found in a range of religious and cultural traditions, he recognizes his discussion of specific virtues is always framed through his Turkish Islamic understanding. But at the same time he is convinced that engaging other traditions deepens and refines his ongoing exploration of the virtues. Central to Gülen writings, initiatives and institutions are the virtues of tolerance/hospitality, compassion, and love. And for this reason they are given featured consideration in this study. However, Gülen's references to specific virtues are wide ranging and extensive; comments on numerous other virtues beyond these three prominent ones can be found throughout his writings. The following discussion will focus on a limited number of such additional virtues which are repeatedly emphasized in his writings, central to the Gülen initiatives, and informed by the pivotal virtue of hospitality, so central to this movement.

Other Virtues Emphasized in the Hizmet Movement

Because of the practicing of the virtue of hospitality by members of the Hizmet movement, we are able to learn of other virtues practiced by them. Aristotle and Gülen both recognize the unity of the virtues. The virtuous person exercising some virtues is well disposed to developing additional virtues since the virtuous person loves what is good and noble. Gülen agrees with Aristotle's emphasis on developing virtuous persons who truly love what is good and seek to develop all the virtues as best they can over a lifetime. The virtues do not stand separate and isolated from one another but rather, as closely linked, bear upon each other. Being disposed toward one virtue helps one become disposed toward other virtues; so too lacking a virtue or having a vice prevents one from developing dispositions toward other virtues. For example the person who cares about the unjust oppression of people will need courage to expose and resist injustice. Kindness will help a person avoid hurtful expressions of justifiable anger. A person lacking courage may not be able to be truthful in trying circumstances. An overly ambitious person may be drawn toward dishonest means of attaining status and praise. Intemperate persons may squander their wealth and be unable to be generous, even when they desire to be so. Therefore, developing a disposition toward a virtue or vice matters significantly.

The strong emphasis on a wide range of virtues in Gülen schools and institutions, explored in the following chapter, is not surprising given the frequent references to the virtues in his writings. Gülen stresses the moral formation of students in a way similar to the approach of the Enlightenment philosopher, Immanuel Kant. In the *Metaphysics of Morals* (6:478), Kant discusses education as intellectual and moral formation rooted in respect for students as persons. He maintains that students should not be passively taught thoughts, but learn *to think*; teachers should encourage and lead them to be *both* thinkers and moral agents, so that they may continue to be lifelong inquirers and engaged moral agents. Like Socrates he describes the teacher as a midwife who facilitates the moral and intellectual development of students, encouraging them to higher and higher levels of perfection. In the same way for Gülen, education entails a formation of both intellect and character. Gülen's writing are full of commentaries on a wide range of interrelated virtues. Most emphasized in his writings are the virtues of tolerance/ hospitality, compassion and love which receive focused attention in this study. In addition the following specific virtues also receive noteworthy attention in his writings and can be seen as holding special places in the lives of his followers. The strong impact of Gülen's writings is shown by the fact that the practicing of these virtues is so evident in members of the Hizmet movement. In reflecting on these virtues, one can begin to discern their interrelatedness—how the practicing of one entails the practicing of others and how they shape the distinctive ethos of the Hizmet movement.

Humility

The intellectual virtues of mind (theoretical and practical wisdom) and the moral virtues of character are emphasized throughout the writings of Gülen. The understanding of both kinds of virtue is rooted ultimately in an understanding of God as both the perfect embodiment and ultimate source of wisdom and goodness. The philosopher Thomas Aquinas contrasts a person wise in a particular area of inquiry (such as astronomy or mathematics) and the absolutely wise person, whose inquiry focuses on God as the origin and end of all that exists and is good and true. In a similar way all of Gülen's inquiry takes off from and is directed toward God. Such an account naturally lends to an emphasis on the virtue of humility, for humankind is humbled before God as the plenitude of all perfections. The prostrations of daily prayer remind Muslims of their humble relation to such a perfect being. Gülen stresses that persons are motivated to be their best when they become humbly aware of the greatness of God which evokes emulation. So humbled, persons seek in inquiry and action to model Divine Truth and Goodness as the font of perfection. Such humility before God evokes the aspiration to live a virtuous life and the commitment to grow in the cultivation and practice of the virtues over a lifetime. Gülen is convinced such virtuous living is in the end what is most truly admired and beloved by persons. He encourages persons to assess themselves and others in terms of this aspiration for virtuous living. In *Toward a Global Civilization of Love and Tolerance*, he speaks of assessing "your worth in the Creator's sight by how much space He occupies in your heart and your worth in people's eyes by how you treat them. Do not neglect the Truth even for a moment. And yet still 'be a human among other humans'" (31).

Nursi emphasized that such humility before God and others does not entail a debasing servility. Humility entails an element of righteous pride, for persons recognize they have the capacity for discerning truth and aspiring to live virtuously. As Nursi stated, "humility is a praiseworthy quality superficially resembling but different to the bad quality of servility, and dignity is a laudable virtue superficially similar to but different from haughtiness" (195). In a similar way Kant emphasizes that persons striving to live morally are at the same time righteously proud and humble. Our acknowledged dignity and worth as moral agents having an intellect and free will fills us with justifiable pride. Our capacity to manage our freedom enables us to live ethically. But the humble recognition that we fail to embody the moral law fully and perfectly helps us avoid both arrogance and dejection. The humble recognition of our imperfection is what motivates our endless aspiration to live more ethically.

Humility also influences how persons conduct themselves in inquiry and dialogue. Thus the virtues of humility and hospitality are interlinked. One welcomes dialogue with others if one humbly recognizes one is not all-knowing. Humble encounters with other persons and traditions open the possibility of one's growth in wisdom. Conyers stresses that such listening to others is directed not toward gaining advantage, but rather the expectant disclosure of truth (Capes 213). Such humility involves a willingness to attend to other individuals, traditions, religions and cultures in hope of understanding and learning from them. Humility fundamentally entails a directedness of the self away from the self toward the other. Only with such humility is hospitality possible; only with such humble openness to and welcoming of the other can dialogue commence. Conyers stresses that the hallmark of authentic tolerance is the "open soul" and "listening heart for which the wise kings prayed." The humble, listening heart opens the door to the virtue of wisdom sought by kings such as Solomon. Conyers identifies this "welcoming [of] the stranger rooted in humility as the practice of hospitality itself." Such inclusive and respectful welcoming "involves not only giving but also receiving in a way that gives dignity and honor to the other" (Capes 214). Conyers emphasizes the early Christian communities' humble practicing of such hospitality and views humility as fundamental to the Christian imitation of Christ, citing the Scriptural passage that "God opposes the proud, but gives grace to the humble" (James 4:6; quoting Proverbs 3:34 "When he is dealing with the arrogant, he is stern, but to the humble he shows kindness") (Capes 219).

So too Gülen emphasizes the cluster of virtues, including humility, associated with the hospitality practiced by the earliest Muslim communities. Gülen describes at length the humility of Mohammad who stopped where children gathered, went where others led him, shared the work of laborers, mended his own clothes, tended animals, ate at table with servants, welcomed the poor, and looked after widows, orphans and the ill (*Key Concepts in the Practice of Sufism* p. 78). Gülen explains that, "True humility means that people know the full extent of their worth before God's infinite Grandeur, and then make the fully realized potential an ingrained, essential part of their nature. Those who have done this are humble and balanced in their relations with people" (79). Because of these traits, they can open themselves to the goodness, wisdom and learning of others. So too humility can lead to fruitful exchanges across traditions. Christian philosophers like Aquinas, in practicing the humility needed to pursue wisdom and truth, drew on the works of Christian, Jewish, Islamic and pagan teachers. And in turn the humble openness of Muslim philosophers to the Greek tradition made possible the preservation and re-introduction of the works of Aristotle to the Christian Medieval tradition. Hospitable dialogue across traditions rooted in humble seeking of truth allowed for the mutual enriching of these traditions.

In the same way, humble openness to others in personal encounters enables revelatory and enriching dialogue so deeply valued in the Hizmet movement. Pratt explores the balance of self-righteousness and magnanimity found in some religious communities which enables interfaith and intercultural dialogue (2010, 191-2). This "equilibrium" reveals a resistance against self-assertion and condescension. In such encounters others are neither dismissed nor vanquished, but rather humbly approached in the hopeful expectation that one can learn something of worth from them. In *Toward a Global Situation of Love and Tolerance*, Gülen describes dialogue as requiring that each approach the other in a posture of mutual respect and humble expectation of mutual discovery and understanding. Herein persons come to dialogue as both bearers and seekers of truth, hoping for further disclosures of truth. The aim is not to defeat the other with superior reasoning skill and insight since what is sought is beyond the possession of the interlocutors—the ongoing disclosure of truth through the inquiry.

A humble openness of the heart rather than competitive desire for triumph sets the tone for such encounters. Rather than delighting in the defeat of the other, recognition of one's own inadequacies and oversights is valued. As Rumi emphasizes, "Before you say anything, first listen" and "O, happy is the soul that sees its own faults" (Çitlak 141). Quoting Nursi, Gülen explains, "Those who are happy about their opponent's defeat in debate have no mercy" and gain nothing (*Toward a Global Situation of Love and Tolerance* 74). Nursi outlines how truth must set the rule of debate, stating that,

> Whoever desires, in debate on any subject, that his own words should turn out to be true, whoever is happy that he turns out to be right and his enemy to be wrong and mistaken— such a person has acted unjustly... [S]uch a person loses, for when he emerges the victor in such a debate, he has not learned anything previously unknown to him, and his probable pride will cause him loss. But if his adversary turns out to be right, he will have learned something without any loss, as well as being saved from pride. In other words, one fair in his dealings and enamoured of truth will subject the desire of his own soul to the demands of the truth. If he sees his adversary to be right, he will accept it willingly and support it happily (211).

Gülen similarly reasons that,

> Debate should not be for the sake of [the] ego, but rather to enable truth to appear. When we look at political debates in which the only thought is to vanquish the other person, there can be no positive result. For the truth to emerge in a debate of ideas, such principles as mutual understanding, respect, and dedication to justice cannot be ignored. As a Qur'anic rule, debate can only take place in an environment that is conducive to dialogue (75).

And dialogue itself must be directed toward what lies beyond each interlocutor. Humility is fundamentally rooted in the awareness of our human limitation and endless yearning for truth and understanding. In a lovely passage of the *Nicomachean Ethics,* Aristotle begins an analysis through which he will take issue with the central conception of the Form of the Good of his beloved teacher and friend, Plato. He writes of the difficulty of commencing his inquiry since the view he is challenging has been posed by his beloved friend and teacher. But he concludes, "still, it presumably seems better, indeed only right, to [challenge] even what is close to us if that is the way to preserve truth. We must especially do this as philosophers [literally "lovers of wisdom"]; for though we love both the truth and our friends, reverence is due to the truth first" (1096a).

Ongoing dialogue, be it between friends, strangers or across traditions, requires a focusing on shared matters of genuine concern, and often such shared concerns are what builds and strengthens bonds between dialogue partners. The dynamic of mutual openness to the disclosure of truth about matters of shared concern is only possible if one has a humble and open heart. Thus humility is, as Gülen recognizes, an essential virtue for human inquiry and dialogue.

Courtesy

Such humble interactions build an ethos characterized by courtesy. Courtesy is deeply revered in many non-Western traditions and was once seen as an essential part of virtuous living in Western societies. Rituals of courtesy in various societies are elaborate and numerous, but many are tied to the fundamental recognition of the other as a person worthy of respect. Seemingly minor gestures profoundly manifest this respect for persons as shown in rituals of greeting in various cultural and religious traditions. The Western tipping of the hat or standing upon another's arrival once expressed respectful recognition of the presence of another person. In greeting another person, Buddhists bow their heads (*panama*) and place their hands together (*añjali*) touching their head, lips and heart. This gesture expresses humility before other persons, acknowledging their sublime human qualities. The gesture is also seen as a daily training in mindfulness, calling the other to be always sensitive to others in thought, speech and action. This greeting is seen as imitative of the Buddha who politely and hospitably welcomed all, even those considered by others to be untouchable. In a similar way, Hindus greet their deities and each other by bowing with palms pressed together and fingers pointed upward before the chest. This *Namaste* gesture stems from the Sanskrit root *namah* (reverential bowing) and *te* (to you), expressing the belief that all persons have a Divine spark within them. Thus the greeting conveys the highly reverential salutation "I greet the divine in you." Such a reverential gesture is also found within Islam. Muslims greet each other by wishing peace upon each other—"*Salam*" returned with "*Assalamualaikun.*" In some cultural settings, Muslims touch their hand to their heart expressing a depth of sincerity in the greeting. This greeting references their ritualized daily prayers that end with the greeting of peace to all those who surround them. Such courteous gestures of greeting carry great ethical significance, and as the Buddhists emphasize, promote a mindfulness regarding all human interactions.

In contrast to the current tendency to reduce courtesy to merely proper decorum tied to conventional etiquette, some past philosophers of the Western tradition recognized the moral dimensions of courtesy. In contrast to Rousseau who critiqued the hypocritical dimensions of ritualized courtesy, Kant viewed courtesy as tied to respect for persons. Kant reasoned that moral living occurs in the context of the performance of duties in the company of others. Courteous and polite responses to persons are required in all human interactions because of the respect due persons. Courtesy can be a clear and direct expression of one's respect for persons. Of course, not all polite behaviors involve respect for persons since the performance of ritualized behaviors may be a matter of mere appearance, deception or even illusion. Thus courtesy can be genuine or disingenuous. But true respect for persons requires their courteous treatment. Kant valued courtesy to the extent that he was convinced that even the mere performance of courteous actions (be they genuine or feigned) is useful in paving the way to genuine respect for persons. He was convinced that in behaving courteously we cultivate respectful treatment of persons. Kant reasoned that even if initially empty, these courteous displays of good will and regard can gradually foster genuine dispositions of respect. Kant was convinced such conventions of polite courtesy may be transformed into morally appropriate expressions of genuine respect for persons. For this reason Kant valued the rules of etiquette, courtesy and social grace. Yet he did recognize that these "tokens" of polite social interaction are not equal to the "real gold" of true virtue, which is right action "in accordance with, and for the sake of [moral] law or virtue" (1978, 39).

In a similar way Sufism links courtesy (*adab*) and moral living. *Adab* is associated with courteous, respectful, refined comportment rooted in ethical commitments. Formation in courtesy begun in childhood is wide ranging, extending from ways of greeting persons and comporting oneself in social gatherings to ways of behaving in religious and civic settings. The refinement tied to *adab* stems from a moral awareness, a desire to avoid acting on blind impulse or passion in ways that cause harm. Nasr explains that, "it is also a way of formalizing human actions in such a way that they display harmony and beauty rather than disorderliness and ugliness. *Adab* even disciplines the body and brings out its innate dignity and its theomorphic nature and teaches us to carry ourselves in a manner that is worthy of the human state" (89–90). Nasr sees its goal as promoting the formation of the virtues of humility and charity and the development of spiritual discipline. According to Sufism," No one on the path to the Garden [understood as paradise from the Middle Persian *pardīs*] can be devoid of inward *adab*" (90).

For Turkish people, such *adab* is also combined with a spirit of *komsuluk* or "neighborliness" directly related to the virtue of hospitality. Courteous, hospitable relations between persons were emphasized by the Prophet Mohammad as shaping positive daily interactions of persons. *Komsuluk* disposes people to relations of respect and solicitude. These respectful patterns of daily interaction are seen as enhancing the quality of life in local communities. To cite but one example among numerous daily practices, the ubiquitous Turkish practice of shared tea-drinking embodies a courteous, hospitable welcoming of persons *as persons* prior to attending to the practical matters at hand. The pause and poise of such practice set the respectful tone of encounters. Gülen broadens this understanding of *komsuluk*, extending it from neighborly interactions within local communities sharing values and beliefs, to interactions among all persons as defined by good-will, respect and concern. Ünal quotes the Hadith passage that inspires Gülen's attentiveness of courteous relations,

> Take note and be attentive to behavior that causes you to love others. Then remind yourself that behaving in the same way will cause them to love you. Always behave decently, and be alert (201).

Loving-Kindness

Courteous interactions are strongly emphasized within the writings and life of Gülen and are manifest in interactions with followers of Gülen. Courteous actions are necessary but not sufficient for moral living. Interactions should move beyond mere courtesy in a way captured by the virtue of loving-kindness. As will be discussed later in a separate section, the virtues of compassion and love have ultimate significance in the Hizmet movement. But tied to courtesy is the virtue of kindness that should shape all daily encounters with persons. This virtue, deeply revered and written about in the Buddhist tradition, is associated with the Buddhist practice of *Mettā* (Pali)/*Maitrī* (Sanskrit) often translated as loving-kindness. Loving-kindness is tied to the broad understanding of kindness (*dayā avera* or *sangaha*), a general term for the approach to others characterized by gentleness, friendliness and loving care. The Buddha stressed not only acting kindly but *becoming* kind in our inner character (*dayāpanna*). The daily performance of kind acts develops in persons a kind disposition from which then naturally flows kind thoughts, words and deeds. Buddha saw this virtue as tied to the virtues of patience, humility, and generosity toward others.

Buddhists emphasize the interconnectedness of all beings as the basis of loving-kindness. They envision loving-kindness as one of the heavenly states or abodes (*Brahmavihāras*) persons should aspire to attain. Such a state promises equanimity and inner peace. In most cases persons tend to be lovingly kind to those closest to them—to oneself and those within one's innermost circle of affection. Buddhists seek to extend loving-kindness beyond oneself, one's kin and friends to include strangers, "difficult" persons who fail to show one loving-kindness, enemies and finally all sentient beings. In the *Metta-sutta* ('Teaching on love') passage in the Pali canon, Buddha describes the boundless range of loving-kindness,

Even as a mother watches over and protects her child, her only child, so with a boundless mind should one cherish all living beings, radiating friendliness over the entire world, above, below, and all around without limit. So let him cultivate a boundless goodwill towards the entire world, uncramped, free from ill will or enmity. Standing or walking, sitting or lying down, during all his waking hours, let him establish this mindfulness of goodwill, which men call the highest state! (Conze 186)

The Buddhist call to loving-kindness is rooted in the fundamental ethical principle to do no harm (*adhimsa*) and to resist inflicting suffering on others and self. It stands independent of agreeing with, approving of, or seeking anything in return from the other. Buddhists believe that persons who cultivate loving-kindness will be at ease and peaceful since they harbor no ill-will toward others. Absence of ill-will contributes greatly to the attainment of inner peace. One meditative practice tied to the cultivation of loving-kindness is the imaginative envisioning of oneself in the place of the other. One wills to treat this other being as if the other were oneself, never intending harm of the other. From this starting point, one seeks then to radiate loving-kindness in all directions to all beings. One hereby lives self-aware, or as Gülen says "alert," conscious of acting with loving-kindness in all one's interactions. Describing how one radiates such loving-kindness, the *Nyanaponika* translates the Buddhist *Simile of the Cloth:*

He abides, having suffused with a mind of loving-kindness
    one direction of the world,
likewise the second, likewise the third, likewise the fourth,
    and so above, below, around and
    everywhere, and to all as to himself;
he abides suffusing the entire universe with loving-kindness,
    with a mind grown great, lofty, boundless and
    free from enmity and ill will.

In numerous passages of his work *Old Path White Clouds,* the Buddhist commentator Thich Nhat Hanh describes the effects of loving-kindness: loving-kindness towards others calms anger, brings happiness to others without expecting anything in return, avoids cruelty, evokes sympathetic compassion and triggers empathic joy. The Dalai Lama speaks of loving-kindness as not a luxury to be treasured, but a necessity for survival given the extent to which it is tied to internal and external peace. In numerous works, he describes the influential power of loving-kindness. If there is loving-kindness, then there is hope that we may have real families, real communities, real equanimity, and real peace. But if we lack loving-kindness and see other beings as enemies to be thwarted, then despite the extent of our knowledge, education or material prosperity, only suffering and confusion will ensue.

Similar to the Buddhists, Gülen sees such loving-kindness as central to peaceful living. He stresses the importance of acting generously toward others, avoiding resentment and trying to show both respect and kindness to others. The Qur'an calls Muslims to practice loving-kindness toward all persons who seek to live in peace (60:8). Hospitality toward others is rooted in this call. One cannot be hospitable without gestures of loving-kindness. Gülen extends this call, bidding

Muslims to turn a blind eye when others do wrong, not in the sense of submissiveness to evil but rather non-retaliation to evil in kind. Like the Buddhist, he holds that one should seek to do no harm, even in response to harm-doing. Recognizing the need for self-respect and concern for one's own well-being, Gülen advises persons to respond with a smile to those who display negative attitudes. The Dalai Lama and Thich Nhat Hanh frequently use such imagery, commenting on the power of the smile in affecting both the self and others. In responding so, persons may nullify unkind behavior with kindness, refusing to hurt persons, even if one has been hurt. Loving-kindness fundamentally requires having good-will toward others. While self-respect demands that one not submit passively to injustice and harm-doing to oneself and one's community, the exemplary practice of Muslims is to be one of loving-kindness and just response to all persons. Even in resisting the infliction of harm to self and community, the demands of justice and loving-kindness determine the manner of resisting the wrongdoing of others. As in Buddhism, Gülen's emphasis shapes a virtuous way of dwelling in the world with others which deepens with each spiraling gesture and action. Gülen writes in *Key Concepts in the Practice of Sufism*,

> Consciousness of goodness is like a mysterious key that opens the door on a virtuous circle. [One] who opens that door and steps into that illuminated corridor enters the "spiral" of a mysterious ascension, as if stepping onto an escalator. In addition to being endowed with this virtue, the correct use of one's free will to do good and refrain from evil will result in an advance of two steps for each step taken: *Is the reward of goodness anything but goodness?* (55:60) (134).

Gülen emphasizes that this wishing of others peace and doing good by them (*Ihsan*) as one desires for oneself, brings an unsought joyfulness which increasingly expands, enlivens, and deepens over time.

Patience

An important related Islamic virtue frequently referenced in the Qur'an (2:45, 2:153, 3:200, 8:46, 11:11, 14:12, 16:126, 31:17, 40:55, 46:35) is patience (*al-ṣabr*). Muslims are called to "persevere in patience and constancy; vie in such perseverance; strengthen each other" (3:200). The open, listening heart is a patient heart. Patience entails a willingness to wait, be attentive, reflect, take into consideration the details of situations, to respond thoughtfully especially in trying circumstances. The patient person recognizes the risk of harm-doing entailed in quick and thoughtless responses. Patient attention and reflection characterize the wise person. Not surprisingly, the virtue of patience is revered in all the scriptures of the Abrahamic tradition.

In the Judaic tradition, the Talmud praises the person who has the virtue of patience, especially the one who, as patient, can endure major challenges. The Torah repeatedly extols this virtue: "The patient man shows much good sense, but the quick-tempered man displays folly at its height" (Proverbs 14:29); "Better is the patient spirit than the lofty spirit. Do not in spirit become quickly discontented, for discontent lodges in the bosom of a fool" (Ecclesiastes 7:8–9). So too Christians are called to be patient in their daily lives, especially in response to challenges which weary them. Christians are to be patient, seeing "how the farmer awaits the precious yield of the soil. He looks forward to it patiently while the soil receives the winter and the spring rains. You, too, must be patient. Steady your hearts" (James 5:7–8). Christians are called to be patient, especially in response to suffering and hardship. Drawing on the exemplary lives of others, "[a]s your models in suffering hardship and in patience, brothers, take the prophets who spoke in the name of the Lord. Those who have endured we call blessed. You have heard of the steadfastness of Job, and have seen what the Lord, who is compassionate and merciful, did in the end" (James 5:10–11). They must seek to, "Remain at peace with one another. We exhort you to admonish the unruly; cheer the fainthearted; support the weak; be patient toward all. See that no one returns evil to any other; always see one another's good and, for that matter, the good of all" (1 Thessalonians 5:13–15). The New Testament calls Christians to live in the example of Christ knowing, "Jesus Christ might display his unlimited patience as an example" (1 Timothy 1:16). Such patience draws on a deep trust in and gratitude for God's benevolence, captured well in the words of the Christian mystic Julian of Norwich, "All shall be well, and all shall be well, and all manner of thing shall be well."

In a similar way, the Qur'an urges Muslims to be patient, encouraging them to "seek (God's) help with patient perseverance and prayer. It is indeed hard, except to those who are humble" (2:45) and to persevere through life in patience and constancy (3:200, 11:115). While striving to use their capabilities with effort and determination, Muslims also trust that all things ultimately occur in accordance with God's Infinite Goodness and Wisdom. In his study of Sufism, Gülen quotes the couplets of Shihab,

> Rely on the All-Merciful in all your affairs;
> One who relies on Him is never at loss.
> Confide in God and be patient with His treatment of you (68).

Listing the good traits and actions, the Qur'an calls persons "to be firm and patient, in pain (or suffering) and adversity and throughout all periods of panic. Such are the people of truth, the God-fearing" (2:177). Patience helps persons respond to situations wisely and virtuously, allowing them to grow closer to God and the attainment of peace. Like Aristotle's great-souled person, this person will be more likely to choose wisely in response to both good and bad fortune. And this person will not be broken by grave misfortunes, having the strength, patience and peace of inner resolve to face losses of what is deeply cherished. Gülen reflects on the meaning of such patience or *Sabr* in his study of Sufism, commenting that,

> *Sabr* literally means enduring, bearing and resisting pain, suffering and difficulty and being able to deal calmly with problems. In more general terms it means patience, which is one of the most important actions of the heart mentioned in the Qur'an. Because of its importance, patience is regarded as half of one's religious life (the other half is thankfulness) (*Key Concepts* p. 99).

Drawing on the Qur'anic verse, "Endure, vie with each other in endurance, and continue your relation with God" (3:199), he calls Muslims to, "be steadfast in following the Straight Path without any deviation, even when Divine bounties pour out onto you. Resolve to endure all difficulties and hardships and maintain your connection or adherence to God whatever happens to you," be it good fortune or misfortune (*Key Concepts* p. 101). Referencing the cry of Job, the Qur'an recognizes "Truly distress… has seized me. But you are the Most Compassionate of the Compassionate" (21:83) (101). Gülen sees the virtue of patience as an essential trait of those most advanced in religious belief, spirituality and closeness to God. Rumi holds this patient traveler must be like a grain of wheat,

> In order to be sustenance for man, a source of strength… a "light" for his eyes, and a substance for the maintenance of his life, a grain of wheat must be buried in the bosom of the earth, germinate under it, and grow to emerge… after a fierce struggle with the earth, and then be sown and threshed, and ground in a mill (103).

In his own life Gülen provides strong witness to the power of patience. Even when extreme secularist groups subjected him to accusations and condemnation, Gülen stood patient and firm in his steadfast promotion of dialogue and peacebuilding. Refusing to retaliate in kind, he eventually left Turkey for the United States for medical reasons but also to avoid escalating tensions. Zeki Saritoprak translates a Turkish text in which Gülen compares those who vehemently opposed him with the Kharijites at the time of the early Muslim community. Facing the difficult challenge of refusing to retaliate in kind to vicious attackers, he writes,

> Similar to the logic of Kharijites, this destructive group destroys everything positive; like an anarchist under the control of hatred and revulsion, they attack everything. They run from one wildness to another, destroying the bridges of understanding and making the roads of dialogue impassable, causing despair in the loving spirits and injecting violence and hatred into hearts that beat with love (2010, p. 183).

Rather than despairing of peacebuilding among opposing groups or retaliating to hostility with hostility, Gülen responded by committing himself to exposing the public to his writings through media outreach, patiently hoping his commitment to dialogue and peacebuilding would be understood and capable of enduring over time. Gülen consistently sought to respond to recriminations with patient deliberation directed toward the discernment of right action.

In the same way Gülen's writings on the 9/11 terrorist attacks called for a patient and morally informed response that would react prudently to this grave wrongdoing in a way not risking the repetition of the suffering of innocents, be it from retaliatory harming or maligning by uninformed generalizations about Muslims. In his essay "Real Muslims Cannot Be Terrorists" in *Love and Tolerance,* Gülen emphasizes the importance of the ritualized gesture of daily Muslim prayers (179). Muslims begin their prayer by cutting off ties with the world, humbly bowing and prostrating themselves before God and clasping their hands in respect. They end their prayer directed toward a peaceful way of living, radiating toward their left and right wishes of health, security and peace. Muslims are called in their daily lives to deliberate patiently regarding all their actions so they can discern how to live in light of this final greeting. But the Qur'an is not alone in calling for this. The words of the Torah, New Testament and Qur'an call persons to reflect on, cultivate and practice the virtue of patience in their daily deliberations, actions and reactions.

Mildness, Mercy and Restorative Justice

The virtue of patience calls us to deliberate and respond wisely and virtuously in all human situations, but especially in circumstances of misfortune, tragedy and hostility which burden the human spirit. Our human condition is one of universal suffering, observed and endured. But suffering resulting from the wrongdoing of others is especially troubling. What is the virtuous way to respond to the wrongdoing we critique and even condemn? The demands of this virtuous response lead to considerations of a number of virtues, often discussed under the terms mildness, mercy and restorative justice. The virtuous person is called to respond virtuously even to others' viciousness. Choosing wisely in response to perceived harms is a highly demanding virtue, both rarely practiced and greatly admired.

Aristotle explores our natural human response of anger to perceived wrongs and harms (*Nicomachean Ethics*, IV, 5). Wrongdoing flares our passions even to the extent of evoking visceral reactions (rapid pulse, pumping blood, reddened faces). But wise persons resist reacting in passionate immediacy without deliberation, recognizing the power of passions unchecked by reason. Wise persons seek to do what is right in response to wrong, recognizing this requires discernment and habituation in virtue over time. Aristotle identifies justifiable anger as a virtue situated between the vices of irascibility (excessive anger) and inirascibility (deficient anger). Persons lacking this virtue may not feel anger at all or too weakly in response to actions causing human harm and suffering. With this vice, they show a callous disregard of or insufficient attentiveness to human pain and suffering. The excessive vice has many forms; persons may have an explosive, quick, extreme, bitter or begrudging type of anger. In contrast the wise person recognizes, is troubled by, and responds to harmful wrongdoing in the right way, at the right time, to the right extent and for the right reason. But interestingly Aristotle is convinced this virtue, unlike the others, is situated not exactly at the mean between two vices, but closer to the deficiency. And for this reason such good temper is often translated as "mildness." When angered, this person mildly, calmly, judiciously responds to wrongdoing. And due to this, he or she "is ready to pardon, not eager to exact a penalty" (*Nicomachean Ethics* 1126a). This person takes no delight in retaliatory revenge and does not seek to return evil with evil. The challenges posed by human anger in response to wrongdoing are examined in a wide range of religious and philosophical traditions. Much of world literature explores ways in which persons meet or fail to meet these challenges. The extent of these examinations and explorations speak to the power of anger in human interactions. Much can be said, drawing on these traditions and writings, but only a few points will be mentioned, drawing on different traditions.

Christian scriptures do speak of the justifiable wrath of God and the anger of Jesus toward the defiling of the temple. But, as in Aristotle, strong emphasis is placed on the tempering of anger and the refusal to do evil in response to evil. In the Sermon on the Mount, Christ calls his followers to respond in a new way to those who do wrong, saying,

> You have heard the commandment, "You shall love your countryman but hate your enemy." My command to you is: love your enemies; pray for your persecutors. This will prove that you are children of your heavenly Father, for His sun rises on the bad and the good, he rains on the just and the unjust. If you love those who love you, what merit is there in that? Do not the tax collectors do as much? And if you greet your brothers [and sisters] only, what is so praiseworthy about that? Do not pagans do as much? In a word, you must be perfect, just as your heavenly Father is perfect (Matthew 5:43–48).

As a reflection of God's compassionate nature, Christians are called to compassionate response rather than rage and revenge. The Psalms describe God as, "gracious and merciful, slow to anger and of great kindness. The Lord is good to all and compassionate toward all His works" (Psalms 145:8–9). This God is "good and true, slow to anger, and governing all with mercy" (Wisdom 15:1). As shown in the discussion of courtesy, all persons are seen as having the likeness of God, the spark of the Divine, even enemies whose actions evoke our righteous anger. When persecuted, Jesus responded in actions consistent with his teaching as shown in the Gospel of Luke. As his enemies approached to arrest him, "[His] companions saw what was going to happen [and] said, "Lord, shall we use the sword?" One of them went so far as to strike the high priest's servant and cut off his ear. Jesus said in answer to their question, "Enough!" Then he touched the ear and healed the man (Luke 22:49–51). Jesus bids his followers to resist responding to evil with evil, calling them to, "Love your enemy and do good; lend without expecting repayment.... You will rightly be called sons of the Most High, since He Himself is good to the ungrateful and the wicked. Be compassionate, as your Father is compassionate" (Luke 6:35–36).

The core Christian prayer, the Our Father, calls God to forgive our wrongdoings as we forgive those who wrong us. Peter asked Christ how many times he should forgive his brother, asking if it should be seven times. In response, Christ replied implying an infinite response, "Not seven times, I say seventy times seven" (Matthew 18:21). All the previously cited passages call persons to respond to harmdoing with love, mercy and forgiveness rather than rancor, rage and revenge. As the Catholic theologian Mary Kate Birge emphasizes, Christ's command to love one's enemies draws "attention to an essential attitude of mind and heart and prescribes a practice, both of which are constitutive for those who follow Jesus. He does so because he has taught those who would follow him to '[d]o to others as you would have them do to you' (6:31), and he has practiced it in word and deed throughout his ministry" (Birge 2013, p. 104).

Buddhists are very wary of anger, hesitating to describe it as a virtue, and not without good reason. Thich Nhat Hanh, a Vietnamese Buddhist monk nominated for the Noble Peace Prize by Martin Luther King, captures well the Buddhist concerns about anger in the title of his book, *Anger, Wisdom for Cooling the Flame,* published close in time to the 9/11 tragedy. Anger (*vyapada*) is described as one of three human poisons, the others being greed and ignorance. Anger starts as a strong emotion or "poisonous mental formation" that requires mindful attentiveness if it is to be positively transformed (2). We suffer due to the perceived harm done to us and others, and our responsive anger causes even more suffering within us. In anger we desire to inflict retaliatory suffering, believing it will diminish our own and other victims' suffering. But anger is like a bomb that needs diffusing. Given the pervasiveness of human suffering, each of us carries within the seeds of anger. The question is whether we water the seed of our anger, allowing it to grow strong over time or water other seeds of compassion and love.

Buddhists are concerned about the blindness of anger which may lead to the retaliatory infliction of pain which then causes further suffering. Anger is a natural human response that need not be suppressed, but must be transformed into a virtuous response. Buddhists bid us to be mindful of our anger—to be attentive to both its sources and its effects—and to cool the flames of our anger. Attentive to the destructive power of anger, Buddha himself lived by the words,

> Conquer anger through gentleness, unkindness through kindness, greed through generosity, and falsehood by truth. Be truthful; do not yield to anger. Give freely, even if you have little... Injuring no one, self-controlled, the wise enter the state of peace beyond all sorrow. Those who are vigilant, who train their minds day and night... Use your body for doing good, not for harm. . . Use your tongue for doing good, not for harm. Train it to speak kindly. Use your mind for doing good, not for harm. Train your mind in love. The wise are disciplined in body, speech and mind. They are well controlled indeed (*The Dhammapada* 188-9).

Buddhists seek to resist developing vices through attentively practicing virtues. For Buddhists to live in the realm of non-harming is to love. Living mindfully leads to wisdom (*prajña*), the ability to look and understand deeply and clearly the sources of harm-doing and suffering. The term Buddha comes from the root *budh,* meaning to wake up and understand in a deep and clear way. The awakened one recognizes that harming (*vihimsa*) in response to harm-doing increases suffering. Only non-harming (*ahisma*) ends harming. Thich Nhat Hanh believes, "When another person makes you suffer, it is because he suffers deeply within himself, and his suffering is spilling over. He does not need punishment; he needs help. That is the message. If you are able to see that, offer him what he needs" (*The Heart of Buddha's Teaching* 196). In place of anger, the Buddhist seeks to nurture seeds of understanding, compassion and forgiveness. Thich Nhat Hanh's reflections on anger in response to suffering shaped his own responses to the harms done to his fellow Vietnamese people. In response to the horrors of the Vietnam War, he founded a grassroots relief organization committed to rebuilding destroyed villages, establishing schools and medical facilities and resettling homeless families until his own governmentally forced exile. He subsequently organized efforts to rescue Vietnamese boat people fleeing suffering and eventually wrote over one hundred books on Buddhism from his Plum Village Monastery in France. His prolific writing, speaking, and grassroots organizing of service initiatives parallel the life of Gülen. Like Thich Nhat Hanh, Gülen has written extensively on, encouraged and modeled mercy, forgiveness and reconciliation in his own life.

Of all the descriptions of God in the Qur'an, the most common ones are the Most-Compassionate and Merciful. The Qur'an describes human persons as having been created well, as noble vicegerents with the capacity to live ethically as God intended. As beings with will and discretion, persons can use their powers to act nobly or ignobly (Surah 95, 4–5). But even when they fail to act nobly, humans still bear the imprint of the divine within themselves. Sufis emphasize that this innermost nature is ever present within persons, no matter how much they become separated and distant from their divine origin. God, as Compassionate and Merciful, always, faithfully, albeit often mysteriously, calls persons back to their best stature (*ahsan taqwîm*). Such divine response calls persons to model these virtues in their interpersonal relations.

Throughout their daily prayers, Muslims are ever mindful of God's all-merciful and forgiving nature. Such affirmations bring Muslims to repeatedly reaffirm and recommit themselves to peaceful relations especially when human relations are strained or severed. Muslims are called to swallow their anger, to avoid feeding it, and to move toward forgiving those who have harmed them (Qur'an 45:14–15; 3:134). Harm-doing violates moral norms and laws, but even more fundamentally damages human relations and causes suffering within individuals and communities. In many local communities, Muslims have developed practical ways of bringing together estranged persons who are suffering from anger, with an emphasis on reconciliation and healing. Similar to Aristotle's conceiving of the virtue of mildness, Gülen calls persons to be patient and lenient, rather than aggressive in dealing with wrong-doing. In *Toward a Global Civilization of Love and Tolerance,* he extols God's forgiveness, compassion, mercy, and veiling of our own shame and faults (37). As an example, he describes the call for leniency in response to the slander spread against A'isha, the beloved wife of Mohammad— "Let them forgive and overlook. Do you not wish that God should forgive you? For God is the All-Forgiving, the All-Merciful" (38).

Gülen describes forgiveness as rooted in the fundamental fact that human persons are capable of both greatness and failure, for he recognizes, "For humans, whose natures contain so many highs and lows, even if committing evil is not essential to their nature, it is inevitable. Even if becoming sullied is accidental, it is likely. For a creature which is going to spoil his good name, forgiveness is paramount" (27). For Gülen, to forgive is to begin a process of healing and repairing. Thus, "it consists of a return to our essence and finding ourselves again. For this reason, the most pleasing action in the eyes of Infinite Mercy is any activity pursued amidst the palpitations of this return and search" (27). He believes it is "impossible for people who have given their heart to seeking forgiveness not to think of forgiving others. Just as they desire to be forgiven, they also desire to forgive," citing the example of Jesus telling the crowd awaiting the stoning of an adulterer that the one who is without sin should cast the first stone (27). Jesus' pointed question called the crowd to be mindful of their rancor and hatred in judging others. According to Gülen the greatest gift today's generation can pass on to the next generation, after a century of escalating suffering, is to teach them "how to forgive—to forgive even when confronted by the worst behavior and the most disturbing events" (29). Only forgiveness can heal over time the wounds of human suffering. He often discusses the importance of modeling the healing power of forgiveness for children in families and schools. Quoting the Turkish literary figure, Ziya Pasha, he stresses, "Diagnose the illness, then set out to heal it" (30).

Forgiveness can begin the gradual repairing and healing of fractured relations. Forgiveness shifts the emphasis from retaliatory justice to restorative justice, emphasizing our coming to grips with the sources of harm-doing and the suffering it causes. Here emphasis is not narrowly focused on punitive responses, although some forms of punishment may have rehabilitative possibilities. Rather, the emphasis is placed on the healing of wounds and restoration of damaged relations. The focus shifts from reducing the offender to merely negative traits and past actions to halting the wrong-doing, encouraging positive traits and actions, and restoring broken human relations. Gülen repeatedly emphasizes that vengeful retaliation is not the way of peace. Drawing on the words of the Sufi Yunus Emre, Gülen advises those who have been wronged to respond as if they lacked the hand and tongue needed to strike back in retaliation (*Toward a Global Civilization of Love and Tolerance* 61). In *Pearls of Wisdom*, he calls persons to widen their hearts, "becoming like the ocean. Be inspired with faith and love of human beings. Let there be no troubled souls to whom you do not offer a hand, and about whom you remain unconcerned" (75). Attending to the Qur'an's repeated emphasis on forgiveness (*samah*), dispute resolution (*sullah*), healing and reconciliation (*ihsan*), he stresses that "love, compassion, tolerance and forgiveness are at the very heart of all religions ("Love, Compassion, Tolerance and Forgiving: the Pillars of Dialogue"). For Muslims, Mohammad's frequent role as wise and patient mediator sets the example of peacemaking among persons (see http://en. fgulen.com/content/view/1800/33/ on forgiveness). Throughout Gülen's writing, the leitmotif, literally meaning a motive which guides, remains reconciliation and forgiveness with no place for wrathful revenge. As Nursi had inspired him, "Our heart is so full of love there is no space for hatred to enter." Gülen repeatedly states our only enemies should be poverty, ignorance and enmity between persons.

Islam acknowledges the right of persons to seek retributive justice, understood as righting wrongs through fair and commensurate punishment and restitution. But it emphasizes that restorative justice is always the better response. Rather than focusing on righting wrongs, restorative justice seeks to address the sources of wrong-doing, respond to the needs of the persons wronged, and reconcile persons. Rather than focusing solely on the past, it stresses reconciliation of past grievances in the present and future movement toward peaceful co-existence. According to Gülen, the key question always must be—what can be done to make our shared future together better? In developing his reflections at length in many texts, he repeatedly calls us to emphasize love, compassion and mercy as our noblest human traits and in imitation of Divine attributes. As emphasized in the film, "The Power of Forgiveness" directed by Martin Doblemeier, these virtues enable us to operate at the "higher frequencies" rather than the "lower frequencies" of anger and revenge. Gülen reasons that we should be willing to forgive and be merciful because this is both the way of God and the way that fosters hope and peace. We hope for such forgiveness and mercy in response to our wrongdoing when judged by fellow persons and God. The words from Shakespeare's *The Merchant of Venice* speak powerfully of the effect of and hope for mercy (Act 4, Scene 1). The wise Portia bids the wronged merchant Shylock to be merciful rather than to seek the exact measure of justice due him, for mercy is God-like, blessing both the one who grants it and the one who receives it. While later struggling and eventually failing to live up to her own insight, she beautifully states,

> The quality of mercy is not strain'd;
> It droppeth as the gentle rain from heaven
> Upon the place beneath: it is twice blest;
> It blesseth him that gives and him that takes.
> 'Tis mightiest in the mightiest: it becomes
> The thronèd monarch better than his crown;
> His scepter shows the force of temporal power,
> The attribute to awe and majesty,
> Wherein doth sit the dread and fear of kings;
> But mercy is above this scept'red sway;
> It is enthroned in the hearts of kings,
> It is an attribute to God himself,
> And earthly power doth then show likest God's
> When mercy seasons justice.

Portia bids the accuser to foresee his own plea for mercy before God,

> Though justice be thy plea, consider this,
> That, in the course of justice, none of us
> Should see salvation: we do pray for mercy;
> And that same prayer doth teach us all to render
> The deeds of mercy.

Seeking a steadfast and expansive practicing of these virtues, Gülen consistently voices a strong message of peace and a call for peaceful relations among all persons, even those whose relations have grown distant, tense and violent. Many of the Gülen schools have been built intentionally in areas rife with risks of violence and hostility. These schools have been described by observers as "islands of peace" which, to use the words of Thich Nhat Hanh, can "cool the flames" of anger and resentment. The members of the Hizmet movement recognize that building peaceful relations among persons is the most demanding, and the most important, task. Peace is a divine name—*al Salam*—and Muslims are called to be agents of peace. Surah 25:72 of the Qur'an states, "The servants of God are those who walk on the earth humbly, and when foolish people address them their answer is 'salam.' Individuals cannot determine and control the actions of others, but they can focus on their own doing of good deeds, even in response to those who harm them. The Qur'an stresses that "Peace is better" (4:128); that you should "fear God and make peace among yourselves" (8:1); that persons should greet each other by wishing peace (*as-salamu alaikum*) and that Paradise will be Dar-al-Salam, the abode of peace. Gülen has consistently spoken and sought to live this message of peace. Even when facing personal hardships, including judicial and personal attacks, he stressed, "We are going to respect our character. We will not harm those who persecute us. We will not seek an eye for an eye. We will never curse them. We will not break hearts, and in the manner of Yunus (the Turkish poet) we will invite everyone to love ... I will not persecute those who have transgressed against me" (as quoted by Zeki Saritoprak 184).

Given the misappropriation and misinterpretation of Islam by extremist groups who seek to right perceived harms through violence and destruction, Gülen responds that, "The method of those who act with enmity and hatred, who view everyone with anger, and who blacken others as infidels is non-Islamic, for Islam is a religion of love and tolerance" ("Islam-A religion of tolerance"). In contrast, he views forgiveness and reconciliation as essential traits of the "Golden Generation" and all their efforts at peacebuilding. As he states,

> Forgiveness cannot be separated from virtue, just as virtue cannot be separated from forgiveness. There is a very common, yet very profound, saying: "Errors from the small, forgiveness from the great." How well this is said! Being forgiven means being repaired, returning to an essence, and finding oneself again. Given this, the most pleasing action in the view of the Infinite Mercy is the one-seeking forgiveness-pursued amidst the palpitations of this return and search ("Forgiveness").

And in circumstances where punishment for evil-doing is justified, the emphasis must be on restorative justice rather than retaliatory vengeance. Surah 16:125–126, 128 of the Qur'an exhorts Muslims to be wise, patient, humble and gracious even when they respond to wrongdoing, stating,

> Invite all to the Way of the Lord with wisdom
> And beautiful preaching:
> And argue with them
> In ways that are best
> And most gracious;
> For thy Lord knoweth best,
> Who have strayed from His Path,
> And who receive guidance.
> And if ye punish, let your punishment
> Be proportionate to the
> Wrong that has been
> Done to you:
> But if ye show patience,
> That is indeed the best (course)
> For those who are patient...
> For God is with those
> Who restrain themselves,
> And those who do good.

Mildness and mercy, rooted in humility and patience, benefit both agent and recipient, allowing for the possibility of restorative healing. Such virtues can be highly difficult to practice in situations of rancor, acrimony and hostility, be it in the current tense political interactions within Turkey at the time of this writing or in other interactions on the familial, local and global levels. The challenge is to remain committed to the virtues of mildness, mercy and restorative justice in times that are most difficult and manifest the great demands of the consistent practicing of these virtues. As the Persian proverb states, "When it is dark enough, then you can see clearly the stars."

Hope

In a world full of human suffering, even at times caused today by extremist Islamic groups who have sullied the image of Islam, Gülen seeks to remain committed in his efforts. The virtue of hope sustains his efforts. In numerous passages in *Key Concepts in the Practice of Sufism*, Gülen discusses the Sufi understanding which inspires him. The Sufi understanding of hope or *Raja* means "waiting for that which he or she wholeheartedly desires to come into existence" (38). Such desiring and waiting are not the same as wishing. Aristotle emphasizes that wishing may be for the impossible or possible (1999, 1111b). We may wish to never be subjected to death or to get a good education, but we make decisions about what can possibly come about to an extent through our own agency. With similar reasoning, Gülen emphasizes "that hope or expectation is not the same as a wish" (39). The Sufi ethic requires far more than mere wishing; it focuses on personally striving to make good choices so one may live virtuously in a way that enhances one's own life and the lives of others. At the same time, Sufis humbly recognize human imperfections and failings. For Gülen, hope is rooted in the conviction that one is responsible for one's own action as one faces the challenge of doing the best one can to make wise choices that have a positive impact. Hope inspires one to work for a better world and to be an agent of the change one seeks. The playwright and Czech President Vaclav Havel describes this spirit-oriented conception of hope in an essay originally published in *Esquire* in October 1993,

> Hope is a state of mind, not a state of the world. Either we have hope or we don't; it is a dimension of the soul, and is not essentially dependent on some particular observation of the world or estimate of the situation. Hope is not prognostication. It is an orientation of the spirit, and orientation of the heart; it transcends the world that is immediately experienced, and is anchored somewhere beyond its horizons. Each of us must find real, fundamental hope within himself. You cannot delegate it to anyone else. Hope, in this deep and powerful sense, is not the same as joy that things are going well, or willingness to invest in enterprises that are obviously heading for success, but rather an ability to work for something *because it is good*, not just because it stands a chance to succeed. The more propitious the situation in which we demonstrate hope, the deeper the hope is. Hope is definitely not the same thing as optimism. It is not the conviction that something will turn out well, but the certainty that something makes sense, regardless of how it turns out.

In hope we make choices and do actions because they embody moral meaning and significance. We marshall all our efforts to do what we judge to be right, hopeful our works will be fruitful, but at the same time recognizing both our human limitations and imperfections.

For Gülen this understanding of hope is fundamentally theological. As a theological virtue, hope has two dimensions—one tied to humility regarding our human efforts and the other tied to confidence in the ultimate triumph of goodness in a world designed by God. Such a conception of hope is found in the words often voiced by Martin Luther King, "The arc of the moral universe may be long, but it tends toward justice." Such hope motivated and sustained his efforts in support of human and civil rights. Similarly Dorothy Day, the founder of the Catholic Worker movement which currently runs over one hundred and sixty Houses of Hospitality for the poor and homeless, emphasized the significance of daily efforts to show love to persons of all races and creeds by working to better the conditions of their lives. And she believed such daily efforts can be sustained only by hope; "People say, what is the sense of our small effort? They cannot see that we must lay one brick at a time, take one step at a time. A pebble cast into a pond causes ripples that spread in all directions. Each one of our thoughts, words and deeds is like that. No one has a right to sit down and feel hopeless. There is too much work to do." In words similar to those of Gülen, she states in "Love is the Measure,"

> What we would like to do is change the world–make it a little simpler for people to feed, clothe, and shelter themselves as God intended them to do. And, by fighting for better conditions, by crying out unceasingly for the rights of the workers, the poor, of the destitute–the rights of the worthy and the unworthy poor, in other words—we can, to a certain extent, change the world; we can work for the oasis, the little cell of joy and peace in a harried world. We can throw our pebble in the pond and be confident that its ever widening circle will reach around the world. We repeat, there is nothing we can do but love, and, dear God, please enlarge our hearts to love each other, to love our neighbor, to love our enemy as our friend (Day 98).

So too, according to Gülen, Sufis seek actively to avoid vices, cultivate virtues and to make wise choices as best they can on their journey—to live a good human life bettering humanity and pleasing God. But this moral striving is balanced with the recognition of humans as finite beings with limited capacities and resources in particular conditions. On their journey of seeking to live a good human life, Sufis are always sensitive to both human striving and Divine forgiving. Such a balance motivates and protects persons from both conceit and despair. As Gülen states, "such people undertake as many good deeds as possible, and then turn to God in expectation of His mercy" (*Key Concepts* p. 38).

Thus for Gülen hope is a theological virtue ultimately focused on the benevolent mercy of God. "Hope is the belief that, like His Attributes of Knowledge, Will and Power, God's Mercy also encompasses all creation and the expectation that he or she may be included in His special mercy: *My Mercy embraces all things* (7:156)... and *God's Mercy exceeds His Wrath*" (*Key Concepts* p. 39). Hope sustains Sufis as they seek ways to reach God in ultimate reliance on His being All-Munificent and Loving. Such Divine kindness is limitless and sustains persons in times of misfortune and weariness but also in times of human inadequacy and failure. Because of the human person's reliance on such a God, "when there are no means left that can be resorted to, and all of the ways out end in the Producer of all causes and means, hope illuminates the way, like a heavenly mount that carries one to peaks normally impossible to reach" (39). Gülen draws on the words of Imam Shafi'i to emphasize his point,

> When my heart was hardened and my ways were blocked,
> I made my hope a ladder… (40).

For this reason, Christians speak of faith as the substance of things hoped for and not yet seen or accomplished (Hebrews 11:1). Hope is not just an anticipation of the future, but a drawing of the future into the present as not-yet. For this reason hope is closely related to patience which entails a willingness to wait, be attentive and persevere. Hope is an action of the heart that both motivates and comforts persons in their efforts. Gülen links hope to patience, gratitude and zeal; "In this context, zeal means constant hope and continuing to serve without becoming dispirited or losing one's energy. It also means seeking an aspect of Diving mercy even in the most distressing conditions, and then relying upon Him alone for His help and victory" (159). Hope keeps anxiety and despair at a distance. In this state of hope the heart rests and can thus be expanded. Gülen draws on the Sufi term *inbisat* which means the "relaxing of one's heart" (115). This relaxing allows for an expansion of the heart, "so that it can embrace everybody and please them with gentle words and pleasant manners…." (115) Living in this state of hope, deeply connected to God and Truth, "we live in our community as one of its inhabitants, being open with and showing respect to everyone" as we seek to do good works (114). In *Essays-Perspectives-Opinions,* he describes the sustaining power of such hope,

> People live in perpetual hope, and thus are children of hope. At the instant they lose their hope, they also lose their "fire" of life, no matter if their physical existence continues. Hope is directly proportional to having faith. Just as winter constitutes one-fourth of a year, so the periods in a person's or a society's life corresponding to winter are also small. The gears of Divine acts revolve around such comprehensive wisdom and merciful purposes that just as the circulation of night and day builds one's hope and revivifies one's spirit, and every new year comes with expectations of spring, and summer, so too the disastrous periods are short and followed by happy times in both an individual's life and a nation's history (22).

Gülen's faith inspires his hope which creates a dynamic that has not faltered or lessened. It is the force underlying and sustaining all the educational and charitable initiatives inspired by his life. The words of Rumi fittingly capture this faith-sustained hope, "Hard work and earning are not obstacles to finding a treasure! Continue to work hard, if it is God's will, the treasure will find you."

The writings and initiatives of the Hizmet movement are wide ranging and have been extensively analyzed from a range of scholarly perspectives—political, economic, sociological, theological and historical—in the past decade. But what fundamentally underlies this movement is a faith-inspired commitment to living virtuously and a focused practicing of key virtues. This is not surprising given the movement's repeated return to the wisdom of Rumi whose "Seven Pieces of Advice" focus directly on the cultivation of the virtues:

> In generosity and helping others
> be like the river.
> In compassion and grace
> be like the sun.
> In concealing others' faults
> be like the night.
> In anger and fury
> be like the dead.
> In modesty and humility
> be like the soil.
> In tolerance
> be like the ocean.
> Either appear as you are or
> be as you appear (Çitlak 140).

Rumi's virtue-focused words shape and sustain the Gülen-inspired educational and service initiatives which have been transformed in an amazingly short period of time into a global force making possible and furthering dialogue and understanding across cultures. All such initiatives are conceived as ways of living and fostering the virtues; their origin and telos thus rest with the virtues.

References

Aristotle. (1999). *Nicomachean ethics* (2nd ed.), (T. Irwin, Trans.). Indianapolis: Hackett.
Birge S. J., Sr. & Mary, K. (2013). WWJD? Jesus, the death penalty, and U.S. Roman Catholics. In V. Schieber, T. Conway, & D. McCarthy, (Eds.), *Where justice and mercy meet*. Collegeville, MN: Liturgical Press.
Capes, D. B. (2010). Tolerance in the theology and thought of a.j. conyers and Fethullah Gülen. In J. Esposito & I. Yilmaz, (Eds.), *Islam and peacemaking, Gülen movement initiatives*. New York: Blue Dome.
Çitlak, M. F. & Bingül H. (Eds.). (2007). *Rumi and his sufi path of love*. Somerset, NJ: The Light
Conze, E. (1969). *Buddhist scriptures*. New York: Penguin
Day, D. (2005). *Dorothy day. Selected writings By Little and By Little*. Maryknoll, NY: Orbis
Easwaran, E. (Trans.). (2007). *The dhammapada*. Tomales, CA: Nilgiri Press
Gülen, M. F. (2006). *Pearls of wisdom*. Somerset, NJ: The Light.
Gülen, M. F. (2004a). *Essays-perspectives-opinions*. Somerset, NJ: The Light.
Gülen, M. F. (2004b). *Key concepts in the practice of sufism, Emerald hills of the heart*. Rutherford, NJ: The Light.
Gülen, M. F. (2004c). *Toward a global civilization of love and tolerance*. New Jersey: The Light.
Gülen, M. F. *Forgiveness*. http://en.fgulen.com/gulens-works/recent-articles?start=70.
Gülen, M. F. *Islam-a religion of tolerance*. http://en.fgulen.com/contentview/1808/33.
Gülen, M. F. *Love, compassion, tolerance and forgiving: The pillars of dialogue*. http://en.fgulen.com/content/view/1339/13.
Hanh, T. N. (2001). *Anger, wisdom for cooling the flames*. New York: Riverhead Books.
Hanh, T. N. (1999). *The heart of Buddha's teaching, transforming suffering into peace and liberation*. New York: Broadway Books.

Hanh, T. N. (1991). *Old path white clouds*. Berkeley, CA: Parallax Press.

Kant, I. (1978). *Anthropology from a Pragmatic point of view*. Carbondale: Southern Illinois University Press.

Kant, I. (1996). *Metaphysics of morals*. New York: Cambridge.

Nasr, S. H. (2007). *The garden of truth, the vision and promise of sufism, Islam's mystical tradition*. New York: Harper.

Nursi, B. S. (2004). *The flashes collection*. (Trans.) Şükran Vahide. Istanbul: Nur Publishers.

Pratt, D. (2010). Islamic prospects for interreligious dialogue: The voice of Fethulah Gülen. In J. Esposito & I. Yilmaz (Eds.), *Islam and peacemaking, Gülen movement initiatives*. New York: Blue Dome Press.

Saritoprak, Z. (2010). Fethullah gülen's theology of peacebuilding. In J. Esposito & I. Yilmaz (Eds.), *Islam and peacebuilding, gülen initiatives*. New York: Blue Dome Press.

Shakespeare, (1998). *The merchant of Venice*. New York: Signet Classics.

Ünal, A. & Williams, A. (2000). *Advocate of dialogue*. Fairfax, VA: The Fountain.

Chapter 6
Education: Development of the Intellectual and Moral Virtues

Education as Virtue Focused

Since its inception, the Hizmet movement has been essentially an educational and social movement focused on the cultivation of both intellectual and moral virtues in the context of service to community. Intellectual understanding and virtuous living are seen as inextricably linked and mutually supportive. In his *Nicomachean Ethics,* Aristotle stressed the human capacity to attain excellence of both intellect and character. The virtues are such states of human excellence or *arête.* Both intellectual and moral virtues are necessary in living a good life. Aristotle further differentiates two kinds of virtuous states of the intellect. Reason may be directed toward understanding "beings whose principles do not admit of being otherwise than they are," describing such inquiry as scientific reasoning as found in understanding the basic laws of the universe (1139a). Such reasoning is directed toward attaining knowledge of truth for its own sake. Humans, as beings who wonder and delight in knowing the truth of things, naturally aspire to such wisdom. The endless questioning of children regarding what, how and why things are as they are attests to this distinctly human aspiration.

In a similar way Gülen stresses the natural inquisitiveness of human persons and sees reflection as the core of human living and the Islamic way of life. Gülen interprets *Tafakkur* (reflection) as thinking deeply and systematically on a subject, describing it as "the heart's lamp, the soul's food, the spirit of knowledge, and the essence and light of the Islamic way of life" (*Key Concepts* p. 10). Reflection enables the books of creation and revelation to be studied and understood. He cites the words of the Prophet Mohammad that praise this human capacity, while recognizing its imperfections and limits; "No act of worship is as meritorious as reflection. So reflect on God's bounties and the works of His Power" (10). Since reflection on the world, "the book of existence," is equated with reflection on the ways of God, "the believer who studies and accurately comprehends this… and then designs his or her life accordingly, will follow the way of guidance and righteousness…" (12). Created as intelligent beings, human persons seek to discover the meaning and value of existence in all its profound complexity. As beings

T. D. Conway, *Cross-cultural Dialogue on the Virtues,*
SpringerBriefs in Religious Studies, DOI: 10.1007/978-3-319-07833-5_6,
© The Author(s) 2014

capable of understanding, cherishing and promoting all that is true, good and beautiful, humans are called to understand and benefit humankind and nature. Gülen sees the pursuit of such knowledge as affirmed in the revelation of the Qur'an and the exemplary life of Mohammad. To seek knowledge is to be more humanly alive. As Gülen states, "Since 'real' life is possible only through knowledge, those who neglect learning and teaching are considered 'dead' even though they are still alive. We were created to learn and communicate what we have learned to others" (Ünal 79). Since ongoing personal and communal growth is dependent on reflection, education becomes the central human concern. When inquiry is directed toward the knowing of truth valued in itself, what becomes known can provide a guide for one's living and the basis for personal and communal improvement. Strongly affirming the human person as a rational inquirer, Gülen also attends to the finitude of our condition which subjects human inquiry to error and limitation. Such emphasis calls the inquirer to be humble and open to the ongoing demands of inquiry and the insights of fellow inquirers. Genuine inquiry and debate are not directed to the triumph of the ego and the submission of others in defeat, but rather the pursuit of wisdom, an intellectual virtue. In such a spirit, education is a good always worth promoting. Consistent with this understanding, an ethos of collaborative dialogue directed toward the disclosure of truth must shape the pedagogy and context of teaching and learning. Both teachers and students must be oriented toward wisdom, as grounded in the disclosure of truth. Service to the truth and the goods it promotes must be the goal rather than service to self.

In contrast with inquiry directed toward truth, Aristotle also discusses inquiry as directed toward right action. He describes another exercising of the human intellect directed toward what is not determined by necessity, as in the inquiry of metaphysics and the sciences, and therefore within the realm of choice, as in the inquiry of ethics and political science. The virtues of moral character have to do with reason and desire directed toward decision making. Humans are capable of voluntary actions which flow from their desires. But even more importantly humans are capable of making choices or decisions involving desire combined with thought. Humans can function as agents because they have the capacity to deliberate about and choose their actions, and for this reason are held responsible for them. Persons who develop the capacity to choose wisely have developed the intellectual virtue of Practical Wisdom or Prudence. In his *Nicomachean Ethics* Aristotle states that the practically wise person is "able to deliberate finely about things that are good and beneficial for himself [and others and]... about what sorts of things promote living well in general" (1140a). Thus Practical Wisdom "is a state of grasping truth, involving reason, concerned with action about things that are good or bad for a human being" (1140b). Practical wisdom is focused on things which we can to an extent control in specific circumstances. Recognizing the role of deliberation, the practically wise person pauses to explore possible courses of action, developing over time the capacity to reason well in a range of human situations. Aristotle notes that, "Further, one person may deliberate a long time before reaching the right thing to do, while another reaches it quickly. Nor, then, is the first condition necessary for good deliberation; good deliberation is correctness that accords with what is beneficial, about the right thing [to be done], in the right way, and at the right time" (1142b). Such practical wisdom is not cleverness, an intellectual keenness in attaining *any* goal, be it praiseworthy or not. Thus, practical wisdom is not mere "cleverness, though it requires this capacity [a sharpness of intellect directed toward ends]. [Practical wisdom], this eye of the soul, requires [moral] virtue to reach its fully developed state… for this [best good] is apparent only to the good person; for vice perverts us and produces false views about the principles of actions. Evidently, then we cannot be [practically wise] without being good" (1144a).

To aspire to grow in wisdom—both intellectual and practical—is to recognize the unique position of responsibility humans hold within the broad scheme of things due to our having both intellect and will. To exercise the moral virtues requires the development of relevant knowledge and practical wisdom which enable persons to figure out the morally right choices here and now in particular circumstances. This demanding challenge requires formation of both mind and character. So too Gülen holds that humans, created as rational inquirers, have the capacity for right decisions. But these decisions require deliberation informed by right reasoning. As Gülen stresses, "Right reasons depend on having a sound mind and… sound thinking. As science and knowledge illuminate and develop one's mind, those deprived of science and knowledge cannot reach right decisions and always are exposed to deception and misguidance" (Ünal 79). Thus the pursuits of knowledge and virtuous living cannot be separated.

All Gülen initiatives, whether focused on education, media, business or charity, stem directly or indirectly from this pivotal emphasis on cultivating both the intellectual and moral virtues. Gülen often speaks of developing a "Golden Generation" of young persons directed toward such an aspiration. Such development is seen as promoting human flourishing and living as befits human nature conceived as originating from and directed toward God. The central emphasis of all educational initiatives remains consistently focused on service to God and humanity, drawing its inspiration from Mohammad's directive for all Muslims, male and female, to pursue knowledge even to the farthest reaches of the earth. Personal, familial and professional successes are seen through this moral lens. Education, while developing natural human capacities and identifying personal talents and ambitions, is seen as preparing persons for such communitarian service, through the development of their capabilities and character. When asked how to encourage lives of service within Muslim communities, Gülen frequently replies that, "A mosque would be nice; a school would be better; the combination of the two would be best" (as quoted in Ünal and Williams 11).

Gülen believes that passive control of a population can be accomplished simply by starving people of opportunities to grow in knowledge and critical judgment leading to better informed choices regarding personal and civic life. For this reason education is seen as inextricably tied to the long-term promotion of social justice and human development. Such liberating education equips citizens to examine critically their life conditions, envision better possibilities, and solve problems. Gülen repeatedly states that the strategy of force must be replaced by the art of gentle, rational persuasion modeled and refined in education. He emphasizes, "As for getting others to accept your ways, the days of getting things done by brute force are over. In today's enlightened world, the only way to get others to accept your ideas is by persuasion and convincing arguments. Those who resort to brute force to reach their goals are intellectually bankrupt souls" (*Key Concepts* p. vi). For this reason Gülen encourages the well-educated and professionally trained members of society to commit themselves to the generous support of broad based educational initiatives.

Education as Promoting Wisdom, the Intellectual Virtue of the Mind

Growing from an initial hospitable gathering of students, Gülen's vision developed to include the private funding and administering of hundreds of educational institutions—elementary schools, high schools, college preparatory schools, universities and educational dormitories in over fifty countries (Gülen 1998). Independently and locally run, these institutions share a pedagogical philosophy and draw on private Turkish entrepreneurs for material and human resources. Contrasting secular education which emphasizes technological and scientific inquiry in service of human mastery and improvement with Islamic religious education which emphasizes spiritual formation in devout submission to God's will, Gülen's educational philosophy links spiritual and scientific understanding with the humanistic aim of improving the current and long-term human condition in ways that befit and honor humanity's material and spiritual nature. For this reason supporting education is seen as a noble endeavor.

Gülen schools place great emphasis on the study of the natural sciences. Gülen acknowledges the vast scientific and technological development generated by the Western Enlightenment tradition. Following the analysis of Nursi, he views this tradition as producing two strains, a positive strain worth following and a negative strain worth challenging. Western sciences can be seen as dimensions of human inquiry directed toward the attaining of intellectual wisdom and human flourishing. Western sciences can also be seen as asserting a naturalistic positivism which reduces all of reality to a materialism void of ends, values and concern for the metaphysical and spiritual dimensions of reality. Nursi clarified this issue for Gülen, writing that, "It should not be misunderstood: Europe is two. One follows the sciences which serve justice and right and the industries beneficial for the life of society through the inspiration it has received from true Christianity; the first Europe I am not addressing. I am rather addressing the second corrupt Europe which, through the darkness of the philosophy of Naturalism, supposing the evils of civilization to be virtues, has driven mankind to vice and misguidance" (Nursi 160).

While appreciating the West's productivity in science and technology which may be used to serve good ends, his reservations also stem from their philosophical origin in an Enlightenment tradition that valued intellectual enlightenment while often disdaining religious belief. In contrast, Gülen seeks to wed intellectual and spiritual enlightenment, thereby ensuring the human advancement based on the development of both mind/intelligence and heart/spirit. In this conception both the origin and telos of education are grounded in the understanding of God as creator of an inherently intelligible universe directed toward the good. Education focusing on the cultivation of both the intellectual and moral virtues flows naturally from this foundational understanding and is directed to the promotion of human flourishing, but always in the supportive context of peaceful interpersonal, social and international relations. Gülen sees this vision of education as consistent with but not limited to the Islamic religious tradition.

Gülen schools are well known for their strong emphasis on both the natural sciences and moral character formation broadly interpreted to speak to a range of religious traditions. In many regions the emphasis on character formation promotes peaceful relations which in turn allow students to focus on their academic studies in both the humanistic and scientific disciplines. Due to this educational orientation a vast network of schools on primary, secondary and university levels have been established in societies on a number of continents, most especially in countries with highly limited educational resources and rife with the potential for religious, ethnic and political conflict. In building schools, priority was given to regions in which there was potential for escalating ethnic-religious conflict and bloodshed (such as in Albania, Kosovo, Macedonia, the Philippines, Banda Aceh and most recently Northern Iraq) which would undermine hopes for education of young people (Esposito 2010, p. 13). One such example is described by Thomas Michel, former Vatican Representative for Interfaith Dialogue for Northern Africa and the Middle East and Secretary for Inter-Religious Dialogue of the Society of Jesus in Rome, in his first-hand account of the Philippine-Turkish School of Tolerance located in Zamboanga on the Philippine island of Mindanao. He describes the school as enabling students to focus on peaceful relations within a context of conflict. For two decades the city's population, comprised of equal numbers of Christians and Muslims, faced Moro separatist groups locked in aggressive armed struggle with government military forces. Impressed by the extent to which the school lives up to its name, Michel acknowledges that,

> The school's affirmation of their school as an institution dedicated to the formation of tolerance was no empty boast. In a region where kidnapping is a frequent occurrence, along with guerilla warfare, summary raids, arrests, disappearances, and killings by military and paramilitary forces, the school offers Muslim and Christian Filipino children an excellent education and a more positive way of living and relating to each other (Michel 2003, p. 70).

So too in the war-torn Aceh region of Indonesia, the Aceh Fatih School brought together students of the Javanese, Batak and Acehnese communities in ways that promoted regional peacebuilding efforts and resisted extremist radicalization (Kalyoncu 303-5). Schools in regions at risk of escalating tensions play a significant role in diminishing hostilities. As H.D. Forbes explains, "more contact between individuals belonging to antagonistic social groups tends to undermine negative stereotypes and thus to reduce prejudice and improve intergroup relations" (7).

Familiarity and interaction through educational, commercial or civic organizations assist in undermining destructive prejudices and antagonism over time. Gülen schools can be seen as a small scale prototype of the pluralistic, inclusivist dialogue and peacebuilding initiatives that define the movement overall. Such schools create zones of peace in which students can further their intellectual exploration in scientific and humanistic studies.

Gülen's educational initiatives have consistently maintained an integrated emphasis on cultivation of the intellectual and moral virtues. The virtue of hospitality initially defined this dual emphasis. Houses of hospitality focused both on the development of the intellect through rigorous study and communal support for the living of an Islamic life focused on spiritual values and practices. These houses enabling and supporting Turkish students' pursuit of education naturally led to the establishment of free-standing educational institutions. Rooted initially in the practice of hospitality, the ethos of these institutions developed and modeled a robust understanding of this virtue. In contrast with religious *madrasas* in some regions which focused solely on religious education, often in a narrow parochial way closed to scientific inquiry, all Gülen schools encourage free, rigorous, rational dialogue across a range of scientific and humanistic disciplines, but always as focused on the collaborative disclosure of truth and inquiry directed to the enhancement of human well-being.[1] Gülen states that, "disciplines that conduct their own discourse largely in isolation from each other, and the prevailing materialistic nature of science that has compartmentalized existence and life, cannot discover the reality of things, existence, and life" (Ünal and Williams 2000, p. 355). The pursuit of the intellectual virtue of wisdom and the social virtues of justice and charity demand an ongoing, broad education of the populace, especially the rising generation of youth who will assume positions of civic leadership and responsibility over time. The schools are designed to equip students with skills enabling them to continue lifelong learning, address the current needs of their society, cultivate habits that build good character, and raise personal and societal standards of living.

The founding commitment to the virtue of hospitality continues to define the dialogical approach and ethos of Gülen schools. Hospitality also requires a practicing of related virtues. On a fundamental level, the hospitable openness of inquiry is rooted in the related virtue of humility since no one person, discipline or tradition is seen as having the full embodiment of truth. Humbling recognizing both our human and individual limitations and fallibility, inquirers are called to open themselves to ongoing collaborative inquiry and dialogue with the aim of furthering enlightenment. Inquirers actively engage the points of view of a range of persons, disciplines, perspectives and traditions, so that inquiry may be rigorously strengthened, broadened and deepened. Gülen claims that, "A sensible person is not

---

[1] Historically *madrasas* under the Abbasids and the Ottomans taught the natural sciences and mathematics. Some contemporary *madrasas*, as found, for example, in some regions of Afghanistan and Pakistan, exclude such studies, solely emphasizing the study of a more puritanical strain of Islam.

one who claims infallibility and therefore is indifferent to others' ideas. Rather, a truly sensible person is one who corrects his or her errors and uses others' ideas in acknowledgment of the fact that human beings are prone to error (Ünal 367). Ünal and Williams gather comments testifying to Gülen's emphasis on engaging persons with whom one does not agree and in ways that do not lead to conflict,

> Mature people never make a difference of idea and opinion a means of conflict. People who do not think like you might be very sincere and beneficial, so do not oppose every idea that seems contradictory and do not scare them off. Seek ways to benefit from their opinions and ideas, and start up a dialogue with them.
>
> People must learn to benefit from other people's knowledge and views, for these can be beneficial to their own system, thought and world. Especially, they should always seek to benefit from the experiences of the experienced (149).

Dialogue rather than combative triumph must be at the center of education, for this educational focus will shape the possibility of civil discourse in society.

Gülen schools emphasize the enduring influence of rational discourse and persuasion rather than the passing triumphs of power, brute force and domination in bringing about societal change. Gülen stresses that Islam upholds the fundamental principle that, "Power lies in truth, a repudiation of the common idea that truth relies upon power" (*Essays—Perspectives—Opinions* 15). Islam "recognizes right, not force, as the foundation of social life... Relationships must be based on belief, love, mutual respect, assistance and understanding instead of conflict and realization of personal interest" (19). Education ensures the protecting of such principles and the promoting of "virtues bring[ing] mutual support and solidarity" (19). Thus education is the only vehicle capable of ensuring the establishing and enduring of democracy, a form of civic order and government seen by Gülen as consistent with Islamic principles.

Contrary to the assumptions of many persons in the West, there is no theoretical tension between Islam and democracy. Gülen maintains, "It's wrong to see Islam and democracy as opposites. In periods when Islam wasn't practiced fully, perhaps it was more backward than today's democracy. For example, human rights were stepped on and despots headed the state" (Ünal and Williams 2000, p. 150). At the same time, democracy required continued development and progress, "Just as [democracy] has gone through many different stages, it will continue to go through other stages in the future to improve itself. Along the way, it will be shaped into a more humane and just system, one based on righteousness and reality" (as quoted in Yilmaz 224). Gülen repeatedly maintains that, despite the shortcomings of democracy, it is the only viable political system capable of ensuring individual rights and freedoms and promoting equal opportunity for development. He also maintains that the Islamic principles of equality, justice and tolerance are consistent with and strengthen democracies. The aspirations of the 2011 Arab Spring evidence the longing of Middle East Muslims for more democratic forms of government. In their introduction to *Islam and Peacebuilding,* Esposito and Yilmaz draw on the Gallup World poll of 35 Muslim societies representing a billion Muslims to confirm this aspiration, noting that the majority of Muslims respond positively to democratic political systems affirming the rule of law, gender equality and respect for human rights and freedom of speech, assembly and religion (7). In the end, Gülen affirms the will of the people which is at the core of democracy, stressing that, "Islam does not propose a certain unchangeable form of government or attempt to shape it. Instead Islam establishes fundamental principles that orient a government's general character, leaving it to the people to choose the type and form of government according to time and circumstances" (Gülen 2001, p. 134).

Gülen's linking of liberal education and democracy resonates with Thomas Jefferson's understanding that, "In a republican nation whose citizens are to be led by reason and persuasion and not by force, the art of reasoning becomes of first importance." An educated populace will both demand and strengthen democratic civic and political life. Hospitable, reasonable dialogue fostered in education is essential to a robust democratic polity that welcomes all persons as equals and encourages their active and informed participation in the political life. Gülen frequently draws on the saying of the Prophet that "all persons are as equal as the teeth of the comb" to emphasize the democratic teaching of Islam. In "A Comparative Approach to Islam and Democracy," he discusses how the fundamental principles underlying the social contract theory of democracy stem from this foundational principle, maintaining that Islam assigns to community members all the duties entrusted to citizens in modern democratic political systems. Democratic civic discourse ideally should allow for the engagement of viewpoints and counterpoints and consultation among persons struggling to address complex matters of civic concern. Gülen views such a collaborative approach as the hallmark of educated, wise persons. He emphasizes that, "Consultation is the first requirement for reaching the right decision. Decisions reached without due reflection or proper consultation usually come to nothing. Individuals and even geniuses who depend only on themselves, who are disconnected from others and unconcerned with their opinions, are at considerable risk of error as compared to those who offer and receive opinions. Simply put, "wise people know who to consult and how to get the most benefit from their opinions" (Unal 115). Such hospitable educational emphasis on open collaborative inquiry, humility, dialogue and persuasion as furthering the long term pursuit of truth does more than embody an educational philosophy. It models for all human interactions, be they personal, societal and international, respectful relations enabled by the distinctly human power of rational persuasion, and providing the best means for furthering the ends of justice and peace.

The philosophical approach underlying Gülen's educational philosophy also emphasizes the integrated unity of human knowledge in contrast with current tendencies toward overly specialized and fragmented inquiry. For this reason interdisciplinary dialogue is seen as essential to the activity of learning. Hospitable inquiry requires openness to a range of disciplinary perspectives and contexts, rather than a narrow, highly specialized training or fragmented learning. It also requires an awareness of the different methodologies, truth-claims and limits of particular kinds of inquiry. Thus it emphasizes meta-questions regarding the nature and relation of different types of inquiry. What characterizes scientific inquiry; what kinds of question does it ask and can it answer; what are the scope and limits of its inquiry? What distinguishes the inquiry of the humanities; what questions shape their exploration; how is such exploration related to the human quest for meaning? How do these two modes of inquiry stand in relation to each other; how do they order, inform and orient our understanding of the complexity of our world? Why are both necessary? In Gülen inspired schools, curricular programming emphasizes rigorous disciplinary work in science and the humanities but always as complemented by interdisciplinary integration. Education narrowly emphasizing the empirical sciences or solely focusing on moral, religious and spiritual values is viewed as equally problematic.

Confidence in the unity of knowledge is shown in the approach Gülen takes to the study of Islamic faith in relation to both the sciences and other religious traditions. Emphasis is placed on respect for persons as they seek to understand the human condition and universe through both religious belief and rational inquiry. Islamic religious belief is also not set in an oppositional dynamic in relation to other religions. Dialogue across traditions is emphasized as being consistent with the human goal of attaining wisdom. The wise person is seen as valuing exploration of the various wisdom traditions. Early in his education, Gülen became well read in the classics of Western philosophy, religion and literature and Eastern religious classics. Influenced by Nursi's beliefs, followers of Gülen never envisioned Islam in confrontation with other religious traditions. Islam's only enemies are identified as ignorance and poverty which challenge human development and internal human dissension which produces debilitating enmity. Such openness opposes a close-minded type of dogmatism which resists and shuts down inquiry and a relativism which undermines the point of inquiry. Whereas many people have come to associate Islam today with the dogmatic and fanatical tendencies of fundamentalism, Gülen counters these tendencies as being truly inimical to Islam. At the same time, an extreme post-modern relativism which skeptically levels all human inquiry to mere opinions not worth debating or defending is equally eschewed. For Gülen the point of all human inquiry is to grow in wisdom, both theoretical and practical. Rejecting dogmatism as blind acceptance without thought, he argues there is no such dogmatism in Islam. Knowing and believing are seen as complementing each other as shown in the Quran's call for each person to develop the powers of reasoning through pondering, evaluating and critiquing.

At one end of the spectrum Turkish secularists, under the influence of Atatürk, viewed religion as backward and irrational; at the other end anti-modern traditionalists, seeing modern science and technology as based in a positivistic materialism, viewed both as non- or even anti-Islamic. Nursi's approach, critical of the purely religious focused *madrasas* system of Islamic education which appeared after the 16th century, was more consistent with the earlier *madrasas* that emphasized Islamic sciences, natural sciences and mathematics. Under his influence Gülen was convinced scientific-rational inquiry is compatible with religious belief. Consistent with Nursi's thinking, Gülen took issue with the narrowly positivistic epistemology which assumed that modern inquiry required the severing of the self from religious traditions and beliefs. He also challenged the assumption that extensive study of science would lead to atheism, arguing that,

"Avoiding the positive sciences fearing that they will lead to atheism is naiveté, and seeing them as contradictory with religion and faith and as vehicles for the rejection of religion is prejudice and ignorance" (Gülen 2006, p. 49). Rather than assuming the dichotomies of religion vs. science and modernity vs. tradition, Gülen claimed both faith and rational inquiry are rooted in the human person's desire to render intelligible the lived world of human experience. The Qur'an is seen as neither contrary to scientific inquiry nor the source of scientific discovery. Through its empirical exploration, the natural sciences reveal dimensions of the truths affirmed in the Qur'an. Science manifests the intelligible order of nature which believers affirm to be rooted in Divine Wisdom and Governance.

Both Nursi and Gülen challenged both polar extremes (anti-science and anti-religion), affirming Islam's positive view of science and its humanistic possibilities. Recognizing the historical leadership Islamic civilization played in the development of the natural sciences, Gülen asks, why should contemporary Muslims fear science? (Ünal 2000, p. iv). He traces a misreading of al-Ghazali's writings as the source of the suspicious distancing of religion and science, resulting in the eliminating of scientific inquiry within religious schools. Such exclusion of the sciences lowered the academic standards of *madrasas* and restricted their humanistic contributions. According to Gülen, the decline of the Islamic world's influence in the modern age is traceable to such regrettable bifurcation.

The Islamic view of science producing its rich historical development centered on human persons, equipped with intellect and will, as the vicegerents of God capable of enhancing the human condition and world through the development and application of knowledge. Given that the inquiry of science is rendered possible by the rule of natural laws, Gülen conceives of science and religion as not inherently antithetical. When freed from positivistic metaphysical presuppositions, science is to be highly valued and promoted, as manifest in the strong scientific legacy of the Islamic historical tradition. In a 1995 interview Gülen explained his conception of the basis for the complementary character of religious and scientific principles, stating,

> God has two collections of laws: one, issuing from His Attribute of Speech, consists of the principles of religion, also called the Shari'a…. The other, issuing from His Attributes of Will and Power, consists of the principles to govern the universe and life, "the laws of nature" that are the subject matter of science. In Islamic terminology, this is called *al-Shari'a al-Fitriya*. Respecting these two collections of laws will make us prosperous in this world and the next, while opposing them will lead us to ruin. The Muslim world remained behind the West because it neglected *al-Shari'a al-Fitriya* (Ünal 2000, p. 27).

Gülen repeatedly expresses confidence in the compatibility of faith and reason. He states, "If there is an apparent contradiction between these two sources [Qur'an and Sunna] and human reason or established rational or scientific facts, such people [humble inquirers] seek to learn the truth of the matter" (*Key Concepts* p. 79). Herein the ongoing demands of exegesis (*ijtihad*) and scientific inquiry reveal both the finitude of human inquiry and its endless search for integrated truth. Hope in such integrated inquiry rests in the conviction that the books of both Revelation (revealed truths) and Nature (discovered truths) find their origin and end in an Omniscient and Benevolent Divinity.

Having been educated initially in the *madrasa* system of religious education, Gülen sought to replace solely religious-focused education with an integrated emphasis on the unity of inquiry encompassing spiritual, ethical, scientific and technological knowledge. Raised in a religiously devout family, he was at the same time well educated in modern science and Western literature and philosophy. Exposed to science teachers who held deep faith commitments, Gülen challenged the dichotomous divorce of science and religion. He frequently states that the two books of the Qur'an and the Universe are two faces of the same truth. Through such emphasis and inspired by such hope, Gülen sought to educate a new "Golden Generation" who might serve as "educated representatives of the understanding of science, faith, morality, and art who are the master builders of those coming after us" capable of using science to serve the good of humanity.

For Gülen, to separate religion from science weakens its comprehension of and influence in the world; to separate science from the moral reflection of religion risks producing human disasters, such as the bombing of Nagasaki and Hiroshima. Gülen often stresses his agreement with Einstein's comments on the fundamental compatibility of science and religion. Einstein writes that,

Even though the realms of religion and science in themselves are clearly marked off from each other, nevertheless there exist between the two strong reciprocal relationships and dependencies. Though religion may be that which determines the goal, it has, nevertheless, learned from science, in the broadest sense, what means will contribute to the attainment of the goals it has set up. But science can only be created by those who are thoroughly imbued with the aspiration toward truth and understanding. This source of feeling, however, springs from the sphere of religion. To this there also belongs the faith in the possibility that the regulations valid for the world of existence are rational, that is, comprehensible to reason. I cannot conceive of a genuine scientist without that profound faith. The situation may be expressed by an image: science without religion is lame, religion without science is blind. (Einstein 2000, p. 26)

Gülen's educational influence is extensive and multi-faceted. Educational trusts inspired by his practices and beliefs have produced worldwide, non-profit voluntary organizations, associations and foundations which support the continuing education of students on all levels through scholarships and school funding. The Gülen movement places educational initiatives at its very center due to its belief that social reform and the human well-being primarily come from an education nurturing the human mind and spirit and promoting universal human goods. Underlying all Gülen initiatives is the conviction that human development cannot be autonomously attained or coerced, but stems from free collaborative inquiry and dialogue that can only be encouraged, facilitated and supported. The community's support is what makes possible the education of individuals, and through such education individuals can play a role in bettering their community and humankind.

Education as Promoting the Moral Virtues of Character

The virtue of hospitality is essentially rooted in an orientation toward the other rather than a narcissistic self-absorption. So too education can be viewed as hospitably oriented toward the well-being of the human community rather than egotistically focused on personal acquisition and achievement. Repeatedly educators in Gülen schools emphasize the important formative role they play in the intellectual and character development of their students. In these schools, educators are not selected solely on the basis of their command of disciplinary knowledge and expertise, but equally importantly on the extent to which they can model the intellectual pursuit of truth and the moral striving to live an ethical life. Teachers are seen as inspiring in students the distinctly human pursuit of both intellectual and moral virtues. As Gülen emphasizes, "Those who are truly human continue to learn, teach, and inspire others. It is hard to regard as truly human those who are ignorant and have no desire to learn. It is also questionable whether a learned person who does not pursue self-renewal and self-reform, and so set an example for others, is truly human" (Unal 2000, p. 79).

Gülen sees the teacher in a way similar to Kant's account. Kant maintains that "The experimental means for cultivating virtue is good example on the part of the teacher (his exemplary conduct).... A teacher will not tell.... his pupil: take an example from that good, orderly, diligent boy! For this would cause him to hate that boy, who puts him in an unfavorable light. A good example (exemplary conduct) should not serve as a model but only as a proof that it is really possible to live ethically" (Kant 1996, 6:479). Emphasis is not placed on comparing one human being to another (teacher/pupil, pupil/pupil) but on revealing that virtuous living is possible. So Kant goes on to say that the teacher who embodies the virtues models how human beings ought to act, and thus through his or her behavior brings students to better understand the ideal of a moral law, which persons can strive to follow. Thus, Kant says, "So it is not comparison with any other human being whatsoever (as he is), but with the idea (of humanity), as he ought to be, and so comparison with the [moral] law, that must serve as the constant standard of a teacher's instruction" (Kant 1996, 6:480). With such an emphasis, one avoids comparison with others, but through exposure to moral persons, one is inspired to strive to live more virtuously. Herein the teacher is like a magnet drawing students to a love of virtue, and then furthering their understanding of the virtues and their commitment to ethical living.

This educational model on many levels is informed by the virtue of hospitality. Teachers live their beliefs, convictions and values and when admired, draw students' emulation. In Book II of the *Nicomachean Ethics,* Aristotle discusses how persons develop the virtues. He stresses that the intellectual virtues are formed by teaching and learning while the moral virtues are shaped by habituation. Persons have the natural aptitude for virtue but develop the specific virtues through practicing virtuous choosing. Comparing such formation to the development of a musician, he emphasizes the modeling and encouraging of parents and teachers.

Persons become courageous by witnessing and doing courageous actions; they become just by witnessing and doing just actions; they become generous by witnessing and doing generous actions. Because of this, "It is not unimportant, then, to acquire one sort of habit or another, right from youth. On the contrary, it is very important, indeed all-important" (1103b). Recognizing the important role of parents and teachers in the formation of mind and character, Aristotle asks, how can we ever repay our teachers and parents, for what they have done cannot be measured in money or equivalent honors (1164b). Repeatedly in his writings, Gülen emphasizes the importance of family and school in the promotion of human well-being. Recognizing the role of teachers in character formation, Gülen schools take great care in selecting teachers on the basis of the quality of both mind and character. Exposure to others in daily living plays a major role in the formation of children and young adults. Persons vocationally called to play a transformational role in the lives of others must have first undergone personal transformation. He writes,

> Those who want to reform the world must first reform themselves. In order to bring others to the path of traveling to a better world, they must purify their inner worlds of hatred, rancor, and jealousy, and adorn their outer world with all kinds of virtues. Those who are far removed from self-control and self-discipline, who have failed to refine their feelings, may seem attractive and insightful at first. However they will not be able to inspire others in any permanent way and the sentiments they arouse will soon disappear (*Essays-Perspectives-Opinions* 112).

The image of Islam known primarily in the West is the image of Islam as having been spread by the sword. Rarely emphasized is the fact that exposure to Islam was occasioned to a great extent by persons witnessing the exemplary virtuous lives of Muslims especially on the vast network of the Silk Road. Witnessing lives embodying virtues drew many persons to Islam. So too Gülen schools do not teach a religious curriculum emphasizing Islamic doctrinal and ethical belief but rather emphasize their teachers embodying core virtues central to Islam and other religious traditions. Honesty, patience, generosity, kindness, respect for persons, self-discipline and sacrifice, just and compassionate treatment of persons, and integrity—these are sought as the hallmark of Gülen educators. Virtuous example (*temsil*) draws emulation rather than indoctrination. In numerous works Gülen stresses the power and value of *temsil* rather than proselytizing. And yet the aim of such modeling is formation in virtues common to all religious traditions, rather than formation in Islamic virtues per se. The focus remains on developing good character and living virtuous lives, worthy of respect and admiration.

So too the schools' curricular programming does not promote indoctrination or passive reception of knowledge, often associated with the pedagogy of *madrasas*. Hospitable educating welcomes students into inquiry, enlivening them to its energy, power and delight. For this reason Gülen schools strive to awaken curiosity and wonder and dialogical exchange fostering the development of skills of inquiry, but always with the aim of serving the community in socially responsible ways. All human inquiry is seen as serving the pursuit of knowledge and truth in ways that promote socially responsible behavior in the context of community. Education of the mind, heart and spirit is necessary to pursue this end. Gülen stresses that,

Neglect of the intellect... would result in a community of poor, docile mystics. Negligence of the heart or spirit, on the other hand, would result in crude rationalism devoid of any spiritual dimension... It is only when the intellect, spirit and body are harmonized, and man is motivated towards activity in the illuminated way of the Divine message, that he can become a complete being and attain true humanity (Gülen 1998, p. 105-6).

Gülen shared Said Nursi's concern that the Kemalist orientation originating under the influence of Ataturk would replace what was cast as backward and antiquated religious thinking with an aggressive implementation of value-free, positivistic thinking. Taking a strongly anti-positivistic approach, Gülen refused to bifurcate the pursuit of rational inquiry, especially through the natural sciences and normative ethical inquiry. While recognizing the differences in methodologies and types of truth-claims, he held that human inquiry seeks integration, and thus science cannot be divorced from normative issues, and ethical inquiry cannot be divorced from the empirical insights of the natural and social sciences. Gülen's reflections consistently challenge dichotomies and fragmentation, emphasizing spiritual *and* intellectual development, reason *and* faith, mind *and* heart, belief *and* action.

At the center of this educational approach is the emphasis on the cultivation of the virtues—both the intellectual virtues of mind and the moral virtues of character. Running through all aspects of Gülen schooling is an Islamic emphasis on ethical formation, scientific proficiency, personal discipline and service to others, all directed toward a pro-active furthering of a more humane and just world. While undeniably Islamic in origin and orientation, this broad educational initiative promotes a rationally persuasive kind of discourse that opens the possibilities of lifetime inquiry and exchanges with others on shared matters of human concern. Analogous to the cultivation of a thriving plant, education provides a supportive environment that nurtures the natural human capacities for wonder, inquiry and development. So for Gülen, "[a] young person [is]... a sapling of power, strength and intelligence. If trained and educated properly, he or she can become a 'hero' who overcomes obstacles and acquires a mind that promises enlightenment to hearts and order to the world" (Ünal 2000, p. 117).

With such an account, teaching becomes an esteemed, even holy, vocation furthering the development of the virtues of both intellect and character. The philosopher Martha Nussbaum speaks of all teachers as being literally "philanthropists," lovingly committed to human well-being and flourishing. As modeled by Gülen himself, education evokes a spirit restlessly engaged in the pursuit of what is true and good and leads to endlessly revising and deepening one's understanding and insight and the ways one can further these ends. Recognizing the central role education plays in our human condition and the Islamic call to all men and women to pursue education "to the ends of the earth," it is not surprising that the Gülen movement has been so successful in tapping into the generous philanthropic orientation of so many Muslims. Whereas Muslims traditionally supported the building of mosques and other directly focused religious initiatives, Gülen convinced his followers that efficacious philanthropy should be focused primarily on educational support. Such philanthropy is affirmed as one of the highest humanitarian services persons can perform. All Muslims are called by God and community to such *hizmet* (the holy duty of service to others). Gülen followers are noted for their practically wise, pro-active, creative seeking of ways of providing service to others, especially through educational outreach. As Gülen succinctly stated, "Just as education and teaching are the most sacred professions, the best service to a country or nation is made through education. Our Prophet esteemed teaching more than another way of serving people" (Ünal 2000, p. 325).

Educational Outreach Through Media Channels

Gülen's educational initiatives focus on human development and well-being. Education develops human capacities and encourages the formation of intellectual and moral virtues that enhance personal and communal well-being. Gülen is convinced such development also allows for informed and responsible citizenship, central to democracy. Education enables democracy and a robust, free public media strengthens democracy. Based on observations internal to Turkey and comparative studies of contemporary societies, Gülen is convinced that societal efforts to suppress the exchange of ideas are never successful. Rational persuasion is the only true way of engaging others and bringing them to come to see the basis of one's convictions and commitments. Coercion and censorship stifle inquiry and breed resentment. Democracy's primary strength, rendering it a truly viable political system in his estimation, is that it builds its institutions and practices on the human capacity for inquiry and desire for truth. Central to democracy is the free, open exchange of ideas and the exposure of citizens to robust debate and dialogue. Gülen recognized the role the mass media can play in developing robust dialogue about important matters of local and human concern. Often the media dummies down complex issues and moves with speed from one sensational, superficial handling of an issue to another, diminishing exposure to inquiry and offering no deep or sustained reflection.

Over the past three decades, the range of media outreach of the Hizmet movement has been staggering; broadcasting companies, publications houses and presses dedicated to promoting inquiry on scientific, religious and ethical issues have been established. In 1979, it began publishing to a broader audience *Sizinti,* a journal dedicated to the integration of scientific knowledge and Islamic inquiry. Its newspaper *Zaman* was acquired in 1986, growing later to include *Ekoloji,* an environment oriented magazine; *Yeni Ümit,* a theological journal; *The Fountain,* an English publication focused on religious and ethical issues, and *Aksiyon,* a weekly magazine. New publishing houses have emerged to broaden the range of scholarly publications. Media outlets grew to include *Smanyolu* TV and *Burc* FM. These outlets inform readers and listeners about the movement's ideas as related to current social issues and concerns. Consistent with the emphasis on rational inquiry and informed discussion, they seek to expose persons to a range of positions and dialogue regarding substantive issues of public concern in and outside Turkey.

The Rumi Forum of Washington D.C. provides an excellent example of such educational outreach through public forums. On a weekly basis, the Rumi Forum organizes gatherings of inquirers to discuss important issues of current concern with prominent scholars and spokespersons from a range of organizations; recordings of such gatherings are then circulated to a wide public through their television media outlet.

Committed to the furthering of inquiry and dialogue, Gülen worked to establish the Journalists and Writers Foundation in 1994. This foundation organizes conferences and dialogue symposia, primarily focused on exploring problems faced in Turkish society, such as the relation between Islam and secularism, democracy and human rights, pluralism, and social reconciliation. Gülen continues to be a prolific writer, composing editorials and articles for a range of journals and magazines. He has authored over forty books, hundreds of articles, and his sermons and speeches have been recorded and made available to a wide public. His website (www.en. fgulen.com) continually updates postings of his reflections. Such emphasis on the dissemination of information and promotion of dialogue on issues of current concern is seen as tapping into the natural human yearning for understanding and truth. It also promotes the democratic well-being of a civic polity by fostering civility in public discourse. And importantly it builds a web of relations that furthers dialogue and understanding. Fethullah Gülen sees such broadly interpreted educational outreach as furthering the pursuit of wisdom and virtues central to living in community with others. Thus at the center of such outreach is the promotion of both intellectual and moral virtues.

References

Aristotle. (1999). *Nicomachean ethics*. 2nd ed. (Trans.), T.Irwin. Indianapolis: Hackett.
Einstein, A. (2000). *Out of my later years*. New York: Citadel.
Esposito, J., & Ihsan, Y. (2010). *Islam and peacebuilding, Gülen movement initiatives*. New York: Blue Dome Press.
Gülen, M. F. (1998). *Prophet Muhammad as commander*. Izmir: Kaynak.
Gülen, M. F. (2004a). *Essays-perspectives-opinions*. Somerset, NJ: The Light.
Gülen, M. F. (2004b). *Key concepts in the practice of Sufism, Emerald hills of the heart*. Rutherford, NJ: The Light.
Gülen, M. F. (2001). A comparative approach to Islam and democracy. *SAIS Review, 21*(2), 133–138.
Gülen, M. F. (2006). *Pearls of wisdom*. Somerset, NJ: The Light.
Kalyoncu, M. (2010). Building civil society in ethno-religiously fractured communities: the gülen movement in turkey and abroad. In J. Eposito & I. Yilmaz (Eds.), *Islam and peacebuilding*. New York: Blue Dome.
Kant, I. (1996). *Metaphysics of morals*. New York: Cambridge.
Michel, T. (2003). Fetullah gülen as educator. In M. H. Yavuz & J. Esposito (Eds.), *Turkish Islam and the secular state: The Gülen movement*. Syracuse: Syracuse University Press.
Ünal, A. & Williams, A. (2000). *Advocate of dialogue*. Fairfax, VA: The Fountain.
Yilmaz, I. (2003). Ijtihad and tajdid by conduct. In M. H. Yavuz & J. Esposito (Eds.), *Turkish Islam and the secular state, the Gülen movement*. Syracuse, NY: Syracuse University Press.

Chapter 7
Service to Humanity: The Virtues of Compassion and Charity

For good reasons Gülen calls the movement he inspired a *Hizmet* movement, a movement of service to humanity. The virtues of compassion and charity play a major role in shaping this movement's understanding of service. Joined to hospitality, these two virtues form the triadic core of this movement.

The Virtue of Compassion

The virtue of compassion has been given much attention in religious and philosophical traditions. Philosophers have made fine distinctions between a number of related virtues—sympathy, compassion and pity. The philosophers Max Scheler and Edith Stein describe sympathy as being broader than compassion for it connotes "fellow-feeling" among persons. Being with others, I may feel, on some level and in some way, as they feel. I share the exuberant joy of the runner finishing the marathon; I feel the fear of family members searching for kin after an earthquake; I feel the excitement of the graduates as a new phase of their lives commences. Compassion is a specific type of "fellow-feeling" that involves feeling the pain, sadness and suffering of others. In English it is distinguished from pity, a response many persons do not welcome since in most circumstances persons prefer not to be pitied. Pity involves a looking down upon—a condescension or even disdain. Pity has a vertical dynamic whereas compassion has a horizontal dynamic wherein I feel one with others in sharing their pain. At times in different languages the equivalent terms are interchanged. Rousseau attends closely to the virtue of compassion, identifying its attentive caring for others as the very root of all the social virtues. So too Martha Nussbaum identifies compassion as the basic social emotion and virtue—our species' way of connecting the interests of others to our own personal goods. Through compassion I see myself in the other. One cannot command compassion, but it can and must be nurtured and encouraged at an early age if we are to develop morally. Failures of compassion diminish our capacity for moral response. For this reason Rousseau places its cultivation at the center of the education of youth.

T. D. Conway, *Cross-cultural Dialogue on the Virtues*,
SpringerBriefs in Religious Studies, DOI: 10.1007/978-3-319-07833-5_7,
© The Author(s) 2014

Situated as a mean between two vices, one contrary vice of compassion would
be taking delight in the suffering of another, whether inflicted or observed. Vicious
cruelty would be the extreme of this vice; the contrary vice would be a type of
insensibility to the suffering of others—a cold-hearted, callous indifference or
blindness to others' pain. Aristotle develops a detailed analysis of compassion. In
The Rhetoric he describes compassion as "a feeling of pain at an apparent evil,
destructive or painful, which befalls one who does not deserve it, and which we
might expect to befall ourselves or (someone we care for), and moreover to befall
us soon" (Aristotle 1947, p. 2207). Compassion is thus a powerful emotional state
that grips us in such a way that we put ourselves into the situation of others, feeling
their suffering and envisioning ourselves in the same state. We recognize, as
human, we too could so suffer.

Aristotle emphasizes that compassion is evoked when suffering has "weight,"
that is, is centered on things that matter to us as humans. We feel compassion in
response to another's bodily injury, sickness, impairment from aging, loss of
family, friends, home or homeland and the like. Seneca illustrates how we do not
feel compassion in relation to trivial matters, for example an aristocrat's lamen-
tation about the delay in his shipment of peacock tongues for a dinner party
(Nussbaum 2003, p. 309). Aristotle also claims that we feel compassion when we
believe persons are not at fault for their sufferings or when their suffering is
disproportionate. To respond compassionately, we must recognize that the suffering was not caused primarily by the person's culpable actions or that the suffering is out of proportion with the fault (such that the person is culpable, but not
deserving of this *degree* of suffering). He holds that we tend not to feel compassion
for those who are responsible for their suffering, for example persons whose
negligence, avoidable ignorance or recklessness brought on their own suffering.
We feel compassion when we witness communities devastated by natural disasters
or when someone's singular wrongdoing results in excessive public ridicule and
the ruining of an entire lifetime's career in one swoop.

As fellow persons, we can envision, feel the suffering of others; we can imag-
inatively place ourselves in their life situations. We envision our own suffering in
such a case; thus "awareness of [our] own weakness and vulnerability is a necessary
condition for compassion" (Nussbaum 2003, p. 315). Compassion entails both the
recognition of another's suffering and our judgment that our own life is also vulnerable to such misfortune. I recognize that this suffering person could be me at
some time. Herein I perceive the other's distress, uprootedness, loss of shelter,
hunger or support, and affirm basic human goods which would alleviate their
condition. In doing so, I recognize the other's good *as* my own good. So compassion entails the exercising of the moral imagination, enabling me to envision
myself in this person's shoes or, more aptly, in this person's skin. In encountering
suffering others, even strangers or foreigners, I recognize them to be persons who
share with me basic human needs, desires and goals; I generously recognize our
commonality, our need for circumstances of prosperity, external goods that promote human flourishing. Because of this recognition, I can enter and feel the other's
pain in its depth, breadth and significance, for I realize I too am at risk. Compassion

thus focuses on the vulnerability of human life, on the fact that we are dependent in many ways on external conditions we cannot fully control. It brings us to face the fragility of our well-being. In the compassionate response we register that "man is the same in all stations" (Rousseau 1979, p. 225). Adam Smith's passage capturing this compassionate realization is worth quoting at length:

> By imagination we place ourselves in his situation, we conceive ourselves as enduring all the torments, we enter as it were his body, and become in some measure the same person with him, and thence form some ideas of his sensations, and even feel something, which though weaker in degree, is not altogether unlike them. His agonies, when they are brought home to ourselves, when we have adopted and made them our own, begin at least to affect us, and we then tremble and shudder at the thought of what he feels. For as [being] in pain or distress of any kind excites the most excessive sorrow, so to conceive or imagine that we are in it, excites some degree of the same emotion, in proportion to the vivacity or dullness of the conception (Smith 1984, p. 9).

Because of our human commonality—because we are all "patients" (ones who suffer)—we can literally "suffer-with" others (*com-pashein*).

Compassion in Religious Traditions

It is not surprising that all major religious traditions emphasize the virtue of compassion. Judaism identifies compassion as both a Divine attribute and a core human virtue. Judaism speaks of God as the Compassionate (*Rahman*). In Exodus 34:6, as God passed before Moses, God proclaimed: "The Lord, the Lord, God, a Compassionate and Gracious God, slow to anger, and abundant in loving-kindness and fidelity." The biblical roots of compassion disclose its meaning. *Riham* comes from the root term *rehem* meaning a mother's womb. Persons feel compassion for and desire to relieve the sufferings of others, as a mother responds to the child in her womb whom she has not yet seen. She feels for the child as an extension of her own self. Talmudic scholars identify compassion as one of the distinguishing virtues of a truly righteous Jew. In being compassionate, persons "walk in God's way" (Deuteronomy 8:6). Jeremiah speaks of those who lack compassion and therefore are prone to acting cruelly. Seeing those who,

> bow and javelin… wield, cruel and without compassion are they.
> They sound like the roaring sea
> as they ride forth on steeds,
> Each in his place, for battle, against you…
> We hear the report of them;
> Helpless fall our hands,
> Anguish takes hold of us,
> Throes like a mother's in childbirth. (6:23-24)

Judaism calls persons to be compassionate to all persons who suffer. An old Hasidic tale discloses the wide range of compassion. It relates how a rabbi asked his students how they could tell when night had ended and the day had begun. "Is it when you can see an animal in the distance and can distinguish whether it's a sheep or a dog?" asked one student. "No," replied the rabbi. "Is it when you can look at a tree in the distance and tell whether it's a fig or peach tree?" asked another student. "No," replied the rabbi. "Then what is it?" the students asked. "It is when you can look upon the face of *any* person and see this is your brother or sister. Because if you cannot see this, it is still night." Compassion must be extended without limit or condition. Judaism even goes so far as to extend it to all living creatures, including animals, who suffer. The enduring challenge is to see and respond to the suffering of any and all beings who suffer and not be selective in our awareness and response.

So too Christians are called to be compassionate because God is the "Father of Compassion and the God of all comfort, who comforts us in our suffering, so that we can comfort those who suffer in trouble with the same comfort we ourselves received from God" (2 Corinthians 1:37). For Christians, Christ embodies fully the essence of compassion, as one who responds compassionately to all who suffer. The Gospels recount numerous examples of Jesus' compassionate responses, revealing how he was moved to act to lessen the suffering:

of the weary	"At the sight of the crowds, his heart was moved with compassion. They were lying prostrate from exhaustion, like sheep without a shepherd" (Matthew 9:36),
of the sick	"[H]e withdrew by boat from there to a deserted place by himself. The crowds heard of it and followed him on foot from the towns. When he disembarked and saw the vast throng, his heart was moved with compassion, and he cured the sick" (Matthew 14:14),
of the hungry	"My heart is moved by compassion for the crowd. By now they have been with me three days and have nothing to eat. I do not wish to send them away hungry, for fear they may collapse on the way" (Matthew 15:32),
of mourners	"Soon afterward he went to a town called Naim, and his disciples and a large crowd accompanied him. As he approached the gate of the town, a dead man was being carried out, the only son of a widowed mother. A considerable crowd of townsfolk were with her. The Lord was moved with compassion upon seeing her and said to her, 'Do not cry.' Then he stepped forward and touched the litter… [and] said, 'Young man, I bid you get up.' The dead man got up and began to speak. Then Jesus gave him back to his mother" (Luke 7:13–14).

The Parable of the Good Samaritan (Luke 10:25–37) embodies the ideal of compassion in its account of the Samaritan's response to a man robbed, beaten and abandoned. While others passed him by, either not noticing or caring about his suffering, the Samaritan, moved by compassion, dressed his wounds, carried him to an inn and cared for him, requesting others to continue his care as the man continued to heal. After relating the parable, Christ calls his listeners to, "Then go and do the same." Such compassion has no limit and also cannot rest with mere "fellow-feeling." The parable makes explicit the call to respond to suffering so as to lessen or eliminate it. In imitation of Christ, Christians are called to "clothe themselves with heartfelt compassion, with kindness, humility, meekness and patience ... Over all these virtues put on love, which binds together and makes them perfect" (Colossians 3:12–15).

Based on this call to do as Christ did, Christians practice the "Works of Mercy." Mercy, compassion and charity are linked in these practices which respond to human suffering and distress of the soul and body. The corporal works of mercy are: to feed the hungry, give drink to the thirsty, clothe the naked, shelter the homeless, visit the sick and imprisoned, and bury the dead. The spiritual works of mercy are: to instruct the ignorant, counsel the doubtful, admonish sinners, bear wrongs patiently, forgive wrongs willingly, comfort the suffering, and pray for the living and deceased. The works are rooted in the will to treat others as one wishes to be treated, but more importantly in imitation of Christ. Christ calls persons to treat others as they would treat him, "For I was hungry, and you gave me not to eat; I was thirsty, and you gave me not to drink. I was a stranger, and you took me not in; naked, and you covered me not; sick and in prison, and you did not visit me." Christ's actions encourage Christians to seek out opportunities to perform such acts of compassion and to do so with kindness, respect and attentiveness to persons' human dignity and worth. As Dorothy Day realized, Christians compassionately and hospitably see God in the commonplace, frail, ordinary suffering of humanity (Day 2005, p. 97). For Christians, hospitality toward those who suffer leads seamlessly to compassionate works of mercy. Dorothy Day believed that persons devoted to such compassionate works were striving to create a world in which it will be easier to be good.

With its emphasis on the lessening of suffering, Buddhist ethics center on the virtue of compassion, developing an extensive understanding and practicing of this virtue, more so than other traditions. Throughout his lifetime, Buddha maintained that he taught *only* suffering and the transformation of suffering. Buddhism identifies the path to human well-being as the path of *Metta* (Loving-kindness) and *Karuna* (Compassion). The Pali word *Karuna* literally means experiencing a trembling or quivering of the heart in response to another's pain. The virtue of compassion can only develop if this quivering of the heart occurs; this experiential response is the seed of the settled disposition to respond compassionately to others' suffering.

The Dalai Lama explains that in Buddhism, "compassion is defined as the wish that all beings be free of their suffering. Unfortunately, it is not possible for us to rid the world of its misery... Yet we can develop our own minds in virtue and thereby help others to do the same" (Dalai Lama 2002, p. 1). Having endured intense suffering through persecution and exile, he focuses on how one can develop an open heart, capable of moving from self-centered to compassionate responses. This begins with the simple act of attentiveness to others. Often the frenetic pace of our lives prevents us from *even noticing* the suffering before us. Attentiveness opens further the possibility of responsibility, grounded in our

capacity to respond caringly to others. Such simple attentiveness requires closeness to others, not merely in the sense of physical proximity but in recognition of
others as fellow-sufferers. Only with such human proximity can compassion take
root. The Dalai Lama explores ways we can develop this "closeness" by:

- reflecting on the virtues directed to the well-being of all others,
- coming to see how these bring inner happiness and peace,
- noticing how others cherish persons practicing them,
- contemplating the shortcomings of self-centeredness,
- being grateful for the kindness and compassion of others,
- becoming aware of the mutual interdependence of each other's well-being and
  suffering,
- desiring to lessen all suffering.

This requires an intentional directedness toward compassion—a daily mindfulness of this central virtue. The Dalai Lama recommends our beginning by
meditating on our self, then persons for whom we feel compassion, leading to
meditating on those for whom we don't initially feel compassion, and expanding
our compassion to include all persons, even our enemies, and finally all sentient
beings until we attain the "great compassion" which is boundless. In contrast with
Aristotle's excluding culpable suffering, the Buddhist maintains "genuine compassion must be unconditional" (110) and extended to all beings who suffer in any
way (110).

The Dalai Lama never minimizes the challenges of doing this. He recognizes
our tendencies to reify people, reducing them to single, unchangeable traits and
categories that keep them at a distance, so that we do not even see their suffering.
For this reason we must intentionally foster awareness that not just I but all persons
suffer and aspire to overcome suffering. Buddhists believe that a life full of
compassion naturally flows into a life of service to others. While loving-kindness
is directed toward the increasing the happiness of others, compassion is directed
toward the lessening of their suffering. Buddhism speaks of the four Heavenly
Abodes that must be cultivated: *Metta*/Loving-Kindness, *Karuna*/Compassion,
Mudita/Appreciative Joy, and *Upekkha*/Inner Peace. Surprisingly, when asked
whether the cultivation of loving-kindness and compassion is *a part* of Buddhist
practice, Buddha responded negatively. Pausing, he clarified that this is *the whole*
of our practice. The Buddhist way *is* the way of compassion.

In a similar way, to walk the path of Islam is to esteem and practice the virtue of
compassion (*Rahmah*). With only one exception, each of the hundred and fourteen
chapters of the Qur'an begins with the invocation of the *basmala*—*Bismillah al-
Rahman al-Rahim*, "I begin in the name of God the Compassionate, the Merciful."
These are the most repeated descriptions of God in the Qur'an and in the daily
lives of Muslims. Muslims consecrate every ritual and significant action through
the utterance of these words. In the same way the Five Pillars of Islam draw
Muslims toward compassionate acts. *Salat*, Muslims' daily prayer, repeatedly
affirms the compassionate nature of God. Through the annual *Zakat,* Muslims
share their material assets with those who suffer from need and poverty. During

Ramadan fasting they commiserate with and act to relieve the sufferings of the less fortunate. In practicing compassion, Muslims reflect the Divine Compassion that encompasses all things (*Qur'an* 7:156). In practicing compassion, they also revere Mohammad as the ideal embodiment of compassion. As an orphan, he was attuned to the most vulnerable members of society. Numerous accounts of Mohammad in the Hadiths highlight his compassion. Similar to the Judaic account which ties the roots of compassion to a mother's response to her child, the following two, frequently referenced, accounts manifest God's infinite compassion as linked to maternal love and mercy.

> There was a woman running frantically in search of her infant; finding him, she nourished him at her breast. In response Mohammad asked his Companions if this woman could cast her child into a fire. After their affirming this impossibility, Mohammad affirmed that God is even more compassionate to His servants than this woman was to her beloved child.

> Mohammad was told that a woman brought before him was a sinner deserving punishment. Instead of questioning her about her sins, the Prophet asked her to name an act of compassion she had done to a fellow person. Not remembering such an act, he then asked her if she had ever shown compassion to any living being. Upon thinking, she recalled how she once felt for a thirsty dog and from compassion removed her sock, filled it with water and brought it back to the dog. Mohammad responded that she could go since God would forgive her sin due to her compassion.

Both accounts illustrate the need for compassion in relation to the sustenance of life. Compassion brings us to connect our needs to the needs of other beings. The Qur'an exhorts persons to give to others in need whatever is not needed to meet their own needs and to never benefit from the suffering of others. A range of acts are forbidden (*haram*) for these reasons, for example: making a profit from others' sufferings (e.g. the selling of burial cloth for profit), producing things harmful to persons, wasting of goods needed by others, leading an overly consumptive lifestyle or hoarding wealth. The Qur'an emphatically states, "if you have enough and there are hungry people, and you take one piece of grain above your need, that is *haram*" (2:219).

Compassion is the inner core of Sufism, generating the image of Sufis responding to those who suffer and are in need. Numerous Sufi practices focus on compassion. To cite only one, many Sufi communities continue to open common kitchens (*langar*) to any and all persons who hunger, drawing inspiration from the Hadith Qudsi 18 account of God's words at the Final Judgment Day. God so speaks,

> I was hungry and you did not feed me, I was thirsty and you did not quench my thirst and I was naked and you did not clothe me. The person being held to account would say O! Allah you are the Provider of food how could I feed you? Allah would say my servant (*abd*) was hungry and you did not feed him. If a human person is hungry it is as I am hungry and if a human person is thirsty it is as I am thirsty, and if a human person is naked it is as I am naked.

The Qur'an warns that devotions without compassionate acts are empty; "Prayers are meaningless if one does not have regard for orphans, the poor and neighborly needs" (107:1–7). The 13th century Sufi poet Saadi goes so far as to say in his *Gulistan* that persons who lack compassion do not deserve to even be called human.

Adam's children are limbs of one another.
Each of the selfsame essence as his brother.
So while one member suffers pains and grief,
The other members cannot find relief.
You who are heedless of your brother's pain
It is not fitting to call you "Human."

                                     Saadi, *Gulistan*

Compassion and Charity in the Hizmet Movement

Hospitality, compassion and charity form the triadic core of virtues of the Hizmet movement. These three virtues flow from each other. Because of hospitable openness to others, members of the movement can draw close to others, making possible interpersonal encounters. Through such openness to others, they are able to recognize human suffering, rendering compassion possible. Feeling compassion, they can seek ways of responding to suffering. Thus being disposed to encounters through hospitality prompts being disposed to compassion and charity. Gülen's robust understanding of tolerance as hospitality opens itself to wide and capacious compassion and charity without limits. As he states in his *Key Concepts of Sufism,*

> Be so tolerant that your bosom becomes wide like the ocean.
> Become inspired with faith and love of human beings.
> Let there be no troubled souls to whom
> you do not offer a hand and about whom
> you remain unconcerned. (iv)

Similar to Saadi's reasoning, Gülen affirms the Sufi welcoming to be expansive, non-conditional and all-inclusive; "Our Prophet said: "The person most beloved by God is the one who has faith in Him and is beneficial to others." Ali, who has an important place in our religion, said, 'Muslim are your brothers in religion and non-Muslims are your human brothers' We are all human" (Ünal 2000, p. 331). Gülen frequently refers to Islam as the religion of universal compassion and Mohammad as the Messenger of God's Infinite Compassion. At the same time he recognizes that the virtue of compassion is affirmed by all religions and identifies compassion as a virtue distinctive of being human. Compassion is often what draws people from across the world to respond quickly to human disasters. Compassion, at the very core of our humanity, is tied to our basic human capacities (sensing, recognizing, imagining, feeling, reflecting) and our human possibilities for moral goodness or evil. Compassion is thus an index of human morality. For these reasons, Gülen stresses that a "human being must show compassion to all living beings, for this is a requirement of being human. The more people display compassion, the more exalted they become; the more they resort to wrongdoing, oppression, and cruelty, the more they are disgraced and humiliated. They become a shame to humanity" (*Essays-Perspectives-Opinions* 49–50).

Gülen repeatedly returns to Mohammad as the exemplar of compassion revered for practicing this virtue, even before receiving his revelations. In his community he was known for protecting and supporting the vulnerable, weak and needy, especially widows, orphans, the poor and the disabled. For these reasons, Mohammad is described in the Qur'an as the one who draws close to others in their suffering, "There has come to you a Messenger from among yourselves; grievous to him is your suffering; anxious is he over you, full of concern for you, for the believers full of pity, compassionate" (33:6). Recognizing the emphasis placed on compassion in all religions, Gülen is deeply troubled by the cruelty inflicted by persons of these traditions, especially his fellow Muslims who practice a violence-perpetuating distortion of Islam. Often propelled by what they interpret as righteous indignation before injustice, such persons remain blind to the immense toll of human suffering stemming from their "righteous" violence. Gülen emphasizes that both ends and means of action must be righteous.

For such reasons Gülen is highly attentive to cultivating compassion in young people and addressing barriers which prevent persons from developing compassion. In keeping others at a distance, be it through intolerance or even a very minimal kind of tolerance, we learn little of others and thus can fall prey to ignorant prejudices and misinformation spread about them. Persons can thoughtlessly and carelessly spread malign characterizations of others not grounded in direct experience or knowledge, thereby fueling hostilities. Such failures of the intellectual and moral virtues set the stage for acts of both cruelty and blindness to the suffering cruelty causes. Recognizing this, hospitality is rightly cherished by Gülen and his followers. Hospitality makes possible encounters through which we can come to know others directly. And direct encounters help disable prejudices, preventing their festering and spreading. Thus hospitality fundamentally helps prevent the formation of malice which often leads to cruelty and suffering. And compassion helps us to respond when we witness suffering. But compassion requires that we abide with others, attending to them sufficiently so that we can notice when they suffer due to human or natural causes. And hospitality is the virtue that first teaches us how to abide with others as fellow-persons. Closing ourselves off from others and keeping others at a distance prevents compassion and charity from ever developing.

For Gülen, hospitality deserves central prominence, since it is necessary for virtuous living. But hospitality is not truly hospitality unless it flows into other virtues. One cannot truly open oneself to others without becoming compassionate and charitable. Gülen's call to God, "By Your Graciousness, assist those who are in need!"(Gülen 2006, p. xvii) is transformed into a call for Muslims to assist those in need, out of compassion for all forms of human suffering. As Buddhists recognize, we cannot rid the world of suffering, but we can and should act to diminish suffering. So for Gülen compassion can never rest with feeling the pain of others, but must produce efficacious actions to address human suffering and its sources. Not surprisingly, his followers have shaped a worldwide *Hizmet* movement highly committed to lessening human suffering. With good reason, both Gülen and those inspired by his work and life, emphasize that this movement should rightly be called the *Hizmet* movement, shifting emphasis from a singular person to the service oriented life of its members. For Gülen the virtue of compassion naturally flows into the virtue of charity, for both are dimensions of human benevolence ultimately traceable to Divine Benevolence. The virtues, attuned to human well-being and flourishing, flow into service to members of the human community.

The Jewish philosopher and Rabbi Moses Maimonides outlined various levels of the interdependent virtues of compassion and charity. At the lowest level we recognize and respond to those in need, but unwillingly and hesitatingly. The contrasting highest level is when we respond to the needs of others in ways which enable persons to address their own needs in sustainable ways. In providing resources, developing partnerships, facilitating training and providing educational support, one helps persons develop their own capacities to address their needs and promote their own thriving and those of their community members over time. Such compassionate response mitigates current suffering, but more importantly addresses the sources of human suffering and supports ways of breaking the chains of such need and suffering. In this sense, all Gülen-inspired initiatives, but most especially educational ones, further this highest level of compassion and charity. They seek to anticipate human needs and aspirations in ways which diminish the current actuality and future possibility of suffering. Gülen does not direct these initiatives, but his account of the virtues seeds all Hizmet initiatives. He encourages the practicing of generosity and charity which motivates followers to open schools, voluntarily financed by local Turkish entrepreneurs and professionals who contribute land, buildings, personnel and financial support as needed. Such educational initiatives help lessen the gaps of social and economic inequality which are common sources of human suffering. The inequitable distribution of wealth sets up conditions eliciting charitable responses; these in turn focus on initiatives promoting long-term economic justice in efficient, enduring ways. Prosperous Gülen followers support charitable initiatives with no expectation or desire for material gain, at times evoking cynical responses from those who hold such actions are too good to be true. Such benefactors see their efforts as simply furthering justice and human flourishing which in turn reflects the Benevolence of God.

Gratitude to God and responsibility for using one's talents and prosperity virtuously inform this understanding of service (*hizmet*). All that persons have is traceable ultimately to God, so persons are called to be generous as God is Generous. As Gülen states in *Pearls of Wisdom,* "Whatever we own is entirely by Your gift and favor" (xvi). And thus, "The most meritorious of the acts or services of worship [are] knowing and loving God Almighty and being beneficial to humanity" (12). Material prosperity is valued when used under the guidance of wisdom and good character. Wealth must be united with philanthropy, a loving, generous service to others. Thus the Hizmet movement supports free enterprise leading to material prosperity, so long as both serve humanity and God. Such benevolence actively resists wealth accumulation being sullied by greed, vanity, and selfish interest. Gülen is convinced all positive initiatives have as their source inner virtues. As Gülen stresses,

Those who want to reform the world must first reform themselves. If they want to lead others to a better world, they must purify their inner worlds of hatred, rancor, and jealousy, and adorn their outer worlds with virtue. The words of those who cannot control and discipline themselves, and who have not refined their feelings, may seem attractive and insightful at first. However, even if they somehow manage to inspire others, which they sometimes do, the sentiments they arouse will soon wither (Ünal 112).

The Hizmet movement has produced a vast range of transnational, faith-inspired initiatives that have amazing potential to respond to human needs. Turkish Muslims throughout the world, who may not even know each other, voluntarily unite in solidarity to address the needs of others on the basis of their shared convictions. These initiatives are grounded in their religious commitments, sustained by a moral ethos that centers on hospitality, compassion and charity, and directed toward the needs and suffering of *all* persons. Hundreds of charitable organizations founded by Hizmet movement members mobilize efforts to respond to the situations of the weak, marginalized, oppressed and needy throughout the world.

Grassroots local gatherings (*cemaats*) promote fellowship, idea exchange, activity and service project design, and financial support development. Often these groups form around shared professions (entrepreneurs, doctors, lawyers, factory workers) residing in the same community. Persons are drawn to these circles primarily for fellowship which in turn shapes their communal identity and lives. Lacking any centralized, hierarchically organized, bureaucratic structure, these circles collaboratively form and direct initiatives. They loosely coordinate with each other on the basis of shared commitments and goals, forming a constellation of local networks. Out of gratitude for this fellowship and a sense of shared responsibility for the sustained success of their initiatives, members contribute generously to fund schools, hospitals and specific service projects. In many cases, members trace their own professional success to the support of these institutions and welcome opportunities to reciprocate by supporting the next generation as benefactors. Surprisingly no hierarchically designed, bureaucratic structures organize such giving. Individuals craft or seek out ways of generously sharing their material goods so as to benefit other members of their own local community, society and global human community.

In her work, *The Gülen Movement, A Sociological Analysis of a Civic Movement Rooted in Moderate Islam,* Helen Ebaugh analyses the generosity that sustains Gülen-inspired projects. In chapters four and five, she explains in detail a number of Turkish practices that foster a joyful, beneficent generosity that seeks to avoid instilling in recipients a sense of obligation and indebtedness to benefactors. Persons generously share their material prosperity, investing in the well-being of others and enhancing the possibility that recipients will thrive and, in turn, be generous to others. Such charitable generosity is practiced in ways that ensure persons in need do not sacrifice their honor and dignity. Voluntary charitable giving (*Sadaka*), religiously mandated sharing of one's wealth with needy relatives, neighbors and other needy persons (*Zekat*), interest-free loans to those in need (*Karz-I hasen*) and charitable trusts ensuring an enduring legacy of generosity (*Vakif*)—all provide well-established, traditional ways of practicing benevolent generosity. In such practices emphasis is placed on the act of generous sharing with others for their welfare. The emphasis is on the recipient rather than the agent in a way that does not draw attention to the agent's virtuous action. In this sense the acts, as other-oriented, are truly altruistic. Generous acts are often done in secret or anonymously, consistent with the Islamic guidance that the left hand should not see what the right hand is doing. Such generous practices are part of the ethos of Turkish culture and Islamic faith which shape the daily lives of families and communities.

Given these Turkish-Islamic practices, it is not surprising that over time well-funded trusts have been established to support local Gülen institutions and service initiatives. These trusts reinforce the virtue of charity as understood in Islam and strongly emphasized by Gülen and effectively channel the generosity of bene-factors in collaboratively effective ways. Such generosity is also tied to the Islamic *Zakat/Zekat* practice whereby a percentage of one's material goods is tithed annually to meet the needs of others who are less fortunate. Such generosity is seen as improving persons' lives in the short-term but also promoting long-term goals of human development. In this sense such generosity is seen as furthering the goals of both charity and justice.

These Gülen-inspired associations take pride in the success of their ventures which in turn generates deeper commitment and new initiatives. What is note-worthy is the extension of this generous outreach to all persons needing support, consistent with core virtues of hospitality and compassion. Gülen repeatedly emphasizes that the diversity of races, ethnicities, customs and traditions enrich our human and local communities, and for this reason service initiatives are directed to the promotion of the common good through respectful and peaceful relations. This approach is also sustained by hope that the practicing of such virtues will reduce poverty, ignorance and enmity which cause human suffering. Members view the movement as primarily concerned with the developing of magnanimous hearts formed in virtues and directed to the promotion of human well-being, alleviation of suffering and praise of God. Such service is viewed as part of their vocation as good persons, good citizens, and good believers.

Kimse Yok Mu

Especially impressive is the movement's grassroots networking capacity to mobi-lize rapid responses to unforeseen situations of grave human need and suffering. Gülen describes these amazingly enthusiastic and effective responses; "In fact our people have a spirit of enterprise. But in order to display this, they have to believe. If someone like me even whispers something like a bee's buzzing, the collective conscience can become active immediately" (Ünal 328). Their faith and formation in virtues shape their "collective conscience" which moves them to act quickly to assist others, affirming what their "Prophet said: 'The person most beloved by God is the one who has faith in Him and is beneficial to others" (331). These responses mobilize local people in response to local needs. And these responses are only possible because of strong, pre-existing, local fellowship networks.

These local service projects, labeled *Kimse Yok Mu*, are traceable to the suffering experienced by Turkish people following the devastating earthquake of August 17, 1999. As volunteers rushed to rescue people, they heard a child's voice cry out from the rubble *"Kimse Yok Mu?"*—"Is anybody there?" Deeply moved by this cry for help, volunteers encouraged the movement's Samanyolu television network to broadcast their call for assistance and funds; their call was rewarded immediately by an overwhelming outpouring of support. Following this experience, a television program entitled *Kimse Yok Mu* was established to coordinate rescue and relief projects and a benefactor support system. In light of growing demands, the *Kimse Yok Mu* Association was formed and was eventually transformed into a NGO humanitarian aid association in March, 2004.

Pre-existing social networks and regular interpersonal contacts provided the greatest resource for mobilizing volunteers for urgent, short term service projects then taken to an international level with earthquake relief efforts in Pakistan (2005) and tsunami aid in Indonesia (2004). Volunteers rapidly designed appropriate actions and marshalled resources, capital and labor. These international responses increased over time, with aid projects in Palestine-Lebanon, Peru, Sudan-Darfur, Georgia-Ossetia, Myanmar, China, Gaza and Haiti. *Kimse Yok Mu* continued to expand to its current state as a member of ECOSCO, a United Nations organization coordinating international humanitarian aid groups. This vast service network mobilizes Hizmet movement supporters and welcomes any and all volunteers to support and participate in its global service projects. This network has broadened to include:

- disaster search, rescue and emergency relief projects responding to natural disasters, famines, and war conditions,
- health projects, such as rural health clinics and eye clinics,
- educational projects meeting local educational needs, especially of underserved regions,
- aid logistical support focused on stocking and shipping supplies for service projects, and
- publicity support, preparing and disseminating materials for *Kimse Yok Mu.*

In addition, information sharing among social networks lends to ongoing identification of service needs in specific locales. This organically developed, globalized network of information-sharing, exchange and interaction allows for quick, effective responses to human needs. Current *Kimse Yok Mu* projects focus on Syrian Refugee Support Campaign; Hunger and Thirst Relief Campaigns in Somalia, Uganda, Ethiopia and Kenya; Pakistan *Ikbaliye* Village Housing Campaign; Haiti Hospital Complex Campaign; Darfur Cataract Campaign; Sudanese Orphans Campaign; Orphaned Palestinian Children's Scholarship Campaign; Water Wells Campaigns in Palestine and Niger; Van (Turkey) Earthquake Emergency Aid

Campaign and the Ontepe (Iraq) School Campaign (www.kimseyokmu.org). Gülen frequently reaffirms his belief that such altruistic services and charitable trusts are the most honorable ways of respecting and serving God and humanity.

Such charitable initiatives are only possible because of the Hizmet movement's strong emphasis on the virtue of generosity. Gülen repeatedly emphasizes that the acquiring of material prosperity through professional success is commendable, so long as it is used to serve the common good and to address the basic human needs of disadvantaged persons. In contrast with competitive striving to amass wealth so as to feed the consumptive lifestyle so encouraged in our age, emphasis is placed on persons' using their material prosperity to meet the needs of others and their doing so wisely in a way that ensures ongoing generosity. The Qur'an encourages persons to "Vie with one another in doing good deeds. Whatever you may be, God will gather you unto him" (2:148). And the doing of good deeds is aided by one's having the means of doing good. Aristotle's discussion of the virtue of generosity, which he describes as the most beloved virtue, speaks to the approach found in the Hizmet movement.

Generosity has to do with the giving and acquiring of wealth or material prosperity, with emphasis placed on the giving. Aristotle considers the virtue of generosity as a mean situated between two extremes which are vices. The deficient vice is "ungenerosity" or miserliness. Herein persons take their wealth more seriously than is right, being overly preoccupied with protecting and increasing their material wealth and refusing to share it with others. Such persons, pained by giving, resist doing so. The excessive vice of prodigality characterizes those who waste their wealth, depleting resources in ways that prevent their continuing generosity. Wasteful persons soon outrun their resources, exhausting their wealth in ways that prevent them from meeting their own needs, let alone the needs of others. Aristotle also emphasizes that wealth can be acquired through commendable or questionable means. Virtuous persons earn their wealth rightly, share it rightly, and take pleasure in doing so. As Aristotle states, "Actions in accord with virtue are fine, and aim at the fine. Hence the generous person will also aim at the fine in his giving, and will give correctly; for he will give to the right people, the right amounts, at the right time … and will do this with pleasure" (*Nicomachean Ethics* 1120a). And generosity, as a state of character disposed toward giving, is not measured by the amount given. All persons can be generous in some way and to some extent, for, "What is generous does not depend on the quantity of what is given, but on the state of character of the giver, and the generous state gives in accord with one's means. Hence one who gives less than another may still be more generous, if he has less to give" (1120b). Nursi similarly stressed that a poor person can enjoy, and take pleasure in sharing, a piece of black bread in response to hunger even more so than a rich person, who overcome by luxury, takes no pleasure in having or sharing the choicest piece of baklava (Nursi 2004, p. 194). Nursi brought Gülen to understand that generosity requires both the avoidance of miserliness and wastefulness. Frugality, or wise management of one's material resources, as "one of the elevated qualities of the Prophet (PBUH) and indeed one of the things on which Divine Wisdom in the order of the universe depends, bears no relation to stinginess, which is a mixture of baseness, avarice, miserliness, and greed" (195). Greed brings endless preoccupation with growing acquisition resulting in dissatisfaction and discontent. In contrast, generosity requires wise management of goods which carries the promise of increase and plenty that can be shared (198).

The philanthropic generosity of Gülen supporters sustains and expands an amazing worldwide network of highly successful hospitals, schools, dialogue centers and service initiatives. Such disposition toward giving is consistent with Gülen's encouraging persons to resist actively the pull toward endless self-centered accumulation of wealth spent on over-consumptive lifestyles that fail to satisfy the human spirit. Heeding the Qur'an's chastening of those who "hoard up gold and silver and spend not in God's way" (9:34), persons are encouraged to develop their talents through education in ways that allow them to meet their responsibilities, share the fruits of their professional accomplishments, and excel in doing good deeds (istibq al-khayrāl). Such generosity is seen as contributing to the common good, addressing economic disparities which breed hostilities, and responding efficiently to conditions which cause human suffering. In this sense generosity is clearly linked to other virtues such as justice, compassion and charity. The outpouring of financial support, the prudent management of financial resources, and the timely and efficient response to situations of need are all highly commendable. But in the end, as Aristotle recognized, what is most striking is the pleasure such persons feel in generously supporting the doing of compassionate and charitable deeds. And for Aristotle, joyful pleasure in doing good acts is the sign of virtuous character. This is one of the most poignant characteristics of members of the Hizmet movement. Without hesitation, without regret, and with joyful enthusiasm, they seek out and welcome opportunities to give so that good might be done. This trait reveals most powerfully that this is literally a *movement*. Often we think of movements as being organized, directed and structured to attain particular pre-determined ends. But returning to the root meaning of the term movement clarifies why this *Hizmet* associative network is rightly called a "movement." It is rooted in faith-based actions that move people to develop habitual ways of choosing and living; these actions shape associative relationships and a shared way of living which are identifiable and distinguishable, and these in turn produce events which bring about change in the lives of other persons. The amazing proliferation of Gülen schools, hospitals, dialogue centers, publications and public gatherings within a few decades attests to the energy and impact of this dynamic service movement.

References

Aristotle. (1947). *Introduction to Aristotle*. (R. McKeon, Trans.). New York: Modern Library.
Aristotle. (1999). *Nicomachean ethics*. 2nd ed. (T. Irwin, Trans.). Indianapolis: Hackett.
Ebaugh, H. (2009). *The Gülen movement: a sociological analysis of a civic movement rooted in moderate Islam*. New York: Springer-Verlag.

Gülen, M. F. (2006). *Pearls of wisdom*. Somerset, NJ: The Light.
Gülen, M. F. (2004a). *Essays-perspectives-opinions*. Somerset, NJ: The Light.
Gülen, M. F. (2004b). *Key concepts in the practice of Sufism, Emerald hills of the heart*.
    Rutherford, NJ: The Light.
Lama, D. (2002). *An open heart, practicing compassion in everyday life*. New York: Back Bay
    Books.
Nursi, B. S. (2004). *The flashes collection* (Ş. Vahide, Trans.). Istanbul: Nur Publishers.
Nussbaum, M. (2003). The cognitive structure of compassion. In *Upheavals of thought, the
    intelligence of emotions*. New York: Cambridge University Press.
Rousseau, J.-J. (1979). *Emile or on education* (A. Bloom, Trans.). New York: Basic Books.
Smith, A. (1984). *The theory of moral sentiments*.. In D. D. Raphael & A. L. Macfie (Eds.).
    Indianapolis, IN: Liberty Fund.

Chapter 8
Love as the Ultimate Virtue

Love in Relation to Other Virtues

The terms "charity" and "love" are often used interchangeably to speak of the same virtue. But it can be argued that charity is a type of love. The virtue of charity as discussed in the preceding chapter focuses on attentive responsiveness to the well-being of those who suffer and are in need. Charity, so understood, is greatly emphasized within the Hizmet movement. But this virtue is part of a broader ethic of love which pervades Gülen's writings, life and the movement he inspired. In describing this movement as creating a *dar al-hizmet*, an abode of service to others for the sake of God and humanity, Gülen reveals how this service ethos is ultimately a practicing of the virtue of love. Hospitality, compassion and charity flow from this deeper, most fundamental virtue. In a sense all virtues originate in and are sustained by this foundational virtue of love. Love is what animates ethics, moving it beyond a merely scrupulous following of commands and obligations. For Gülen, the love of God flows naturally into the love of all humanity willed into existence through God's benevolent creation. This love grounds and motivates the ethical orientation to refrain from doing harm, but more importantly to pro-actively promote the doing of good.

Such a distinction is illuminated by Phillip Hallie's writings on the moral goodness of the people of Le Chambon, discussed in the opening segment of this book. In reflecting on encounters with members of the Hizmet movement, Hallie's account of these people often came to mind. In discussing the efficacious goodness of the people of Le Chambon, Philip Hallie speaks of two kinds of ethics—a negative and positive ethics (Hallie 2000, p. 86). A negative ethics, found in all religious and ethical traditions, focuses on moral *prohibitions* of acts of wrongdoing. These prohibitions require one to avoid acts of harm-doing which inflict suffering on others. To live by such an ethics is to guide one's life by a series of "Thou Shalt Nots". These negative imperatives bring one to refrain from murdering, lying, stealing, etc. thereby producing a decency of behavior. Hallie also describes a positive ethics, similarly found in these traditions, which demands more than mere refraining from prohibited actions; such an ethics requires the very

T. D. Conway, *Cross-cultural Dialogue on the Virtues*,
SpringerBriefs in Religious Studies, DOI: 10.1007/978-3-319-07833-5_8,
© The Author(s) 2014

active, robust, efficacious *doing of good*. Keeping one's hands clean of wrong-doing by refraining from certain acts is not enough; one must actively be doing good and be doing good willingly, even joyfully, to live by this positive ethics.

Hallie turns to the people of Le Chambon as a shining example of such efficacious goodness. Not only did the members of this community not harm persons during periods of intense persecution in Occupied France during World War II, but they actively committed themselves as a community to *doing good*—to saving the lives of thousands of people, most of them young children. They hospitably sheltered refugees in their homes and educated them in their schools, and when possible, guided them to safety in neutral Switzerland. Their spiritual vision and power enabled them to join together to secure the well-being of those in harm's way. They obeyed the negative *and* positive commandments of their faith, avoiding wrongdoing and doing good. Hallie argues that the center of their communal life was a love of God and humanity that produced a powerful ethic focused on the virtue of hospitality. These people actively welcomed and sought ways to cherish and promote the well-being of other persons, especially at-risk strangers and foreigners. Hallie concludes that the opposite of the cruelty of evil-doers is the loving goodness and hospitality lived by the people of Le Chambon. Such a community inspired people during this time of moral darkness and continues to fill people with hope in our current age. Rumi recognized our insufficiency in defining the nature of love, noting that in our attempt to do so, the pen breaks and we cease to write. And yet we recognize and are deeply moved by the powerful witness of those who live an ethic of love. They *show* what cannot adequately be expressed in words.

Just as compassion is not the same as pity, so an ethic of love transforms the virtue of charity. With compassion, one suffers with the other and is moved to relieve the others' suffering. One does not stand at a distance, looking pitifully down upon others. And such compassion has no limits: "My loving compassion encompasses all things" (*Qur'an* 7:156). So too charity does not involve a condescending dynamic between haves and have-nots, with charitable acts reaping praise and self-satisfaction. Gülen often emphasizes that service to others must not be concerned with direct or indirect material and political gain. Sincerity and purity of attention are required for true service. The Qur'an speaks of charity as the unselfish, joyful giving of one's self and one's goods (2:274). Such giving renders what is right, thereby establishing a relationship between the virtues of charity and justice. Charity enriches both the giver and the receiver. And true charity, informed by love, works to address the current needs of persons and their long-term well-being. This linkage of charity, justice and love clarifies the strong emphasis on education as furthering human development in the Hizmet movement. All initiatives—educational, philanthropic, and charitable—serve the end of human flourishing. And all such service is grounded in an ethics of love.

The people of Le Chambon, like members of the Gülen movement, drew no sharp line between the love of God and the love of human persons. God's love brought forth the human community, and love of others manifests gratitude for such Divine love. And thus their love had no limits or conditions, extending even to those who intended their and others' harm. And this community's moral goodness was sustained by the theological virtues of faith (in a God yet unseen), hope (for a never-ending happiness not yet attained) and love (of God and the human community).

In the *Summa Theologica* (Part I–II, Questions 26–27) Thomas Aquinas writes of an order of love that speaks to this understanding. Building on Aristotle, Aquinas develops a detailed account of the moral virtues and then turns to the three theological virtues of faith, hope and love, the greatest of which is love. He calls these virtues theological because their origin and telos is God, and they direct persons to supernatural happiness with God. For Aquinas, there is an order of love flowing from the love of God. According to Aquinas, we first love God as the source and principle of good and the basis for the virtue of love. We then love ourselves not in a selfish, narcissistic way but as creatures of God sharing in God's goodness and capable of living virtuously. We are then called to love all others within the human community. With deepest affection, we love those closest to us—our parents, children and extended family. We naturally love more deeply those united to us by ties of kinship and affection. Our love for them is intense and abundant, for we have many reasons for loving them. We are then called to love our friends, for whom we also have deep affection, and then the members of our local community and society—our neighbors, literally those near to us. And then we are called to love *all* our fellow human persons—near and far—wishing them well in thought, word and deed. And finally, and most challengingly, we are called to love our enemies who fail to wish us well and thwart our well-being. In loving enemies, we wish them well, refusing to retaliate against their wrong-doing with wrong-doing. Aquinas maintains that God is ultimately the reason we should love our enemy since our enemy is loved by God. And we should love our enemy for, in doing so, we manifest the depth of our love of God and God's creation. The strength of our love of God is thereby shown by our loving those most distant from us. Aquinas writes, "Our love for God is proved to be all the stronger through carrying man's affection to things what are the furthest from him, namely the love of enemies, even as the power of the furnace proved stronger according as it throws its heat to more distant objects" (Aquinas 2007, Q. 27, Article 8). But the intensity of our love is rightly directed to those closest to us. Aquinas goes on to explain,

> Hence our love for God is proved to be so much stronger, as the more difficult are the things we accomplish for its sake... Yet just as the same fire acts with greater force on what is near than on what is more distant, so too, [love] loves with greater fervour those who are united to us than those who are far removed; and in this respect the love of friends, considered in itself, is more ardent... than the love of one's enemy.

Gülen also speaks of the love of God shaping the love of others. As Rumi recognized, the human response to God, the initiator of love, is love. The love of God transforms hearts in such a way that persons no longer categorize each other as "they" and "we", "others" and "ours" (*Toward a Global Civilization of Love and Tolerance* 100). And he is convinced such love of God and others frees persons from the narrow prison of the self, making them more joyful, grateful and hopeful. Charity flowing from such love neither waits to be earned or deserved nor is restricted to me and mine; it flows naturally and gratuitously to those who simply are in need.

This order of love, affirmed by Sufis, originates in and flows from the love of God, who loves the beings of creation intentionally willed into existence. Thus all beings of the universe are touched by such Divine love. Human love stems from the love of the Divine and gives rise to the love of all beings derived from the love of God. Such love issues forth in a love of God's Prophets and Messengers and holy persons who live the way ordained by God. And such love extends to all beings as creatures of God. Thus love is the crowning moral virtue as wisdom (truth) is the highest intellectual virtue. For Rumi, love and truth bring one into the Beloved's Garden which ultimately and eternally refreshes the human spirit. The way of love in our daily lives with others points toward this ultimate state.

In Gülen's understanding, persons are in their nature communal, social beings. We find ourselves existing in a network of families, friendships, and civic, societal and global associations. Our ethical obligations always begin locally in the context of family and community but spread universally to include the entire human community. We live in a network of reciprocal relations with responsibilities stretching out from our closest to our most distant relations. The ancient Greek philosopher Diogenes spoke of our living in two communities—the community of our homeland and the wider community of our humanity. In this sense we are both a citizen of a native land and a citizen of the world. Diogenes emphasized the importance of cultivating ties with and concerns for the local and the universal. Influenced by this conception, the Stoic philosophers stressed that we live in the local community of our origin (our *polis*) and in the world community (*kosmopolis*).The philosopher Seneca recognized the importance of education fostering this understanding that each of us belongs to two communities, "one that is… truly common… in which we look neither to this corner nor to that, but measure the boundaries of our nation by the sun; the other, the one to which we have been assigned by birth" (as quoted in Nussbaum 1997, p. 58). Such understanding brought Cicero to emphasize our duty to treat all humanity with respect and to be especially attentive to treating foreigners with honor and hospitality in our homeland (59). He understood the importance of avoiding tension-generating partisanship and factionalism that foster hostilities and can be manipulated to serve negative political ends. The Stoics conceived the self as surrounded by a series of widening concentric circles, extending from family, kin, neighbours, compatriots to all humanity. Nussbaum, in her study of an educational approach emphasizing these points, describes this circular imagery in a way that speaks to the writings of Gülen. She argues that such education should pull the outer circles toward the center, drawing all human beings into fellowship without sacrificing ties to our local communities. Nussbaum writes, "In other words, we need not give up our special affections and identifications, whether national or ethnic or religious; but we should work to make all human beings part of our community of dialogue and concern, showing respect for the human wherever it occurs, and allowing that respect to constrain our national or local politics" (60–61).

Unquestionably the members of the Hizmet movement have deep ties to their Turkish homeland, the Turkish people, the Turkish cultural tradition and the Hizmet movement. Much of their service is directed parochially to family, local associations, Hizmet projects, and Turkish initiatives. Their familial and associative relations are distinctly Turkish, and they identify themselves as members of a particular moderate Sunni sect of Islam. And yet the *dar-al-hizmet* (abode of service to humanity) they foster is never directed only to the local and parochial. In respect to their practicing of the moral virtues—be they compassion, charity, tolerance/hospitality, justice, generosity—they are citizens of the world, for like the Stoics they believe "we should regard all human beings as our fellow citizens and local residents" (Nussbaum 1997, p. 52). The charitable associations of the Hizmet movement reveal that often we are called to meet the very dire needs of strangers in ways that may even take immediate precedence over the local, familial and societal responsibilities of our daily lives. Unquestionably in our actions we always have a deeper responsibility to our familial and local community members, but Gülen is convinced we must also always take into consideration the moral claims other persons, including future generations, make on us. Living an intentional ethical life requires such broad focus. Gülen often speaks of "servanthood" as living with a consciousness of being God's servant and a willingness to serve God through service to others near and far and to do so joyfully. *Dar-al-hizmet* (the abode of service to humanity) is *Islam* (submission to God).

The ancient Greek philosophers spoke of *philanthropia*, a love of humankind which evokes benevolent charity. Epicurus speaks of charity as "less intense perhaps than the love of God but broader in scope..., as though open to the universal and 'dancing around the world' like a light of joy and gentleness shining on all men, known and unknown, near and far, in the name of a common humanity, a common life, a common fragility" (Comte-Sponville 1996, p. 280). Gülen is convinced this philanthropy—this love of humanity—is what brings persons to focus on "how they can be useful to society and how they can avoid disputes with the society of which they are members. When they detect a problem in society, they take action like a spiritual leader rather than a warrior, leading people of virtue and lofty spirituality, abstaining from any sort of... dominance or thought of rule" (*Toward a Global Civilization of Love and Tolerance* 100). Such love produces acts of efficacious goodness. Both Gülen and Christian commentators on love develop in detail how a multitude of virtues both require and flow from love. St. Paul writes,

> Now I will show you the way which surpasses all the others. If I speak with human tongues and angelic as well, but do not have love, I am a noisy gong, a clanging symbol. If I have the gift of prophecy and, with full knowledge comprehend all mysteries, if I have faith enough to move mountains, but have not love, I am nothing. If I give everything I have to feed the poor and hand over my body to be burned, but have not love, I gain nothing. Love is patient; Love is kind. Love is not jealous, it does not put on airs; it is not snobbish. Love is never rude; it is not self-seeking; it is not prone to anger; neither does it brood over injuries. Love does not rejoice in what is wrong, but rejoices with truth. There is no limit of love's forbearance, to its trust, its hope, its power to endure... There are in the end three things that last: faith, hope and love, and the greatest of these is love (1 Corinthians 13).

So too Gülen describes at length how numerous virtues both require and flow from love. As he explains, persons who love and are faithful to God are,

> humbled with gratitude and… joy. They know how to be patient… and are tensed with determination. They start their journey anew with sharpened will. They do not become arrogant or ungrateful in the face of bounty nor do they fall into despair when they suffer deprivation. They carry a prophet-like heart in their exchanges with people. They love and embrace everyone; they turn a blind eye to the faults of others… They forgive the faults of those around them, not only under normal conditions, but also at times when they feel angered; they know how to live peacefully with even the most irritable souls. In fact Islam advises its followers to forgive as much as possible, and not to fall prey to feelings of rancor, hatred or revenge… [I]n all their acts they seek the means by which they can benefit others, they wish for the good of others, and they try to keep alive the love in their hearts, waging a never-ending battle against rancor and hate… They start their work willingly and prepare the ground for the seedlings of good… even when approached with hatred,… they repel the greatest armies with the indefatigable weapon of love (*Toward a Global Civilization of Love and Tolerance*, 98–99).

Gülen's ethics is clearly a virtue-based rather than a duty-driven ethics. Duty issues commands and constrains our actions. Whereas the virtues produce states of character from which settled dispositions to choose virtuously in particular ways emerge. The more one is hospitable, the less hospitality seems a duty required of one; the more one is generous, the less generosity is felt as an obligation restraining one's actions. One simply becomes a type of person who acts hospitably and generously and finds joy in being so. Duty obliges us to do what we would naturally do if we were acting from love. And duty commands actions even when we fail to be motivated by love. For this reason moral commands are required since persons can and often do lack love. Kant stresses that love of persons is no doubt possible,

> but it cannot be commanded. For it is not in the power of any man to *love* anyone at command… To love God means, in this sense, to like to do His commandments; to love one's neighbour means to like to practice all duties towards him. But the command that makes this a rule cannot command us to have this disposition in actions conformed to duty, but only to *endeavour* after it. For a command to like to do a thing is in itself a contradictory (Kant 2008, p. 58).

In a way similar to Gülen's account of the "Golden Generation", Kant writes of persons striving to live an ideal of holiness. The moral saint has developed moral dispositions to do all that the love of God and neighbour entails. The Sufi-inspired path of love calls persons to aspire to such an ideal of holiness. From Gülen's love of God and love of humanity flow virtuous actions which in turn develop habits, or settled dispositions, to act in ways benefitting and serving the good of human persons. And such love produces the joyfulness of virtuous actions associated with the truly virtuous person. St. Augustine calls persons "to love and do what you will"—in the sense that love truly motivates the doing of virtuous actions. In his commentary on 1 John 4:4–12, Augustine writes, "Once for all, then a short precept is given you: Love, and do what you will, whether you hold your peace, through love hold your peace; whether you cry out, through love cry out; whether you correct, through love correct,...: let the root of love beat within, of this root can nothing spring but what is good" (Augustine 2009, p. 504).

As we have seen in many religious traditions, the etymological roots of specific virtues are tied to the love often displayed by a mother toward her child. In so acting for the good of the child, a mother acts from love rather than duty. As André Compte-Sponville succinctly states, love "is the alpha and omega of all virtue" (1996, p. 226). Interactions with members of the Gülen-inspired movement disclose that the movement is fundamentally a faith-inspired philanthropic *Hizmet* movement. For this reason it is best understood through this lens of the virtues rooted ultimately in love. From its beginnings in the establishing of houses of hospitality through the establishing of schools, hospitals, media outlets, charitable associations, and dialogue centers across the world, its identity and dynamic have been formed and sustained by the practicing of core virtues and a constellation of related virtues ultimately traceable to love so emphasized by Rumi.

Persons are not born virtuous; they become virtuous through communal affiliations that model and foster the virtues—families, schools, and associations. And, as argued in this book, the Hizmet movement in all its complexity can be best understood through its emphasis on such formation in virtue. The Western tradition speaks of the cardinal virtues of courage, temperance, wisdom and justice. References to these and a wide range of virtues affirmed in philosophical and religious traditions are found in the writings of Gülen. But the cardinal virtues of this movement are clearly hospitality, wisdom, compassion, and charity as grounded in love; these virtues shape the movement's orientation and ethos and sustain its energy and expansion. And its expansion is truly amazing, radiating out from Turkey to span one-hundred and twenty countries and encompass hundreds of thousands of members in a network of informal voluntary associations dedicated to philanthropic service.

Three Current Challenges

The Hizmet Movement as a Non-political Initiative

Yet despite its impressive growth and enthusiastic support, the Hizmet movement continues to face challenges. Repeatedly it has had to address suspicion that it is a political movement seeking to amass political power and influence within Turkey and through its global outreach. Such suspicions surfaced repeatedly at the end of 2013. Gülen repeatedly emphasizes that he has no interest in political power, and in fact strongly opposes the use of religion to serve personal ambition or political ends. And yet in a deeper sense the Hizmet movement is truly "political" in an indirect way. Modern conceptions define politics as the art or science of government concerned with guiding or influencing governmental policy and winning and holding control over a government (*Merriam-Webster Dictionary*). Politics thus has to do with competing groups or individuals vying for power and control in government. Gülen repeatedly eschews such politics. But based on a deeper understanding of politics as closely related to ethics, it makes sense to describe Gülen as "political" in this more fundamental sense. "Politics" in the ancient Greek sense understood by Aristotle has to do with persons living well together in the polis, the social community. In the *Nicomachean Ethics,* Aristotle identifies the highest ruling science tied to ethics as political science, for this inquiry prescribes which of the sciences ought to be studied in society and identifies what ought to be done, preserved and avoided to promote the human good for people living together as social beings (1194b). In this sense "politics" has to do with reflections and policies about how to bring about virtuous living and flourishing within communities. Gülen's inquiry has consistently maintained such an ethical focus, seeking to discern how persons and communities can live well and flourish. Socrates was "political" in this sense, as captured in his description of himself as the gadfly of Athens. Socrates distanced himself from political roles, but sought to promote dialogue that encouraged reflection on important issues concerning shared civic life especially in its moral dimensions. Like a gadfly waking up a sluggish horse, he sought through his dialogues to encourage citizens to live more examined lives so they could better cultivate and serve humanity. And like Fethullah Gülen, his inquiry and dialogues focused on the virtues and the role they play in living a good life. In defending himself against charges of impiety and corruption of the youth of Athens, Socrates explained why he could not refrain from dialogue, even if it resulted in such false accusations. Recognizing his accusers' lack of understanding, he stated in the *Apology,* "If I say that it is the greatest good for man to discuss virtue every day and those things you hear me conversing and testing myself and others, or the unexamined life is not worth living for men, you will believe me even less" (Plato 2002, 38a).

Gülen repeatedly describes the associative network he has inspired as a *Hizmet* (service) movement. Consistent with this, Gülen is best understood as continuing the long Sufi tradition of serving the spiritual needs of people, educating them, and assisting them in meeting their basic physical needs. And he primarily does this through speaking and writing as forms of dialogue. As Ebru Altinoğlu argues, this suspicion of being political in the former sense of seeking to amass power is not surprising since Gülen stands in a long line of Sufis, including the highly renowned Rumi, who have been suspected of seeking political power, despite repeated denials (Altinoğlu 1999, p. 102). What remains obvious in direct encounters with members of the Hizmet movement is that this charismatic figure has inspired a grassroots social movement of persons dedicated to cultivating and practicing virtues that promote human well-being. And it is this practice, rather than the acquiring of power and control, that attracts admirers.

Perhaps the suspicious response to the *Hizmet* movement on the part of some individuals says more about the cynicism and distrust found in our contemporary age than it does about Gülen and the members of this movement. Some persons participating in the Rumi Forum programs in Turkey never had previous contact with Islamic societies. They had not previously experienced the depth of joyful graciousness, hospitality and generosity shown them by their hosts in cities across Turkey. They were baffled by the service ethic which defined the lives of so many individuals they encountered. At times suspicious questions were raised about the self-serving interests that had to underlie the seemingly altruistic acts of generosity and good-will. Some initially questioned whether the movement's focus on tolerance, service and peaceful relations masked a hidden nefarious, power amassing agenda. Could there truly be people who sought to live virtuously and delighted in doing so?

In response to such queries, the words of Aristotle, echoed in the writings of Gülen, often came to mind during such conversations. Aristotle claims that happiness is tied to virtue, and the life of virtue is a pleasant life in itself. He writes in the *Nicomachean Ethics*,

> For being pleased is a condition of soul. Further each type of person finds pleasure in whatever he is called a lover of; a horse, for instance, pleases the horse-lover, a spectacle the lover of spectacles. Similarly what is just pleases the lover of justice, and, in general what accords with virtue pleases the lover of virtue... Hence these people's life does not need pleasure to be added [to virtuous activity] as some sort of extra decoration; rather it has pleasure within itself (1099a).

In a 2012 article entitled "Virtue and Happiness" Gülen reaffirms this conviction regarding the role virtues play in a well-lived, happy life. He states that "Those who promise happiness to people must equip them with the virtues first. Happiness is not out of reach for those whose hearts have been saturated with virtue. From the past to the present, sound minds have always accepted it as so. Felicity and virtue are twins" (4). Gülen recognizes that virtue itself cannot guarantee a life free of spiritual and physical need, loss and deep suffering. He references individuals who suffered on a number of levels, but yet on a deeply human level maintained happiness and well-being. As he notes in this same article,

> A virtuous person can be ill, poor, or in a wretched condition. Such a person may suffer the oppression, insults and betrayals of other people, and may even undergo torture, convictions, and exiles. Jesus was betrayed. Socrates was convicted, and Epictetus was oppressed—but they all remained happy in a deep sense. In this respect, we believe that happiness resides in the heart, in the form of the breezes of an inner paradise, reinforced by the practice of virtues that cannot be shaken... We have learned this deep relation of virtue with true happiness from the most honourable figures of humanity. This is the very felicity which makes hearts find contentment, and which sets minds at rest. This felicity is based on the soundest pillars of virtue such as having no arrogance, being mature and tolerant, overlooking faults, and holding no grudges or hatred. To put it directly: this felicity is in the heart and spirit. It is so deep-rooted as never to be replaced by anything else. It is related to the essence of humanity. Materialistic pleasures in the superficial, selfish ambitious sense can add nothing to this type of felicity, nor can they substitute for it. How fortunate are those who exalt their souls with belief and refine their hearts with virtue! (5)

It may be the case that the suspicions of power acquisition and self-serving motivations regarding the Hizmet movement speak to the lessening of belief in the conviction that happiness and virtue are truly linked. All of Gülen's writings focus on the cultivation of the virtues as serving God and humanity and contributing to a well-lived human life. Human flourishing remains the core of his ethic and religious servanthood. Gülen offers to work with any and all persons to support educational and charitable initiatives fostering the practicing of the virtues and enabling sustainable human development. These efforts seek to promote the preparation of successful professionals who can further these initiatives and work to create public spaces for civic associations fostering dialogue, understanding and human flourishing. For this reason and in light of this understanding of "politics", the movement is best understood as a religiously inspired, grassroots communitarian movement. Gülen has never deviated from the conviction of Nursi that human efforts should be unified to combat ignorance, poverty and conflict. Marshalling the power to defeat *these* enemies remains his central concern. Amazingly abundant resources of social and financial capital have been dedicated to combating these and furthering the interlinked ends of peaceful relations and human well-being. But the means of doing this has always been through direct dialogical encounters which build mutual trust, understanding and concern rather than the acquiring of political power, force and influence.

The Hizmet Movement as a Modernist, Moderate Islamic Movement

The Hizmet movement also faces a second challenge of being rightly understood as a moderate Islamic movement. This movement avoids the polar opposites of a privatized secularism which marginalizes and silences Islam and fundamentalist extremism which produces a militant politicized Islam. The movement has sought to carve out a space for an alternate narrative and practice—a modernist, moderate, peaceful Islam that engages and seeks to contribute to contemporary life, not as a political movement, but as a faith-inspired social movement. Gülen supports neither the relegation of religion to a merely private sphere stripped of civic influence nor an Islamic system of government heavy-handedly regulating all aspects of life. While not advocating any specific form of government, he has always supported democratic principles ensuring a separation of religion and government. This support is grounded in his convictions that religious belief and practice can never be coerced and that both thrive in a context of religious liberty. Such liberty is seen as granting religion a role in public life, allowing religion to promote virtuous living in a civil society, respect for persons and human rights, and hospitable interactions between persons in the public sphere. But such civil society and public life require a minimum of tolerance, liberty, civility and rational discourse. Gülen is convinced the virtues at the core of his movement promote and enhance the discourse and practice of democracy.

The Hizmet movement prides itself on being a social movement initiated by Muslims with a modern orientation. This movement supports democratic principles and sees itself both engaging and contributing to the contemporary world. Its followers stand in a line of Muslims confident about the resourcefulness and adaptability of Islam which enable it to engage varied cultural contexts and respond to changing historical circumstances. Gülen places strong emphasis on the role of on-going *ijtihad* or hermeneutical interpretation of Islam in light of the opportunities and challenges of the contemporary age. To freeze *ijtihad* would be to stultify Islam and deny its capacity for addressing changing human circumstances and evolving needs. Drawing on the on-going interpretation of the Qur'an, Hadiths and Sunna and the use of analogical reasoning (*qiyas*) to apply these sources to new realities, Islam is seen as having the capacity to thrive as it faces current circumstances, conditions and contexts. This capacity renders possible the ongoing renewal and vitality of Islam. The Islamic tradition over time envisioned each age producing such "renewers" who would remain committed to the inner core of Islam while envisioning ways in which Islam could address the needs and challenges of the current age. Then Islam could continue to bring its central texts to life in evolving cultural and historical contexts.

While being faithful to the inner core of Islam, the Hizmet movement members pride themselves on following a distinctive Turkish Islam in regard to aspects of Islam that are open to interpretation. They are committed to keeping alive a vibrant Islam that can serve the contemporary globalized world. The members of the movement seek to model the intellectual and moral virtues they identify as the core of the Islamic ethos (wisdom and tolerance/hospitality, compassion, charity/love) in order to be faithful to Islam and also to resist the proliferation of highly distorted images of Islam which fuel hostility and intensify suffering. Gülen recognizes that, "the present, distorted image of Islam has resulted from its misuse by both Muslims and non-Muslims for their goals scare both Muslims and non-Muslims (Gülen, "Jews and Christians").

The Hizmet Movement as a Communitarian Service Movement

The Hizmet movement also faces a third challenge associated with its initial description as the "Gülen Movement". Gülen has consistently sought to shift emphasis from himself to this communitarian movement creating an ethos of service (*dar al-hizmet*). But it is his inspiration that created and sustains this movement and ethos. Perhaps more than any other trait, he is esteemed by supporters for his integrity, his consistently living the beliefs he expresses in his writings and speeches. This trait draws interest and sustains loyalty, building trust and confidence in him as a revered and honourable person. While never explicitly developing an account of integrity in his writings, his own integrity bears witness to this virtue and is frequently alluded to by those who admire him. Gülen's and Nursi's frequent references to the importance of sincerity speak to the virtue of integrity.

Nursi recognizes the great importance of sincerity noting that it "is the spirit and foundation of all good deeds" (Nursi 2004, p. 210). Sincerity as tied to truthfulness reveals how the moral virtues are illuminated by the intellectual virtues. The aspiration for truthfulness is one of the highest human aspirations, tied to our human capacity to know, understand and love what is true. Sincerity has to do with seeing, recognizing and remaining committed to truth. Such commitment to truth results in our being honest in expressing ourselves in thoughts, words and actions even when challenges and difficulties arise. Sincerity (al-ikhlās), understood as the avoidance of hypocrisy and deception, is a hallmark of Sufis. Thus "the book of Sufi is not black and ink words, it is none other than a pure heart white like snow" (as quoted in Nasr 2007, p. 165). To be sincere entails seeking out hidden, distorted intentions within the self and hypocrisy in one's words and deeds. As sincere, one seeks to be truthful about oneself to oneself and to others. Such self-honesty is required if one is to strive to grow in the practicing of virtue and to build trustworthy relations with others.

A number of contemporary philosophers' commentaries on integrity incorporate such points regarding sincerity. Integrity is more easily identified than defined. A number of studies of integrity, including Stephen Carter's *Integrity* and Bernard Williams' "Integrity", identify a cluster of traits associated with integrity, making it easier to discern what it means to have or lack integrity. Integrity is fundamentally tied to honesty in relation to oneself and others. It requires that there be a self to whom one can be true. Integrity has to do with a person having deeply held beliefs, commitments and convictions that are essentially tied to who the person is. To violate these is to violate the self. Persons with integrity have a noticeable depth and unity of character. The term "integrity" itself references these traits. The English word comes from the latin root *integri* meaning a whole, as in the term "integer" or whole number. Thus integrity entails a state or quality of wholeness or completeness. A person of integrity is one whose self and life reveal an integrated wholeness. There is a self to which this person can be true; there is no gap between the inner person and the outer person; there is no discrepancy between the person's thoughts, beliefs and actions. Thus persons of integrity are honest in their dealings, sincerely expressing themselves in word and deed. For this reason integrity is tied to courage, for persons of integrity stand their ground, being willing to speak their mind, express their convictions and commitments in both word and deed, even when this proves challenging and difficult. For this reason, persons of integrity can be counted on and trusted. They have consciously formed commitments affirming certain beliefs and principles, and these commitments are manifest faithfully and consistently in their choices, actions and projects. They have developed settled dispositions which shaped their character. Therefore even when persons like Socrates, Martin Luther King and Nelson Mandela were imprisoned and publicly vilified, they remained true to their convictions, commitments and character. Integrity is thus tied to fidelity and sincerity which enable trust. Persons of integrity maintain their commitments, living their convictions rather than casually and easily compromising and abandoning them.

But such steadfastness does not imply a rigidity or refusal to continue to think. Persons of integrity listen to others and are willing to discuss disagreements, exhibiting what Nietzsche described as having the courage to face an attack on one's convictions. Persons of integrity continue to reflect on their convictions and commitments, but never abandon them lightly. And such persons do not resist critical self-examination, seeking to avoid self-deception and welcoming the insights of others about them. The philosopher Bernard Williams maintains integrity is tied to the belief that each of us is responsible for what we do and how we live. Thus our actions flow from convictions and commitments which are taken seriously at the deepest level, comprising the inner core of our lives. Persons with such integrity are understandably deeply admired, for this trait reveals a depth of character comprised of so many virtues. Many persons respect Fethullah Gülen because of the integrity they find he manifests in his character and way of living.

The three challenges facing the Hizmet movement appear interrelated and speak to assumptions operative in the contemporary world. It may say much about our contemporary world that persons embodying such integrity are at times suspiciously viewed as having a hidden political agenda tied to the amassing of personal gain and power. Unquestionably, exposed and discredited persons have jaded our perceptions and judgments. But at the same time a moral cynicism today fuels such a quickly applied hermeneutic of suspicion. And this current cynicism may be partially traceable to the fact that many political and religious leaders seek positions of leadership solely to serve their personal ends. We live in a world in which we witness far too often the lack of integrity and glaring hypocrisy of persons in positions of power and authority. We also witness the misuse of religion to serve political ends tied to the exercising and amassing of great personal power and wealth. Perhaps the cynicism of our age has grown to the point that some refuse to believe there exist persons who sincerely and with integrity strive to live ethical lives promoting the well-being of others.

Gülen is respectfully and affectionately spoken of as *Hodjaefendi,* a term reserved for persons highly respected for their wisdom and stature. His stature is that of a sage—respected as wise, perceptive and discerning—and a virtuous person—beloved for his kindness, courtesy, humility, patience, generosity, compassion and hospitality, all traceable to his love of God and humanity. His living of his beliefs inspires and evokes imitation. As Lester Kurtz recognized, for Gülen, "spiritual practice and morality are… more important than ritual and dogmatism. The practicing of love, compassion, tolerance and forgiveness are what most matters. This sets up the possibility for dialogue and peaceful relations (377). And so too Gülen institutions and initiatives educate by witnessing—by modeling an Islamic faith that challenges assumptions, fears, prejudices and anxieties that can build and be fueled, especially for political ends. His followers inspire and teach by witnessing—modeling the virtues esteemed by all religious traditions and identified by them as central to their Islamic way of life. They model and teach by creating through schools, dialogue centers, forums, and cultural trips "islands of peace and dialogue" that value both our commonality and differences. Gülen and his followers always seek to identify and build on the common ground we share, even if it can only be minimally recognized as a common world and human condition. He stresses, "Even though we may not have common ground on some matters, we all live in this world and are passengers on the same ship. In this respect, there are many points that can be discussed and shared with people from every segment of society" ("Tolerance in the Life of the Individual and Society"). With amazing perseverance and dedication, Gülen and his followers consistently seek to find the common ground, even in circumstances where this is most challenging. This is evident in all their institutions and activities, but most noticeably in their intercultural trips to Turkey.

This study of the virtues in the Gülen movement began with an invitation to join a colleague and theologian, Bill Collinge, on a journey to Turkey. In unexpected ways and long before the Rumi Forum trip, Bill's writings and conversations brought me to reflect on the virtue of hospitality, so central to the Gülen movement. In an essay on teaching, Bill quotes the Catholic theologian Henri Nouwen's work on hospitality entitled *Reaching Out*. Nouwen defines hospitality as,

> the creation of a free space where the stranger can enter and become a friend instead of an enemy. Hospitality is not to change people, but to offer them space where change can take place. It is not to bring men and women over to our side but to offer freedom not disturbed by dividing lines... it is the liberation of fearful hearts so that words can find roots and bear ample fruit (51).

Nouwen recognizes that creating hospitable spaces is far from easy, especially in our overly frenetic and preoccupied lives. The philosopher Martin Heidegger captures well a state that increasingly shapes and defines our lives in the German term *Aufenthaltlosigkeit*—the state of never tarrying anywhere. But Nouwen also recognizes that,

> if we expect any salvation, any redemption, healing and new life, the first thing we need is an open receptive place where something can happen to us. Hospitality, therefore, is such an important attitude. We cannot change the world by a new plan, project or idea. We cannot even change other people by our convictions, stories, advice and proposals, but we can offer a space where people are encouraged to disarm themselves, to lay aside their occupations and pre-occupations and to listen with attention and care to the voices speaking in the center (54).

Just as Hallie conceived hospitality as the opposite of cruelty, so Nouwen conceives hospitality as being at the opposite end of the spectrum from hostility (Hallie 2000). Collinge explains that Nouwen's conception of hostility refers "not only to outright hatred and aggression but also—and more pertinently—to all attitudes and behavior which are marked by fearfulness and defensiveness toward others, in which we react to others as threats or rivals" (Collinge 1980, pp. 10–11). Insightfully, Collinge describes hospitality as fundamentally involving a "letting-be of the other", a kind of withdrawing in order to make space for others to be themselves, irrespective of one's own expectations, hopes or fears concerning them" (11). Collinge goes on to emphasize that this "letting-be" is very far from a passive response. He explains that even the most basic form of hospitality—inviting a person into one's home—assumes an interest in the invited guest and a concern for his or her well-being. Thus, hospitality is far from passive; it "requires making an effort to overcome hostility and fear in order to *create* a free space, and resisting the impulse to fill that space with one's own ideas, interests, and preoccupations" (11).

Collinge's reflections focus on his teaching philosophy to undergraduates. But his comments on hospitality and teaching resonate with anyone taking a journey based in the desire to learn. Nouwen, like Plato, believes all education is fundamentally a turning of the soul, a guiding of the soul to questions about why we live, work, love and die and how we should go about doing these well in humanly meaningful ways. Educators, especially teachers of philosophy and theology, invite students on such journeys of exploration. So too, Gülen in his writing, speaking, and dialoguing with others, invites them on what he hopes will be a transformational journey. Followers of Gülen continue on this journey, reading his steady stream of writings and reflections and inviting others to learn about the movement he inspired.

The Rumi Forum trip to Turkey was full of these exchanges over meals, in buses and late into the night in hotel lounges. Our hosts delighted in bringing us to experience sites and scenes they had repeatedly returned to on such trips. Bill Collinge ends his essay on hospitality with the words of St. Augustine on his own teaching catechumens about Christian beliefs and practices. Augustine wrote of returning to subjects in dialogue with them that he had often explored, asking,

> Is it not a common occurrence, that when we are showing to those who have never seen them before certain lovely expanses, whether of town or countryside, which we through often seeing already have been in the habit of passing by without any pleasure, our own delight is renewed by their delight at the novelty of the scene? And the more so, the closer friendship between them and us; for in proportion as we dwell in them through the bond of love, so do things which were old become new to us also (12).

So too, we witnessed these Turkish sites and scenes come alive to our hosts and ourselves as we journeyed and dialogued together throughout Turkey.

It is fitting that this extended reflection on the virtue of hospitality and related virtues practiced by the followers of Gülen ends where it began—with the hospitable invitation to commence a journey with the members of the Rumi Forum of Washington, D.C. From them I learned much about this Turkey-based communitarian network of voluntary associations dedicated to peaceful relations and human flourishing. But even more so, from them and this study, I continue to learn about the soul's exploration of questions of why we live, work, love and die and how we can go about doing these well in humanly hope-and-meaning-filled ways. In the end it seems quite fitting that this work comes to closure with a final response of gratitude. Much of my own life's cross-cultural journeying and the deep long-lasting relationships it produced resonated with this trip and study. So it seems fitting to end this cross-cultural reflection on the virtues with the words of a Sufi poet often translated to me by my husband, Abdolreza Banan. These selected excerpts capture the core meaning of Rumi's poem "Moses and the Shepherd". When Moses harshly chastised a humble shepherd after he overheard his words to God, "Where are you, Allah, that I may be your servant; that I may comb and delice your hair; wash and mend your clothes; lovingly bring you milk, and if you become ill, take care of you as one of my own, sacrificing all for you?", the voice of God spoke to Moses,

> Why are you separating me from my people? You were sent to bring people to me, not to separate them from me. I have given each people a way of seeing, knowing and speaking. Each people have a unique way of expressing their love and worship of God—Hindus as Hindus, San as Sand [a people living in a region between India and Persia]. The lover of God does not recognize nationality or origin. A special gem does not need to be engraved to be valued. Those hearts which have love do not feel sorrow even in the ocean of sorrow. I send you to bring the people closer to me, not to separate them from me. Make a fire of love and burn all thinking about prayer rituals! See inside the person, penetrating to what is inner rather than outer.

The Hizmet movement continues to keep alive the Sufi spirit of Rumi captured in these verses. Drawing on this spirit, the Rumi Forum of Washington D.C. welcomes everyone who wishes to work with them to foster dialogue and understanding among people of different faiths and cultures. Their gracious hospitality and practicing of numerous virtues have given many people hope that moral living is possible and that respectful dialogue among persons is a reality achievable by real persons, rather than a naïve, idealistic pipe dream. Immanuel Kant held that the question "What can we hope for?" is one of the four most essential questions posed by human beings. Kant recognized that a life devoid of hope is a life overwhelmed by sadness (Kant 1978, 7:254). He was convinced the human soul is strengthened and elevated by encountering examples of persons who live a moral life. In the absence of such examples, we can cynically convince ourselves that moral living is either an impossibility or a manipulative deception worth suspicious unmasking. Gülen recognizes that human persons cannot function, let alone thrive, without hope. Moral living is motivated and sustained by hope.

Through encountering members of the Hizmet movement we deepen our awareness of the role a range of virtues play in such on-going dialogue and deepening understanding of our shared humanity. From the movement's practice of hospitality, we come to realize a fundamental insight so needed in our world today, namely that persons from different "nationalities or origins" come bearing gifts which help us to better *understand* the virtues that are so central to our shared human living. And in a deepening spirit of hospitality, such cross-cultural dialogue and understanding may help us to *live* better the virtues so needed if we are to sustain our hope in and work for peaceful relations with fellow persons from richly diverse cultural and religious traditions. This hope echoes the profound statement of the *Qur'an* that inspires and motivates the Hizmet movement,

> Humans, we have created you from male and female and have divided you into nations and tribes that you might come to know one another (*Qur'an* 49:13).

The Hizmet movement provides living witness to the power and efficacy of the practicing of virtues so needed today in our personal and communal lives in local, societal and global settings. And such witness sustains our hope and motivates our determination to live ethically.

References

Altinoğlu, Ebru. (1999). *Fethullah Gulen's perception of state and society*. Istanbul: Bosphurus University.

Aquinas, T. (2007). *Summa Theologica* (Volume I: Part II-II). Charleston, SC: Bibliobazaar.

Aristotle. (1999). *Nicomachean ethics*. 2nd ed. (T. Irwin, Trans.). Indianapolis: Hackett

Augustine. (2009). Ten homilies on the first epistle of John, Homily 7, section 8. In P. Schaff (Ed.), *The Nicene and post-Nicene fathers series* (Christian Classics Edition). Grand Rapids, MI: Eerdmans.

Collinge, W. J. (1980). Hospitality and required philosophy courses. *Contemporary Philosophy, Philosophic Research and Analysis, VII*(12), 10–12.

Comte-Sponville, A. (1996). *A small treatise on the great virtues*. New York: Holt.

Gülen, M. F. (2004). *Toward a global civilization of love and tolerance*. New Jersey: The Light.

Gülen, M. F. (2012). Virtue and happiness. *The Fountain, 85*, 4–5.

Gülen, M. F. *Jews and Christians in the Quran*. http://en.fgulen.com/content/view/1342/13)

Gülen, M. F. *Tolerance in the life of the individual and society*.

Gülen, M. F. http://en.fgulen.com/content/view/1800/33

Hallie, P. (2000). From cruelty to goodness. In L. Pojman (Ed.), *The moral life*. New York: Oxford.

Kant, I. (1978). *Anthropology from a pragmatic point of view*. Carbondale: Southern Illinois University Press.

Kant, I. (2008). *Kant's critique of practical reason*. Radford, VA: Wilder Publications.

Kurtz, L. Gülen's paradox: combining commitment and tolerance. *The Muslim World* 95:373–384.

Nasr, S. H. (2007). *The garden of truth, the vision and promise of Sufism, Islam's mystical tradition*. New York: Harper.

Nouwen, H. (1986). *Reaching out, the three movements of the spiritual life*. New York: Image.

Nursi, B. S. (2004). *The flashes collection* (S. Vahide, trans.). Istanbul: Nur Publishers.

Nussbaum, M. (1997). *Cultivating humanity, a classical defense of reform in liberal education*. Cambridge, MA: Harvard University Press.

Plato. (1992). *The republic* (G. Grube, Trans.). Indianapolis: Hackett.

Williams, B. (1973). Integrity. In J. J. C. Smart & B. Williams (Eds.), *Utilitarianism for and against*. New York: Cambridge University Press.

Works Cited and Referenced

Algar, H. (2001). The centennial renewer: Bediuzzaman Said Nursi and the tradition of Tajdid. *Journal of Islamic Studies, 12*(3), 291–311.

Altinoğlu, E. (1999). *Fethullah Gülen's perception of state and society.* Istanbul: Bosphurus University.

Aquinas, T. (2007). *Summa theologica,* Vol. I: Part II–II. Charleston, SC: Bibliobazaar.

Aristotle. (1999). *Nicomachean ethics.* (2nd ed.), (T. Irwin, Trans.) Indianapolis: Hackett.

Aristotle. (1947). *Introduction to Aristotle.* (R. McKeon, Trans.). New York: Modern Library.

Augustine. (2009). Ten homilies on the first epistle of john, homily 7, section 8. In P. Schaff (Eds.), The Nicene and Post-Nicene Fathers Series, Vol. Christian Classics Edn. Grand Rapids, MI: Eerdmans.

Baumgarth, W. P., & Regan, R. (1998). *Saint Thomas Aquinas on law, morality and politics.* Indianapolis: Hackett.

Benedict, S. (2013). *The rule of Saint Benedict.* Retrieved December, 2013 from http://www.osb. org/rb/text/rbeaad1.html

Birge S. J., Sr. Mary K. (2013). Wwjd? Jesus, the death penalty, and U.S. roman catholics. In V. Schieber, T. Conway, D. McCarthy (Eds.), *Where justice and mercy meet.* Collegeville, MN: Liturgical Press.

Bruckmayr, P. (2010). Phnom penh's Fethullah Gülen schools as an alternative to prevalent forms of education for cambodia's muslim minority. In J. Esposito & I. Yilmaz (Eds.), *Islam and peacebuilding, Gülen movement initiatives.* New York: Blue Dome Press.

Buber, M. (2000). *I and thou.* New York: Scribner.

Camus, A. (1965). L'Incroyant et les chrétiens: fragments d'une exposé fait au convent des Dominicains de Latour-Maubourg en 1948. *Essais Actuelles* 1, Paris.

Camus, A. (1990). The guest. In W. Fowlie (Ed.) *French stories.* New York: Dover.

Capes, D. B. (2010). Tolerance in the theology and thought of a.j. conyers and Fethullah Gülen. In J. Esposito & I. Yilmaz (Eds.), *Islam and peacemaking, Gülen movement initiatives.* New York: Blue Dome.

Carroll, B. J. (2007). *A dialogue of civilization, Gülen's Islamic ideal and humanistic discourses.* Somerset, NJ: The Light.

Carter, S. (1996). *Integrity.* New York: Harper.

Çitlak, M.F. & Bingül, H. (2007). *Rumi and his sufi path of Love.* Somerset, NJ: The Light.

Collinge, W. J. (1980). *Hospitality and required philosophy courses.* Contemporary Philosophy, Philosophic Research and Analysis. Vol. VII, No. 12, Winter: 10–12.

Comte-Sponville, A. (1996). *A small treatise on the great virtues.* New York: Holt.

Conway, G. D. (1989). *Wittgenstein on foundations.* Amherst, New York: Humanities Press International (currently Prometheus/Humanity).

Conway, T., Schieber, V., & McCarthy, D. (Eds.). (2013). *Where justice and mercy meet.* Collegeville: Liturgical Press.

Conze, E. (1969). *Buddhist scriptures.* New York: Penguin.

Dali, L. (2002). *An open heart, practicing compassion in everyday life.* New York: Back Bay Books.

Day, D. (2005). *Dorothy day. Selected writings By Little and By Little.* Maryknoll, NY: Orbis.

Derrida, J. (1999). *Adieu Emmanuel Levinas.* Stanford: Stanford University Press.

Derrida, J. (2000). *Hospitality.* Stanford: Stanford University Press.

Descartes, R. (1985). In J. Cottingham, R. Stoohut & D. Murdock (Eds.), *The philosophical writings of Descartes* (Vol. 1). Cambridge: Cambridge University Press.

Doblmeier, M. (Director). (2007). *The power of forgiveness.* Journey Films, Inc.

Easwaran, E. (Trans). (2007). *The Dhammapada.* Tomales, CA: Nilgiri Press.

Ebaugh, H. (2009). *The Gülen movement: A sociological analysis of a civic movement rooted in moderate Islam.* New York: Springer.

Einstein, A. (2000). *Out of my later years.* New York: Citadel.

Esposito, J. (2011). *Islam, the straight path* (4th ed.). New York: Oxford University Press.

Esposito, J. & Ihsan, Y. (2010). *Islam and peacebuilding, Gülen movement initiatives.* New York: Blue Dome Press.

Fatemi, N. (1977). *Sufism: Message of brotherhood, harmony and hope.* Lancaster: Gazelle Book Services.

Fiala, A. (2002). Toleration and the limits of the moral imagination. *Philosophy in the Contemporary World, 10*(2), 33–40.

Forbes, H. D. (1997). *Ethnic conflict, commerce, culture and the contact hypothesis.* New Haven: Yale.

Gadamer, H. (1989). *Truth and method.* (Revised 2nd ed.), (J. Weinsheimer & D. G. Marshall Trans.). New York: Crossroad.

Galleotti, A. (2002). *Toleration as recognition.* Cambridge: Cambridge University Press.

Grinnell, K. (2010). Border thinking: fethullah gülen and the east-west divide. In J. Esposito, Yilmaz (Eds.), *Islam and peacebuilding, Gülen movement initiatives.* New York: Blue Dome Press.

Gülen, M. F. (1998). *Prophet Muhammad as commander.* Izmir: Kaynak

Gülen, M. F. (2000a). In A. Ünal & A. Williams (Eds.), *Advocate of dialogue.* Fairfax: The Fountain.

Gülen, M. F. (2000b). *Prophet Muhammad: Aspects of his life.* Fairfax: The Fountain.

Gülen, M. F. (2001). A comparative approach to islam and democracy. *SAIS Review 21*(2), 133–138

Gülen, M. F. (2004a). *Essays-perspectives-opinions.* Somerset, NJ: The Light.

Gülen, M. F. (2004b). *Key concepts in the practice of sufism, emerald hills of the heart.* Rutherford, NJ: The Light.

Gülen, M. F. (2004c). *Toward a global civilization of love and tolerance.* New Jersey: The Light.

Gülen, M. F. (2006). *Pearls of wisdom.* Somerset, NJ: The Light.

Gülen, M. F. (2012). Virtue and happiness. *The Fountain, 85,* 4–5.

Gülen, M. F. Forgiveness. http://en.fgulen.com/gulens-works/recent-articles?start=70

Gülen, M. F. Islam-A religion of tolerance. http://en.fgulen.com/contentview/1808/33

Gülen, M. F. Jews and christians in the quran. http://en.fgulen.com/content/view/1342/13

Gülen, M. F. Love, compassion, tolerance and forgiving: The pillars of dialogue. http://en.fgulen.com/content/view/1339/13

Gülen, M. F. Tolerance in the life of the individual and society. http://en.fgulen.com/content/view/1800/33

Gurbuz, M. (2013). Performing moral opposition: Musings on the strategy and identity in the gülen movement. In I. Yilmaz, G. Barton, & P. Weller (Eds.), *Muslim world in transition: Contributions of the Gulen movement.* London: Leeds Metropolitan University Press.

Hallie, P. (1994). *Lest innocent blood be shed, the story of the village of Le Chambon and how goodness happened there.* New York: Harper.

Hallie, P. (2000). From cruelty to goodness. In L. Pojman (Ed.), *The moral life.* New York: Oxford.

Hanh, T. N. (1991). *Old path white clouds*. Berkeley, CA: Parallax Press.

Hanh, T. N. (1999). *The heart of Buddha's teaching, transforming suffering into peace and liberation*. New York: Broadway Books.

Hanh, T. N. (2001). *Anger, wisdom for cooling the flames*. New York: Riverhead Books.

Ignatieff, M. (2000). Nationalism and toleration. In S. Mendus (Ed.), *The politics of toleration in modern life*. Durham: Duke University Press.

Kalyoncu, M. (2010). Building civil society in ethno-religiously fractured communities: The Gülen movement in turkey and abroad. In J. Eposito & I. Yilmaz (Eds.), *Islam and peacebuilding*. New York: Blue Dome.

Kant, I. (1963). Proper self respect and duties to self. In *Lectures on ethics*. New York: Harper & Row.

Kant, I. (1996). *Metaphysics of morals*. New York: Cambridge.

Kant, I. (1978). *Anthropology from a pragmatic point of view*. Carbondale: Southern Illinois University Press.

Kant, I. (2008). *Kant's critique of practical reason*. Radford, VA: Wilder Publications.

Khantipālo, P. (1964). *Tolerance, a study from Buddhist sources*. Eugene, OR: Wipf and Stock.

Kurtz, L. Gülen's paradox: combining commitment and tolerance. *The Muslim World 95*, 373–384.

Levinas, E. (1994). *In the time of nations* (M. B. Smith Trans.). London: Athlone Press.

Locke, J. (1990). *A letter concerning toleration*. Amherst, NY: Prometheus.

Luttrell, M. (2007). *Lone survivor*. New York: Little, Brown and Company.

Mendus, S., & Edwards, D. (Eds.). (1987). *On Toleration*. Oxford: Clarendon.

Michel, T. (2003). Fetullah Gülen as educator. In M. H. Yavuz and J. Esposito (Eds.), *Turkish Islam and the secular state: The Gülen movement*, Syracuse: Syracuse University Press.

Nasr, S. H. (2007). *The garden of truth, the vision and promise of Sufism, Islam's mystical tradition*. New York: Harper.

Nouwen, H. (1986). *Reaching out, the three movements of the spiritual life*. New York: Image.

Nursi, B. S. 2004. *The flashes collection*. (Ş. Vahide. Trans.). Istanbul: Nur Publishers.

Nussbaum, M. (1985). 'Finely aware and richly responsible': Moral attention and the moral task of literature. *Journal of Philosophy, 82*(10), 516–529.

Nussbaum, M. (1988). Non-relative virtues: An Aristotelian approach. *Midwest Studies in Philosophy XIII*, 32–52.

Nussbaum, M. (1992). Internal criticism and Indian rationalist raditions. In M. Krauz (Ed.), *Relativism: Interpretation and confrontation*. Notre Dame, IN: University of Notre Dame.

Nussbaum, M. (1997). *Cultivating humanity, a classical defense of reform in liberal education*. Cambridge, MA: Harvard University Press.

Nussbaum, M. (2003). The cognitive structure of compassion. In *Upheavals of thought, the intelligence of emotions*. New York: Cambridge University Press.

Oberdiek, H. (2001). *Tolerance, beyond forebearance to acceptance*. Rowman and Littlefield

Plato (1992). *The republic*. (G. Grube, Trans.). Indianapolis: Hackett

Pratt, D. (2010). Islamic prospects for interreligious dialogue: the voice of fethulah Gülen. In J. Esposito & I. Yilmaz (Eds.), *Islam and peacemaking, Gülen movement initiatives*. New York: Blue Dome Press.

Radcliffe, T. (2008). *Why go to church, the drama of the Eucharist*. New York: Continuum.

Rousseau, J. (1979). *Emile or on education*. (A. Bloom, Trans.). New York: Basic Books.

Rumi, M. J. (1943). Moses and the shepherd. In *Masnavi* (A. Banan, Trans.). Teheran: Aftab Publisher, (1321, [C.E. 1943], pp. 148–149).

Said, E. (2001). *Orientalism: Western conceptions of the orient*. New York: Penguin.

Saritoprak, Z. (2010). Fethullah Gülen's theology of peacebuilding. In J. Esposito & I. Yilmaz (Eds.), *Islam and peacebuilding, Gülen initiatives*. New York: Blue Dome Press.

Scarry, E. (1998). The difficulty of imagining other persons. In E. Weiner (ed.), *The handbook of interethnic coexistence*. New York: Continuum Publishing.

Shakespeare. (1998). *The Merchant of Venice*. New York: Signet Classics.

Smith, A. (1984). *The theory of moral sentiments*. In D. D. Raphael & A. L. Macfie (Eds.). Indianapolis, IN: Liberty Fund.

Taylor, C. (1994). The politics of identity. In A. Gutman (Ed.), *Multiculturalism, examining the politics of recognition*. Princeton, NJ: Princeton University Press.

Ünal, A., & Williams, A. (2000). *Advocate of dialogue*. Fairfax, VA: The Fountain.

Walzer, M. (1997). *On toleration*. New Haven, CT: Yale.

Williams, B. (1973). Integrity. In J. J. C. Smart & B. Williams (Eds.), *Utilitarianism for and against*. New York: Cambridge University Press.

Yavuz, M. H., & Esposito, J. L. (2003). *Turkish Islam and the secular state*. Syracuse, NY: Syracuse University Press.

Yilmaz, I. (2003). Ijtihad and tajdid by conduct. In M. H. Yavuz, J. Esposito (Eds.), *Turkish Islam and the secular state, the Gülen movement*. Syracuse, NY: Syracuse University Press.

Yurtsever, A. (Ed.). (2009). *When I was in turkey*. Washington, DC: Rumi Forum.

Mrs. Malone sank into her rocker and quickly slit the envelope with a hairpin. Jay pulled out a dining chair, sat down and laid his cap over his knee.

The letter told a tragic story. Uncle Joe had just lost his entire family. George, their grown son who worked in Philadelphia, had come home very sick and died three days later. Then Aunt Martha came down with it (he didn't say what) and she lasted only one week. Uncle Joe said he was managing. But he wondered if maybe they wouldn't like to come stay with him for the duration.

Mrs. Malone and Jay locked stares. That they should leave their comfortable niche in the old home town had not once occurred to either of them.

Jay shook his head and said with finality, "No!"

His mother nodded, agreeing. Yet troubling thoughts disturbed her. Joe was her only living relative. Just they two were left of the family. And he had always been good to her. The poor man doubtless found it terrible hard. She knew what loneliness was.

She spoke only of practical matters. "In a way," she said slowly, "it would be a big help to us for money. Not needing the house rent, we'd be able to save for when Dad comes home."

Jay kept shaking his head stubbornly.

"And the food bills. Uncle Joe wrote one time that their creek was full of fish and crabs for the taking."

Still Jay balked. But Mrs. Malone, against her will, could think of more reasons for going than not. In their present beggarly circumstances (even their modest contributions to the church collection plate had dwindled), they should be thankful for Uncle Joe's generous invitation.

To avoid argument, she said, "We'll have to sleep on it," and folded the letter into her apron pocket. "Perhaps you'd take that pan of peelings down on the lot for me?"

Carrying the heavy dishpan down the boardwalk to the pit they wanted filled up, Jay could see two of his buddies hanging around their fort in the weedlot by the canal. Sight of them fired up his anger at the thought of moving away. He got so mad that when he went to heave in his load, he heaved himself in with it. Sputtering, he crawled out plastered with tomato skins.

His mother standing with her hands on her hips at the screen door saw him and laughed. Venting his fury would take some of the steam out of his resistance to leaving. All she said to him was, "Those loose boards have got to be fixed."

Over the weekend while they "slept on it," she enlisted the aid of Grampa Malone. After church he came home with them for Sunday dinner. They would have everybody's favorite dessert, kasha kuchen—cherry cake. And to salve up Jay, she made his favorite treat, what he called "slop pie." It was simply the pastry trimmings rolled into a crust, covered with milk, and sprinkled with sugar and spices. Jay was fond of it for snacking.

While she was busy washing up, Grampa and Jay had the back porch to themselves. Seeming without guile, the old gentleman said, "I brung you a book I think you'll like. It's cram full of facts and stories about the old war." He handed over a rather dog-eared volume in dark blue covers stamped in gold letters Blue and Gray.

With a little smile Jay politely accepted the relic, studying its cover. Sunk into the fabric were two flags, and in a gold circle two soldiers stood shaking hands. It was thick, more than eight hundred pages, he saw, leafing through.

Grampa added, "Until school begins and you get acquainted down there, you'll have time for reading, I should think."

A shadow passed over Jay's face, but he did not voice his discontent.

Grampa gave him a sharp glance, fingering his beard. "I know you hate to go away. But so did your Dad. Still, he figgered it was his duty. And helping out your Uncle Joe is kinda the same for you and your Ma."

Jay screwed up his face and shrugged. He was not in the habit of arguing with his Grampa.

"Think of all the adventures you'll have. I shouldn't wonder but what you'd learn to ride a horse good as any cavalryman—"

"There ain't no justice," Jay muttered, hardly to the point, but the kids thought the expression so clever.

"Well, mebbe not," Grampa quietly agreed. "But we all have to make sacrifices sometime or other. And fer a young feller, spending time on a farm seems like an easy way to do your part."

Still, Jay was unhappy at the prospect. "We'll be way off in the middle of nowhere," he whispered, "and not know nobody." He had never met his Uncle Joe.

"Oh, you'll make a nice lot of friends in no time," Grampa soothed him. "Let's just pretend that this is your engagement for the duration."

Mrs. Malone, letting it be known that they were leaving, sought to shield Jay from well-meaning adults. She urged that no one mention the move to him, explaining that he was unhappy about leaving all his friends.

Obliging relatives offered temporary storage for their few pieces of furniture, after which, a trunk and two traveling bags held all they had to take. Family and friends saw them off on the train, waving and shouting,

"Good-bye. Good-bye." And, "Don't forget to write often." The Bay Ferry, Jay's first ride on anything bigger than a rowboat, thrilled him so that he was all over the vessel. Finally there was another train ride, quite short, and they reached their destination after dark.

Uncle Joe met them in the dim light of the station platform. And after a hug and kiss for his sister, he took Jay's hand in his leathery palms and said warmly, "I'm right glad you've come." He was a small wiry man with a dark walrus mustache and deeply lined face. To accommodate all their luggage, he had come in the hearse. This was in fact an undertaker's vehicle with the glass top removed by somebody so they could sell it as a spring wagon. It rode most comfortably Uncle Joe said, on account of the good soft springs.

Tuckered out from his day-long excitement, Jay dozed off as the horse jogged out the dark road and his mother related the events of their trip down. Pulling up at the lane gate, they were greeted by a big excited dog, honey-color in the lantern light. "His name is Josh," Uncle Joe said. "He's a Golden Retriever, and he'll be your special friend."

For Jay it was love at first sight.

Uncle Joe let them into the big farmhouse kitchen, put down their bags and lit a lamp. Their trunk could wait for help in the morning. "Now, if you'll just set a minute while I unhitch," he said, "we'll have a little bite to eat."

Jay and his mother sank into a couple of old cozy rockers either side of a big round table cluttered with magazines and letters on top of which lay an open pair of spectacles. Facing them stood a huge, ornate "Acme Sterling" range brightly shining, and to one side, above the woodbox, hung a narrow shelf supporting two kerosene lamps and a mantel clock ornate of case and loud of tick. Cupboards about the room were crowded with china and glassware.

Uncle Joe was back in a trice and Josh came in with him. After that, Jay had eyes for nothing but his newfound friend. His thin arms encircling the eager dog's neck, he was rewarded with a lick on the cheek, which made him chuckle.

Over a quick little fire of paper and kindling wood, Uncle Joe heated up a pot of delicious soup. And he set out thick slices of homemade bread which they lathered with sweet butter. Jay paid hardly any attention to the grown-up talk, being engrossed in sneaking down to Josh tidbits much appreciated.

While Uncle Joe had a pipe, he wanted to reassure his sister that he had not asked her down just to put her to work. His eyes twinkling, he said, "You needn't to worry your head about a thing, Clara. I've got a widow-woman living clost by has been nicely handling the housekeeping."

But Mrs. Malone was not accustomed to playing the lady. She laughed, "We'll just see."

The clock struck ten and Uncle Joe laid aside his pipe. "I guess you're tired out from your trip. We'd better get some rest. There'll be time for talk in the morning."

Reminding Josh that his bed was on the porch, Uncle Joe handed the table lamp to his sister while he carried the bag they needed and led the climb up steep, narrow stairs, their shadows following along the wall.

Jay was given a small, cramped room at the head of the stairs. Its furnishings were sparse: a chipped enamel bedstead covered with a pieced quilt, one small oak bureau with matching washstand supporting suitable crockery in deep blue, one cushionless straight chair, and a pink china lamp standing on a nailkeg. This Uncle Joe lighted. With a wink he departed. Jay sat on the edge of the bed, while his mother unpacked his nightclothes, and studied his little cell. Hardly the comfy bedroom he'd left back home. But then, he would fix it up with his picture of the little drummer boy hanging there between the window and the closet door.

Tired out, he fell asleep at once. When he opened his eyes the next morning, it was at the nudge of a cold nose. Uncle Joe had sent Josh up to waken him. Hurriedly he dressed and together they ran down the stairs.

Mrs. Tarbutton, a stout cheerful woman in clean gingham, her faded hair caught in a egg-sized knot with straggling wisps, her face flushed like she'd been working over the hot stove, was saying as he entered the kitchen, "Yes, indeedy. I had eight childern myself. Six a-livin'." She beamed. "And now we're expectin' our very first gran'child."

It was a shock to Jay and his mother, learning the great distance he must travel to school—two and a half miles! What a difference after living within five blocks of the schoolhouse. But Uncle Joe hoped to pick up a secondhand bicycle somewhere at one of the farm auctions.

In those first few days, Mrs. Malone found little to do but walk about or sit with her fancy work. Mrs. Tarbutton declined her offers to help, urging her to take it easy. But the habits of a lifetime were not easily broken. Always a hard worker, Clara Malone found idleness irksome. She was not sorry when the grandbaby arrived early and Mrs. Tarbutton was needed at home.

For Jay those late summer days passed more quickly than he would ever have imagined. Helping with the chores, many of them new experiences, was fun. In his one-piece fancy stripe bathing suit that showed what a skinny little fellow he was, he worked at learning to swim. Holding his nose, he would jump off the end of the pier and dog-paddle about. Jay never did learn properly to dive. He waded the cove crabbing. And Uncle Joe took him out fishing; they started before sunup, not waiting for regular breakfast but sharing a cantaloupe out of the patch. Learning to ride the docile farm horses—Dewey and Danny—gave him a kindred feeling with Grampa Malone, though his mount hardly matched his vision of the Captain's fiery charger springing into battle. But Jay could make believe. And always Josh was there, eager for any prank his adored one might dream up.

When school started, he found good friends among some swell guys in his class. And his feud with the youngest Willey, which began when little snaggle-tooth tripped him on purpose with her jumping rope, lasted till the end of seventh grade. After their set-to, he never saw the little brat again. To his immense relief, he heard that her folks had moved away.

★ ★ ★

Chapter IV

That winter 1917-18 was severe as to weather. Making ready, the Tarbutton boys had hauled in for them ten two-horse wagon loads of wood. And feeding the fires in the big Acme Sterling became their endless drudgery. "One way to get warm proper," Uncle Joe allowed, "is a workout with the bucksaw." Sometimes he might keep at it way into the night by lantern light, while frigid blasts shook the woodhouse, or snow was blowing. Jay always helped, stacking neatly and keeping his uncle company with small boy talk. They discussed lots of important things,

Invariably impressed with what a fine boy Jay was, Uncle Joe worried about their prospects for Christmas that year. Those were pinching times. But kids needed Santa Claus. And he knew that Jay would be awful lonesome without his home- town friends. What could they do? He tackled his sister across the table with her knitting. Speaking softly so's not to be overheard by Jay abed, he said, "Now, Clara, you and me've got to get our heads together. What's there special that we can buy for Jay's Christmas?"

From long make-do experience, she had an answer, "You know, Joe, it's not what a child gets so much as how it looks. Wrap it fancy, hang it on a tree, and even everyday things are exciting. A new pair of stockings—he complains so about the ones I put new feet in, and gloves he needs. Them I've just about finished." She hadn't realized that a finger was off her son's old pair until the bitterly cold day they offered Mrs. Tarbutton a ride home. And Jay, his body jackknifed tightly into the buggy box, had his one finger next to frostbitten. It hurt so he was in tears.

"Well, mebbe." Uncle Joe frowned, puffing on his pipe. "But I'm of a mind to see that he gets something he don't expect. Now you help me think."

Only after a stroke of remarkable luck was he so easy in his mind that he could joke about it. He and Jay driving home in the buggy came past the abandoned log cabin, and there on the stone chimney sat a big buzzard. Uncle Joe couldn't resist a little fun, "From the looks of things, 'pears like they ain't gonna be no Christmas this year. Santa Claus must've come early and got stuck in the chimney."

Jay gave him a sideways grin. But then he began to worry. Though not a true believer, he still pretended, just to make sure he didn't hurt anybody's feelings.

Uncle Joe never stopped gloating over the power of joy he got from his good luck. On Saturday, though the weather was raw with sullen overcast threatening cold rain, he needed a quick trip to town. Jay, with Josh, had gone over to help Will Price with his boat building. And Mrs. Malone was stirring up her eggless, milkless and butterless cake.

When Joe was gone so much longer than was expected, she began to wonder what could be keeping him. And she felt some anxiety till mid-afternoon when he drove into the lane. The next thing she knew, he burst into the warm kitchen.

"Brrr," he shivered, "It's cold out there."

"Well, now you can get warm. That stove's pret' near crazy," she said, siddling past the waves of heat. "I've been bakin', is why."

He was carrying a spanking new grain bag oddly bulging. Hanging up his cap and coat, he took his easy chair by the table and drew the grain bag up between his knees. His expression was smug. She, by now ready to rest, dropped into her rocker opposite.

"I'm late," he said, "because I ran into my old friend Cap'n Roth at the hardware store. First time I'd laid eyes on him in two, three years. . . for all he don't live so fur away. He's a retired sea captain. Had quite a life travelin' all over the world. Intrustin' old feller. Now he's got him a snug little place on the water about five miles north of town. He invited us all over for some Sunday afternoon music on his phonograph."

He had brought from an inside pocket his pipe and tobacco pouch. You heard phew, phew as he cleared the stem; knock, knock of the bowl on the heel of his shoe. Two pinches of dark brown weed were tamped down, then he folded the pouch and returned it to his pocket. The flame of a splinter lit at the range was sucked into the tobacco, with one puff of smoke from the right side of his mouth, two from the left, and a cloud from his nose. Only then was he ready to satisfy his sister's curiosity.

She, meanwhile, patiently waiting, kept her eyes on the grain bag, wondering what on earth he had been up to.

"Cap'n said he was on his way to an auction, and why didn't I come along. So I went. More out of cur'osity than anything. A crowd of folks was gathered at the old Dryden place where the sale was goin' on. The Drydens are a well-to-do fam'ly hereabouts, and social folk in town. The old folks that jest passed on had lived in the same house—that'n facin' on the harbor—since they was married pret' near sixty year ago. But now they've died off and the young ones ain't wastin' no time gettin' rid of things."

Reaching into the grain bag, Joe lifted out a little military cap, dark blue cloth with gilt cord and buttons, and the kepi's top tilt.

Mrs. Malone's sweet face beamed as she turned the little treasure about in her hands. "Oh, Joe, he'll be thrilled! It's like Grampa Malone's and the little drummer boy's up in his room."

Uncle Joe chuckled. "Looks to me like it's practically brand new. Somebody took pretty good care of it, I'd say. I was lucky too. I started the biddin' at twenty-five cents, and nobody else wanted it." He dug deeper in the grain bag. "And what do you know, I got him somethin' to read besides. Wait till you see." He set on the table a package of four books tied up with twine. "I couldn't be sure what I was gettin', but they come dirt cheap."

Of the four, three dealt with American history, while the last was a picture album. Mrs. Malone began reading the titles: "Glimpses of America, Story of the Wild West by Buffalo Bill . . ."

Joe pushed the books aside. "Let's us wait on them a bit. Fer I've got some-thin' fer you, too. I've noticed, Clara, that you always think of everybody else before you think of yourself." Carefully he extracted the mysterious something that oddly bulged the grain bag. It was a lady's cape. "It's plush, the auctioneer said, and the trim is brown bear fur." He got up and brought it around the table to drape over her shoulders. "I swan, you look beautiful as a sassiety lady."

"Really, Joe?" She stroked the lustrous folds, thinking it was too nice to wear. She had a habit, whenever she received a nice gift, of declaring it "too pretty to use." And so the delicate cambric nightgowns trimmed with wide lace and pink ribbons, the handkerchiefs edged with tatting or embroidery, all the artistic little pincushions and needlecases fashioned for her by the Malone womenfolk remained tucked away, "too pretty to use." Now as she reveled in the luxurious wrap, she knew that she would probably never wear it. After all, where did she go that it would be suitable? But of course she wouldn't for the world hurt Joe's feelings.

"It commence to rain light about the time I left the Dryden house," he said, "and it worried me some that the things might get ruined. A grain bag was the quickest pertection I could think of."

"It's a beauty, Joe, and you're so sweet to think of me." She gave him an arch smile. "But you know, one thing calls for another. Like a new hat, maybe, to pretty up with that pheasant tail Aunt Martha sent me." But such talk was for her only from the teeth out.

Joe was tickled. "I thought mebbe we'd lay it away till Christmas."

Quickly, in order to have time for a peek at Jay's presents before he came home, she ran upstairs to hide the rich garment away in her bedroom.

The books, too, seemed to have had gentle usage. Inside the cover of Glimpses of America they found a folded page from a Sears, Roebuck & Co. catalogue describing the contents of each one. About this volume she read: "Portraying the complete history of the United States and Scenic America by pen and camera, representing the works of leading artists, both of the United States,

Canada and Europe. This work also contains 400 reproductions of photographs. Size 11 x 14. Bound in English silk cloth, stamped in gold. . . 98c."

And Story of the Wild West by Buffalo Bill: "A full and complete history of the renowned pioneer quartet, Boone, Crockett, Carson and Buffalo Bill. Replete with graphic descriptions of wild life and thrilling adventures by famous heroes of the frontier. A record of exciting events on the western borders pushed westward to the sea, massacres, desperate battles, extraordinary bravery, marvelous fortitude, astounding heroism, grand hunts, rollicking anecdotes, tales of sorrow, droll stories, curious escapades and a melange of incidents that make up the melodrama of civilization in its march over mountains and prairies to the Pacific. 766 pages."

Uncle Joe, listening with chin in hand, his forefinger alongside his nose, exclaimed, "Old Buffalo Bill didn't hardly leave out nothin', did he ?"

Jay's whistle in the lane startled them. He with a sweep of his arm gathered up the books; she took in hand the little cap and the grain bag. Frantically they stowed their treasures away at the back of the pantry, and were sitting sociably in their chairs when boy and dog burst in with a gust of cold air.

After supper Jay stretched out on the old leather couch, with a cushion at his head and Josh alongside, intending to read over his history lesson. History was his favorite subject, and he got good grades in it. But soon his eyes grew heavy; so his mother sent him up to bed.

As soon as they thought it was safe, his mother brought the two remaining books and read aloud what the Sears Catalogue sheet said about them.

United States Secret Service of the Late Civil War—Gen. Lafayette C. Baker "Exciting experience in the North and South, peerless adventures, hair-breadth escapes and valuable services of the detectives of the late Civil War. Fully illustrated. 480 pages."

Eagerly they searched out the last one—

Story of American Heroism. "A war gallery of noted men and events, comprising exploits of scouts and spies, forlorn hopes, hand to hand struggles, imprisonments and hair-breadth escapes, perilous journeys, terrible hardships, patient endurance, bold dashes, brilliant successes, clever captures, daring raids, wonderful achievements, magnanimous action, romantic, humorous and tragic, etc. Beautifully illustrated with over 300 original drawings."

Overwhelmed by their riches, they just stared at each other. Then on the back of an old envelope Uncle Joe added up the figures. "Better'n two thousand pages of stories and about seven hundred pictures. Now ain't that somethin'? Enough fer two winter's readin'. All fer jest a dollar."

But the heap of books there on the table seemed like maybe too much. Mrs. Malone had an idea. "What you say we just give him half for Christmas?

With his stockings and gloves, and the little cap. . . just two ought to be enough. Then the others would be good for his birthday."

"Good idee," Uncle Joe agreed. "Mebbe them last two? They sound right intrustin' to me."

She liked them too. Besides, as she leafed through one, there dropped into her lap a homemade scrapbook pasted full of the comic strip Buster Brown and his Dog Tige. She held it up.

"Are we lucky?"

Christmas morning Jay saw at a glance that Santa had not perished down the log cabin chimney. Two stockings, nicely filled, with holly sprigs in the top, hung from the clock shelf. Josh got a large meaty bone and one piece of chocolate fudge; he loved candy but it was not good for him. Jay found a big polished apple, an orange wrapped in tissue, raisin clusters and a handful of various kinds of nuts. Also, four sweets. But he was not allowed so much as one little nibble before breakfast.

Their small tree decorated with tinsel, red balls and paper angels beckoned them to the important things in packages large and small. Watching Jay unwrap his books and exclaim over them, Uncle Joe sat with his fingers laced over his stomach, absently twiddling his thumbs, "a power of joy" on his face. Santa had left him tobacco, heavy sox and handkerchiefs. Mrs. Malone found a pretty hand mirror of imitation ebony, Rose talcum powder and a subscription to the Pictorial Review. Through the mail had come a camisole with crocheted yoke for her but "too pretty to wear" and for Jay a Penny Saver bank.

As he unwrapped the military cap, sunshine spread over Jay's thin little face. Adjusting it on, he clicked his heels, gave a salute and marched across the room to the looking glass. Josh watched him quizzically,

The plush cape, folded into a clean gingham apron and carefully wrapped to appear for Jay's benefit a surprise, brought exclamations of delight. His mother draped it over her shoulders and slowly turned for them to admire. Jay capered about with excitement, shouting, "Gee, Mom, you look like a queen!" And Uncle Joe, puffing his pipe, contentedly watched their clowning.

So it had been a good Christmas after all: but tinged with sadness and longing for their absent ones. Uncle Joe could not forget last year; his sister anticipated Christmas to come when Jay's Dad would surely be home. Passing him as she tidied up, she laid her hand on his arm in wordless sympathy.

All the gift wrappings must be carefully saved. White tissues and satin ribbons would be carefully pressed with a warm iron and laid away to use again next year. Tissues from the oranges were smoothed out for toilet paper and hung on a nail out in the privy.

★ ★ ★

$\sim$

Chapter V

Like all patriotic Americans they were conscientious in their war sacrifices. They changed their eating habits, observing the meatless days and the wheatless days. They conserved sugar. Jay's mother seemed to be evermore knitting socks for the soldiers. Though money was awful scarce, they managed to buy a small bond during the Liberty Loan drives. They pinched every way they could. Still, they managed to be tolerably comfortable.

Letters from Jay's father told that he was not. As he said, living at the front hardly offered the comfort of his bed back home.

"I could have stayed in the dugout," he wrote, "but it was filthy. Men had lived in there too long. Overhead great thick planks support the earth. There are wide cracks between them, and you can poke a finger up into the rotten wood. Great big toadstools grow there, pretty colors—bright reds and golden yellows. Water drips in your face, and if you try to sleep, rats run over you and bite your ears and nose. I figured a shell hit would bury us and we'd smother to death before we'd be dug out; so I sleep outside."

Mostly he posted assurances that he was all right and missed them very, very much. If nothing else, he complained about the mud. Oh, Lord, the mud! When you tried to move equipment, it bogged down, immovable for men and animals together, sunk in the mire up to their knees. There was no use to beat the poor beasts; they couldn't go nowhere.

He lamented the devastation and the sad plight of the refugees, thankful that his loved ones were safe from all the horror. Always he tried to keep them cheerful.

"Up at the front," he wrote, "I found a can. Finding that can meant that I could take a bath. It was a large can. So I went down to the canal and filled it full of water. Then I kindled me a fire, laid some stones around, and put on my can of water. When it was warm I washed up. Then I got it boiling and put in my clothes, I knew that boiling water alone wouldn't kill lice; you have to add salt. I got some salt. When my clothes were clean I put them on. I had a hard time because they had shrunk. That cheap wool they use. But I managed to get into them. They had a million wrinkles. Ay gorsh, I thought I was the only soldier so near the front without any lice.

"But before long I reached down to my ribs and brought him out. There he was. And suddenly I realized how come. We wear our dog tags on a tape. I forgot to boil the tape. When I unrolled it, there they were, a zillion of them, just like horses in a stable, all lined up in a row."

Things like that he wrote, little stories you remembered with a chuckle.

After his hay-time mishap, Jay went through a long spell of moodiness that Uncle Joe considered unnatural for any normal boy his age. It was very troubling. The old gent cudgelled his brain: how to keep the lad occupied and entertained through the summer. When his rheumatism had flared up, he was finally persuaded to let the Tarbutton boys farm his place on shares. But he and Jay took care of the stock, did the milking and kept up with the garden chores. When they worked together, weeding or maybe picking potato bugs, he often tried through innocent remarks to learn what was eating his nephew. He never could find out.

For quite a while they had been needing a new rowboat. But none reasonable enough had turned up at auction. Then, deep in a sleepless night, the idea visited Uncle Joe: he and Jay would build a boat. That was the ticket!

Over his breakfast pancakes he said, "How'd you like to help me build us a boat?"

Jay grinned. "Sure!"

"You got some experience helpin' Will Price with his." (Privately he reckoned Jay's contribution had amounted to little more than fetch and carry, with a deal of chatter, which old man Price seemed to find entertaining). "And I could use some first-rate ideas." He was secretly congratulating himself on his cleverness.

First off, they must decide on the place where they wanted to work. The old wagon shed was not bad for space and they'd be under cover. To make ready took nearly a whole day for clearing accumulations of stuff stored in there. In the afternoon, Jay, going about barefoot, stepped on an old rusty nail. His mother, terrified of lockjaw, applied her turpentine remedy: warm to the wound, cold to the face and neck, then gently rubbed along the spine. To keep Jay's mind occupied, Uncle Joe talked boat. "Mornin', noon and night," his sister said. They worked on plans for size and style (Jay had a knack for drawing pictures), carefully figured quantity and cost of materials they could afford, calculated any new tools they might be needing. It was agreed that they'd not hurry the work but go slowly. This job must be equal to anything turned out by the regular boatbuilders in town.

Through the summer days she gradually took shape, their neat little craft, pristine white with trim a medium brown wood color. She drew compliments from everyone who saw her. And Jay went around bursting with pride. The shine in his eyes brought joy to his elders.

One day Uncle Joe opened a subject that nestled in the back of his mind. "Have you give thought yet to what we'll be callin' her?" He knew already. But it must be Jay's idea.

"No, Sir."

"Well, now, it's high time we figgered on it. Don't you think so? You got any best girls with pretty names?" He fixed his nephew with a stern look over his glasses.

Jay grinned bashfully and shook his head,

Uncle Joe thought differently. "Sure you've got a best girl." He waited, busy filling his pipe.

Jay considered. Suddenly light dawned. "Mom!"

"Of course. We'll call her the Clarabelle. There ain't no prettier name this side the pearly gates."

So they put their heads together drawing stencils for the neatest of lettering. No town boatbuilder was going to find fault with their work.

The Tarbutton boys helping, they brought their treasure down to the pier. Mrs. Malone, standing with her hands folded under her apron, exclaimed over her namesake. And Josh, who had supervised the whole project from his place just inside the wagon- shed doors, capered about, barking excitedly.

Thankful for the miracle of Jay's restored good spirit, his mother looked fondly upon his boat. On her way to the henhouse or the hogpen, she always glanced "seaward" to admire the little beauty out there resting on its reflection. And when her menfolks set forth on their first fishing trip, she watched the trim little craft skimming smoothly over the water, oars dipping and rising, bearing the "fellows," in new overalls and old straw hats, out to the deeps of the creek. They made a picture, and she thought, "If only I had a camera."

Towards the end of August, the old Spencer place on the island was rented to a family from New York named Williams. Nothing much was known about them. A lawyer, Mr. Williams had to give up his offices because of failing eyesight and poor health. Mrs. Williams in times past was a singer on the stage. And they had a young daughter.

Spencer's island once upon a time formed the tip of the peninsula. But erosion had cut that small parcel of land adrift. Now its only connection with the point was a narrow causeway of oyster shells, not too deep even during flood for a horse and buggy crossing, but traversed on foot only at low tide. The tall old frame house, weathered and gaunt, had stood empty for some time, and the whole place, long untended, was wildly overgrown.

Why these big city folks chose to settle down here puzzled everyone. But nothing of their affairs would be learned from any of the family. They were all close-mouthed. It was made quite plain that they intended to live in seclusion. Old man Blades had been hired to fetch their mail and do their marketing. If they needed a trip to town, they would go in his boat.

Though the new folks appeared uppity, Mrs. Malone remarked that their lamp light across the water "seemed right neighborly." And after a proper interval, she put on her good dress and paid a polite call. About her impressions she was mum, never expressing in Jay's hearing her opinion of Mrs. Williams. Their young daughter, she said, was "a sweet little creature".

The newcomers were hardly settled before school started and Marta Williams appeared in Jay's class. She was just beginning eighth grade, as was he.

Shortly afterward, when he caught sight of her walking the road one morning, he waved and called, "Wait and I'll go with you."

As usual, Josh gamboled along beside him as far as the gate, where Marta stood leaning against a post, her strapped books over one shoulder, an orange lunch box in her hand. Dark honey blonde, she had big brown eyes and a nice smile showing small even white teeth. Her crisp sky-blue hair bow matched the tie of her gray middy blouse. Josh got his parting pat on the head and forlornly watched them leave, his tail wagging slower, slower and sagging until it was still.

Already a bit late, they knew they had to step on it. Marta told Jay that she would be rowing across the cove and walking in each day. They agreed to make the trip together. In spite of hurrying, they had not quite reached the outskirts of town when they heard the school bell sounding across the flat farmland. With a gasp of dismay, Jay caught Marta by the hand and they began to run. Though she was a palely plump young lady, she managed to keep up.

In the afternoon, trudging home they had time for improving their acquaintance. And Jay could share with Marta his dread of the cutoff through the woods. About half way to town, it might save you a quarter mile walk, dare you use it. But it was a scary place. More so on dark days. Beginning at a blasted tree with an osprey's ruined stick nest in the top, the narrow track snaking over matted pine needles, low in spots with standing dark water, disappeared into the dense pine woods. Jay had tried this shortcut once. He started in blithely enough, but only a little way along, fear gripped him. He began to feel terribly alone, surrounded by a sinister silence and gloom. In panic he turned and ran back out. After that, walking the road, he hurried past. And in the buggy during the drive home after a picture show, it seemed that Dewey, even at a trot, was too poky slow passing through the pitch black stretch of close woods.

Listening in on the conversations of his elders, he had learned that a crazy man escaped from an asylum was hiding out somewhere in the countryside. A farm woman driving alone claimed to have seen him asleep beside a log, but at the time she told nobody. Jay's fears multiplied. He never heard that the person was captured. But to be on the safe side, as he explained to Marta, it was safest to keep on the far side of the road, hoping to see nothing more terrifying than the brooding woods.

★ ★ ★

Chapter VI

News of the Armistice sped over the wires before daylight that Monday morning, November 11, 1918. The church bells rang, and the town went wild. People forgot everything. They surged through the streets, blowing horns and whistles. They fired off guns. Marta being kept home with a bad cold, Jay rode into school that day so he could pick up a few supplies. Reaching town he encountered such jubilation as made even placid Dewey skittish. Nobody had time for school; there would be a holiday. But Jay hung around awhile with the crowd gathered to hang the Kaiser in effigy. That over, he tore himself away. They'd want the great news at home.

Dewey trotted briskly out of town, but slowed to a walk once they passed the depot. Jay, lost in daydreams of his Dad's homecoming that would soon whisk him back to the old home place, left Dewey to follow his own lead. Inattentive to all but his thoughts, he rocked along, the reins draped loosely over his mount's neck. Once again he would be leading the junior fighting forces in screaming assault along the towpath. With him so long away, the fort must need a lot of repairs. The fellows had probably let the place go to pot. He saw himself again marching in the parades on Decoration Day; though it wouldn't be quite the same now with Dad Seltzer and Mr. Bricker both gone.

Ambling along thusly, they were less than half way home when a big Collie dog suddenly stepped out of the nearby woods and startled Dewey. With a snort the big brute sidestepped his forefeet right into the ditch, and Jay pitched headforemost down over his roached mane. Unhurt, the boy scrambled up, shouting, "Whoa!" But the heedless Dewey took off for home. And Jay was left to follow on foot, lugging his schoolbooks and the bag of supplies which had fallen off with him. Soon he found his saddle blanket in the middle of the road, And further along, there lay the saddle.

When Dewey showed up riderless at the farm gate, Uncle Joe's strength almost failed him. Expecting the worst, he hopped aboard bareback and pushed the wayward rascal at a gallop back to town. Great was his relief to meet the luckless Jay trudging along under the weight of his belongings. And he could hardly smother his mirth when he heard what had happened.

War's end brought back to Mrs. Malone's face, almost as of old, the little smile that even in repose lingered about her dark eyes and the corners of her mouth, as if she were pleased with what she saw or what she might be thinking. Dimmed by heart-ache during the long months past, it shone again. Her thoughts, and Jay's, dwelt upon their return home. Yet that was not mentioned. As she cautioned Jay, they must wait until Dad returned, and that might take some time yet. Meanwhile, to herself she worried about leaving Brother Joe alone.

John Jay Malone II was twice wounded and returned to the battle lines. Then, just two weeks before the war ended, they found only his dog tag.

Mrs. Malone took the news bravely. She was not a weeper in front of others. Jay sat stunned. Their sorrow deeply troubled good, kind Uncle Joe. He said gently, "You know, Clara, you and Jay always have a home here."

His mother's meaningful glance silenced Jay. She said, "You're mighty good to us, Joe. We'll try to make it up to you."

And as time passed, she noticed that Joe, bless his heart, tried to make it up to them. The poor man never spent money on himself. But he kept in mind their need for a little pleasure. The picture show right often was his idea. And he liked to pick out a little bag of fancy candies at the Greek Candy Store so that Clara might enjoy a treat she didn't have to fix herself.

For some time Uncle Joe had talked peach orchard. Just a small one. But it must be a planting of the choicest fruit. Not only was he very fond of peaches—"You know, Clara, just thinking 'big juicy peach' makes my mouth water"—but also he considered the prospects good for a profitable market later on. The field he intended to use was bordered by a growth of cedar trees, some old and hoary, others young. Naturally they would have to go. The big ones, sawed up, might make a nice chest for woolens and such. "One of them little 'uns," he said, "is just about right fer a proper Christmas tree." He and his sister had decided that even though their hearts were not in it, still there should be Christmas for Jay.

Cold rain rattled on the windows, but their evening was cozy, the three of them gathered around the big table: Uncle Joe at ease in his comfort chair, his slippered feet resting on the hassock, Mrs. Malone opposite and busy with her mending, Jay sharing with Josh the leather couch.

Jay had an idea. "How about if we could sell some of the little ones? Folks'll want Christmas trees, same as us. I could take a few orders maybe, and Marta'll help."

Uncle Joe valued gumption in young people. "A capital idee!" He took a couple of puffs on his pipe. "Tell you what. We'll be partners. You take the orders. And I'll help han'le the delivery. Trees are a mite awkard to unload. You and Marta can divide the money. And I'll get my grove cleared away. How's that?"

His sister smothered a smile, thinking, "Only brother Joe could offer such a scheme without blushing."

His impish sideways glance told her that he knew what she was thinking.

Jay was immensely pleased. But sharing the good news with Marta would have to keep till Monday schooltime. After his first few visits he had given up going over to the island. He felt unwanted there. The place gave him the willies, and Marta's parents were so odd. He never saw Mr. Williams. Mrs. Williams he knew only through a window screened with vines. And no matter what he and Marta might be doing—like planting the Grave Privet—her mother kept jawing at them, and Marta went right on with what she was about, paying not the slightest attention, quite indifferent. Even when "the old lady" fell silent, which seemed all too rarely, he had the uncomfortable feeling that she spied on them, grim and disapproving.

From the first, Marta had prattled about a flower garden. She kept remembering Grandmama's back home. One afternoon when she and Jay were crossing the old family burying ground out back of the house, Marta caught the loose sole of her shoe in a creeper and fell down. Jay gave her a hand up.

"What is this stuff?" she asked with a sweep of her arm across the wide reaches of green leaves.

"It's Grave Privet. When it blooms, this whole place is covered with blue flowers."

"Oh, blue is my favorite color." She clapped her hands. "Can I have some?"

"Sure. You can have all you want."

"Right now?"

"M'm," reluctantly. Then with a shrug, "Sure. We'll need to find a shovel. And a basket."

That day, Mrs. Williams seemed even more aggravating than usual, if that were possible. And Jay made up his mind—never again.

But Marta could always count on a warm welcome from his folks. They quickly came to love her like a daughter. Happily the little girl accepted their house as her second home. And very soon it seemed quite natural to include her in everything.

Saturdays the two of them shared the buggy with his mother on her trips to town because she enjoyed their company so. Then, while she shopped, they had time to explore and spend a few cents of their own money. After school, with so much ground to cover, they dare not tarry for long, especially during the short days of winter. But weekends they could indulge their little interests. From the hitching rack they scattered their separate ways.

Marta made a beeline for the small gift shop with red geraniums in the window, and oftentimes the owner's black cat asleep in the sunshine. She enjoyed there a warm friendship with the ancient lady who never hurried her in choosing another of those dinky little flowered doilies she was forever embroidering. Along with that three penny purchase, she selected six chocolate creams that melted in your mouth. They ate them while jogging home. Her parents never cared for sweets.

Jay liked to look through the hardware store that smelled of rubber "and things"; maybe choose a new ball or a few marbles. Then he might wander toward the boat yards or, lured by the clang of the blacksmith's hammer, go and watch a horse being shod.

But now the time was growing short; they must attend to their Christmas tree business. Going door to door of the neat houses bordering the side streets, they hardly realized what a woeful pair they looked, poor patched country kids peddling their fresh-cut Christmas trees at twenty-five cents each. Orders in hand, they were eager for the cutting, which absorbed their whole attention until finally the hearse was loaded and with Uncle Joe driving, they set out in high spirits. The responsibilities were divided: Jay would ring the doorbells and hand over the tree; Marta would take the money, which she carried in her pocketbook. They were dressed for the season, Jay wearing his new red scarf, rosy-cheeked Marta in a red coat and hood made for her Christmas present by Mrs. Malone.

After they'd had chance to count the settlement in full, Jay and Marta swaggered about, proud of their jinglings in the pocket. How wonderful to be rich! And they knew exactly what they intended to buy. Ice skates. Ordered now, they would be on hand for great fun when Marta got back from spending the holidays with her Grandmama in Washington City.

Though his elders tried on Jay's account to make Christmas as happy as possible, it was quiet. Their little tree prettily displayed the paper angels and strings of red holly berries. Underneath Jay found a stag-handle pocket knife (to replace his that got lost), and a book that Uncle Joe picked up someplace called Hot Stuff by Famous Funny Men. A collection of stories by such writers as Mark Twain, Josh Billings, Bill Nye, Petroleum V. Nasby, Artemus Ward, Bret Harte, and the like, it was packed full of humor, wit, satire, ridicule, repartee, anecdotes, bulls and blunders. Uncle Joe smiled over his sox and tobacco (he got the same each year), and Mrs. Malone unwrapped handmade gifts as usual "too pretty to use."

★ ★ ★

Chapter VII

With the New Year, school started. But where was Marta? Jay waited for her till the last moment, then went on to town alone. Each morning he expected to see her. For a whole week he was disappointed. Going it alone, the trip seemed interminable. The road stretched away, long and empty and lonesome. There was no lively camaraderie to warm the spirits. She didn't come, and didn't come. They wondered why.

Then one morning there she was! A sight for sore eyes, as Uncle Joe would say. Bundled up in her red coat and hood, she was waiting at the gate. Jay and Josh broke into a run. In his rapture the dog almost knocked her down.

She was all agog. "Have they come? The skates?"

"Yep."

"You didn't begin without me?" She pretended to pout.

"Course not. I've been waiting. Where you been all this time?"

"Grandmama needed me to help her nurse poor Purvey. He's her parrot. He's real, real old. He kept saying, 'Purvey's hungry. Purvey's hungry.' We were so worried. But we finally got him filled up. Then he laughed."

Though she was late, smart little Marta quickly made up her missed lessons. Jay, inclined to laziness, was glad to occasionally consult her about classwork. Sometimes he felt a twinge of jealousy bearing constant praise of Marta's cleverness. "She's the brightest child and catches on so quickly," his mother would remark after they had figured how to make some intricate fancywork pattern, or Marta picked out a tune on their old piano. Though lessons had been denied her, she could play by ear remarkably well.

But he never said anything, and his irritation soon passed. Marta was such a good sport. If he dared, she dared. And when he was afraid, she trembled with him. In all things she accepted his judgment without question. Such absolute faith nourished his self-esteem, made him feel big and important.

When his mother firmly ruled out the frozen edges of the creek as too treacherous, they skated on a shallow ice-covered pond in the woods. And from supporting each other, with many falls and much laughter, they developed skill in skimming through the sticks protruding. Their antics gave Josh fits.

Success with the Christmas trees encouraged thoughts of other lucrative ventures. And they began shaping ambitious plans. Soon would come the season for huckleberries which they could peddle at twelve and a half cents a quart to the nice fat German lady who lived on a farm near the edge of town. And they had big ideas about how many baskets of tomatoes they could pick.

Marta might look delicate, but she was tough. And Jay respected her courage. He could count on her to join in any scheme, no matter how daring. And if things went wrong, she was no cry-baby.

Only once did he see her cry. Not when they were picking blackberries and a wasp stung her on the upper lip. Nor when she slipped and struck her big painful stone bruise on a sharp stob. Not even when the water moccasin suddenly slithered from the mud between her ankles. It happened when she was given a sad poem to read in a program at school:

"That poor little boy with no cap on his head,

A board is his bed, his mother is dead,

That poor little boy with no cap on his head,

Has never a friend in the world."

Marta got so far and broke down, crying into her blue bow tie. Quickly the teacher consoled her, and later asked her to read another piece that was happier.

In after years, thinking back to those days, Jay wondered: could it be that Marta, who bore up so staunchly under physical adversity, had associated the verse's tragedy with himself and his mother, whom she dearly loved?

He knew that Marta would deny herself if he were in need. But for her, he would have gone hungry that day at school when he left his lunch box on a window sill in the ivy-mantled bell tower, and at noontime found his ham sandwich and chocolate cake full of ants. Marta made him take half of her skimpy cheese sandwich and a ginger cookie.

And when his mother had one of her sick headaches, Marta hovered about, soothing her brow with soft hands and cool moist cloths, afterwards gently combing her long black hair.

Severe sore throat kept Marta home that Arbor Day. And Jay was late picking up his tree. Handing over his two cents, he took the only thing left— a dead-looking switch that had lost its identification tag. Somebody thought it was a peach. Oh, well, he and Marta would do their bit planting it, out of sight in a far corner of his own garden patch.

Sight of the sad thing tickled her immensely. But they pitched in, digging deep for its tiny root ball. Marta said, "I'll just think a little prayer for it."

Daily they watered it, hoping, but not expecting anything. When at last they found a tiny green leaf, they danced a jig.

A couple of report cards that anybody could be proud of were their passports to lazy summer days. For roughing it, they dressed alike; over blue bathing suits each pulled on a pair of old brown pants (Marta's on loan). Barefoot, they wore on their heads, when they remembered, wide-brimmed straw hats.

They went beachcombing, poking through the driftwood left helter-skelter and draped with tatters of seaweed. Marta found half buried in the sand a broken barpin of faceted black glass which she treasured in her trinket box kept hidden under the hay in their barn. Jay discovered a homemade toy boat washed up from who knows what perilous voyage, still carrying its little crooked sail.

They hunted birds' eggs for his collection. Never more than one was taken from a nest. And he displayed them in a box lined with milkweed floss, all neatly labeled. One day they found a hole in the high bank along the shore —a kingfisher's nest. When he recklessly thrust in his hand and was nipped by a sharp beak, Marta danced with glee. Shamefaced, he grinned back at her.

Later, when she crammed a fistful of red raspberries into her mouth and gagged on a stink bug, he nearly split his sides laughing.

Her good-nature was contagious. They might argue, sometimes vehemently, but they never really quarreled. He was usually tolerant of her girlish whims, while she strove to keep pace with his he-man ventures.

When not roughing it, Marta indulged her high-flown ideas of fashionable living. Though Jay preferred other pastimes to games of housekeeping, he humored her imaginings if nothing more exciting offered. When she required a house, he obliged, arranging logs in the woodshed to enclose her parlor. Their inevitable tea party was satisfying as to cold biscuits with jelly, but he balked at lukewarm cambric tea.

So that she might regally ride out in her carriage, they rigged up his red wagon with a top-heavy cover of tow sacks. Jay was always the horse, of course. One afternoon he accidentally upset her in the ditch. Untangling herself from the canopy and lap-robe, Marta came up scolding. But seeing his shocked surprise, she burst out laughing, helped him right the unwieldy conveyance, and calmly resumed her drive.

Through the long summer days they shared whatever games they could think up, inventing their own entertainment. No one their age came to visit. Yet they remained ever hopeful. Whenever a moving object in a small cloud of dust appeared up the road, they, like any backwoodsy folks, climbed to the porch railing, eager to see who was coming. But few and far between were signs of life in the direction of town.

Near time for the Floating Theater to dock, his mother invited Marta to see a play. And the little girl was thrilled to her fingertips. She could talk of nothing else. Thinking about it, she would murmur, "Oh, this is the most exciting thing in my whole life!"

At once there was much ado about what she should wear. The pretty blue mull dress his mother had started, of course. One last fitting and it would be ready. But what about shoes?

Because she was so hard on footwear (after all, twenty miles a week over oyster shell roads scuffed a lot of shoe leather), Marta's parents bought for her heavy boy's shoes. And added copper toes! Those horrid shoes were the bane of her existence. Now she wailed, "A beautiful dress with old ugly clodhoppers!" And unhappiness troubling her gentle soul suddenly mushroomed into rebellion. She would have a pair of lady's shoes. She could buy them with her own money—nickels and dimes hard-earned through hot noons in the berry patches where the chiggers nearly ate you alive, and backbreaking hours filling countless baskets of tomatoes. And she intended to have exactly what she wanted. Her fever of anxiety was calmed only by a trip with Mrs. Malone to the shoe store.

When the eagerly anticipated day came, Uncle Joe, handing them up into the buggy, said, "You both look beautiful." With a satisfied smile Marta smoothed the soft folds of her blue skirt and peeked down at her strapped slippers. She put on more airs than an heiress, Jay thought grumpily, his nose out of joint at being left behind. Sliding down the barn roof, which was forbidden, he had sprained his ankle.

Marta came home bubbling with rapture and wonder. The actresses were so enchanting that she had decided on her future then and there: she would act the heroine of a beautiful story. And one of the actors was ever so good-looking, with his black, black hair and white, white teeth. Her thoughts and prattle skipped from the characters, the clothes, the music, the flowers, to a happening altogether puzzling. How could big snowflakes fall on the stage when outside it was still summertime?

She sighed. "This is the most exciting day of my life!" Dancing a little pirouette and watching the swirl of her full skirt, she danced over and gave Mrs. Malone a kiss, saying, "Thank you, thank you."

School brought an end to their barefoot freedom and Marta faced again those hated copper toes. But she got sick. And Jay learned that she would not be returning. Mr. Williams was seriously ill and needed specialized care; so they were leaving.

Screwing up his willpower, Jay walked over to say good-bye to Marta. Her mother greeted him from the window behind the vines. "Marta's not well enough to see anybody right now. But I'll tell her you came by."

He shuffled his feet, intimidated, but hoping for one last word with Marta. "We'll miss her," he managed to say.

"I'll tell her," old stony-heart replied.

"Mother sent over the paper dolls that Marta likes." He held out the Journal.

"Just leave it on the steps," she told him.

A moment longer he hesitated, then placing the magazine on the nearest corner of the bottom step, he disconsolately turned away.

From the edge of their woods he looked back at the tall gray house rising against overcast sky. There, framed in a small bull's-eye window high up in the peak of the roof, was Marta's face and her little hand waving. With a thrill of pleasure he answered her. And for a long minute they waved to each other. Reluctantly, he started away, then turned back for another lingering farewell. Abruptly he wheeled and fled down the lane between their tall gloomy pines. The tide was rising. High-stepping through the deepening water, he ran across the causeway.

★ ★ ★

Chapter VIII

With the loss of little Marta, Uncle Joe began to worry. He dreaded that Jay's despondency following his haytime accident might return. Ahead stretched Autumn days and the long, lonesome walks to and from school. It might save the situation if Jay could ride Dewey, but livery stable charges were steep. The prices on bicycles dismayed him. He asked around that everybody be on the lookout for a second-hand bike. The Methodist minister happened upon what he needed and could pay for. Though a month early for Jay's sixteenth birthday, that was his present. And he was so thrilled.

Then, before Uncle Joe had time to replenish the till, he splurged again. So that Jay and his mother might glimpse the wide, restless ocean, he stretched his purse to buy tickets for a train excursion to Ocean City. It seemed to Jay that the day would never come. Eager to help make ready, he got so underfoot that his mother finally gave him the task of neatly packing their two small picnic hampers. They would feast on sandwiches of ham and chicken, pickled eggs, cherry tarts and chocolate layer cake. The sight of such goodies tempted Jay to sample with the tip of his finger the frosting on his piece of cake.

Admonishing Josh to look after things, they gaily set forth, plenty early, in the motor boat. Pulling out into the cove, Jay couldn't bear to look back at his pal there on the end of the pier dejectedly watching them leave without him. Chugging around the point through the narrows, they turned up Back Creek. Almost within sight of their destination, the motor died. Uncle Joe frantically tinkered with it. Nothing worked. The moments ticked away. They heard the train blow. It stopped and they could picture a flock of eager people climbing aboard. Soon with clang and clamor it pulled out, gathering steam as it sped away past them up along the shoreline. Meanwhile, there they sat out on the water, with their full picnic baskets, dolefully watching it go without them.

They were stalled just about in front of Price's. Old Will came out to offer help and towed them in to his pier. Then, everybody in the dismals, they plodded home across the fields. Mrs. Malone tried to keep up, but her menfolks strode along so fast, angrily kicking any clods in their path, that she finally quit trying. Stopping to catch her breath, she laughed. Such dour faces! "Oh, come, you two, this isn't world's end." They grinned sheepishly. She said, "We'll just have a nice picnic at home."

Their absence had lasted less than a couple of hours; yet Josh greeted them like they'd been gone forever. Jay's disappointment was the dog's joy, for he shared the sandwiches.

A delayed present for Jay's Christmas that year was a small box camera that his mother got with Octagon Soap. It came five weeks late because of the time she needed to collect enough coupons. Kindhearted Mrs. Tarbutton contributed some. "Here, take mine," she said. "I've saved 'em but I don't know fer what." And Uncle Joe went to the expense of buying extra soap to make up the count. It was his idea to begin with, after he came across a box of coupons on a high pantry shelf.

At first Jay snapped everything in sight, willy-nilly, getting mostly pictures that were awful: Uncle Joe dunging out the stable, his mother at the hog pen, her face half hidden by the shirred hood of her bonnet. Josh figured largely, but too far away or blurred in motion. Then the boy began to realize that he couldn't afford to be wasteful of film. Neither could he expect his magic box to produce a fine photograph of any scene he had given only a cursory glance. He learned to be choosy about his backgrounds, to be critical of the picture he would preserve.

Diligently he worked at refining his ideas of composition and mood, using for one subject a scene that had long intrigued him. In a gut through wide marsh at the far end of Uncle Joe's fields, a Chesapeake Bay skipjack, the Fanny L. Benton, was "laid up for dead." She still carried her mast and boom and wheel, her bowsprit pointing seaward toward the scenes of her heyday. Once trim and neat, her paint had become scurfy, her iron coated with rust. Jay and Josh first approached her by rowboat, maneuvering for just the right angle to express her sadness against stormy sky. Another day, as a snowstorm commenced, his camera stopped time, fixing forever that melancholy moment of her inexorable dissolution.

His camera helped him bear bitter disappointment at being left behind when his mother went home for Grampa Malone's funeral. Jay begged her to bring back pictures of everybody, and she took along one of him on Dewey. Trying to control his tears, he sent a message to the fellows: "Tell everybody I said, 'Hi!'"

Grampa was buried in his Grand Army uniform, with one of his two large flags draped over the casket. The church soloist sang When The Roll Is Called Up Yonder. His other flag and his service pistol he left to Jay when he should come of age. People remarked that Decoration Day would never be the same, now that only two old soldiers were left and they growing ever feebler.

Though never a real robust lad, from the first Jay was a big help on the farm. Obedient and polite, accustomed to doing his chores, he had made himself useful in many ways. Depending upon the season, he (with Marta) searched out wild asparagus along the line fences, picked berries and fruit, even plums from the ancient damson trees along the lane. But they were a wormy lot. He hoed the big garden, and helped his mother tend her flowers, marveling at her preference for a large waxy white rose with no more scent than a tallow candle.

So that the boy's sense of responsibility and pride be nourished by property exclusively his own, Uncle Joe gave him a small fertile garden plot, and half a dozen fine hens with a big bossy rooster. With each hatching of chicks he acquired a nice enlargement of his flock. They left high-stepping Jenny Hen clucking over ten little peeps the cloudless Sunday afternoon they drove over for a musical treat at Captain Roth's.

The Captain was a cheery rotund little man with blue eyes, a snowy fringe around his bald spot and a trim mustache to match. He shared his small white frame house with a dozen or so complacent cats—mostly orange, but some black and a couple of tigers. Mrs. Malone remarked that the place was "neat as a pin." The Captain heartily greeted them, saying, "Welcome, my friends!" shaking hands all around, receiving Jay as cordially as if he were an adult. He ushered them into his parlor. Small and cozy, it contained, besides the polished Victrola, reed chairs with brown corduroy cushions for the comfort of all his guests, as well as a footstool for young people like Jay. The room's chief ornament was a gold hanging lamp decorated with painted flower designs in natural colors and encircled by a wealth of cut glass pendants. And on the stiffly starched lace curtains were pinned paper butterflies.

The old gentleman talked proudly of his large record collection. There was entertainment for all ages. Blissfully he listened, hands clasped over his pot belly, a smile on his face, occasionally closing his eyes and nodding in time with the music. Conversation was not encouraged during the program. But they chatted while changing records and during an intermission for refreshments of ice cream and cake. Mrs. Malone complimented him on his flower beds, and they shared the lore of plants.

Learning that the talking machine cost less than he had imagined, Uncle Joe decided that they should begin to save for one. And perhaps now was the time to make notes on the records they liked. The gospel hymns stirred him, especially a male quartet offering When The Roll Is Called Up Yonder, and a soprano/contralto duet of Whispering Hope.

Mrs. Malone was charmed by a tenor singing Silver Threads Among the Gold. But she would be long haunted by the instrumental pieces: A Perfect Day beautifully rendered by violin, 'cello and piano, and The Sweetest Story Ever Told blending violin, flute and harp.

Intriguing to all of them was something different, clever whistling of Spring Voices.

Jay responded with merriment to the comic songs such as Waltz Me Around Again Willie, Waiting At The Church and a tenor solo of troubles with The Whole Damn Family.

Entertained as never before, they forgot the time. A clock off in the house somewhere faintly striking reminded Uncle Joe to consult his watch, and he was shocked to find it already four in the afternoon. His sister, observing him, leaned forward in her chair and said, with her usual grace, "It's been delightful, Captain, and I'm afraid we've overstayed. We really must be going."

"Thank you all for coming." The Captain gave them a little bow. "For me the afternoon has just melted away. We must do this again."

"And you must come visit us," Mrs. Malone said. "Try one of our Pennsylvania dinners."

Because the music so enraptured them, they had been deaf to the rumble of distant thunder. Now they stepped out on the porch to face ominous black clouds shot with lightning and rapidly rolling in from the west.

The Captain insisted they wait out the storm. "'My friends, I won't let you go. Come quickly, Laddie, and we'll shelter your good horse in the barn." He plucked his cap from the hall-tree, and they ran out to move Dewey from under the tall oak tree already rocking in strong wind.

Uncle Joe looked doubtful, but his sister reassured him. She had thought to close all the windows. Besides, it hardly made sense to start now; they'd never make it home ahead of the storm.

When everybody was again seated in the parlor, Jay politely asked if he might hear Billy Murray sing The Whole Damm Family once more. He wanted to memorize it.

The Captain said, "Oh, but you must take notes." And besides providing pad and pencil, he obligingly stood by the machine to stop the record while Jay, jotting down the lines, was able to catch up:

"Last summer at a watering place, a man named Damm I met/ Who entertained me with such grace, said I, 'Now don't forget./ Next winter come and visit me.' Said he, 'That's what I'll do.'/ And yesterday that man arrived and brought some others too./

"There was Mr. Damm and Mrs. Damm, the Damm kids two or three./ With You be Damm and I be Damm, and the whole Damm family./

"My apartment is a small affair. Just room for two or three./ Since that Damm family landed here, there is no room for me./ The rooms are full of different Damms of every size and shape./ So with the Damm dog I must sleep out on the fire escape./

"There is Mr. Damm and Mrs. Damm, the Damm kids two or three./ With You be Damm and I be Damm, and the whole Damm family."

Suddenly in the doorway appeared an enormous orange cat. He looked up and opened his mouth but no sound came out. The Captain looked down and opened his mouth but said nothing. "Poor Midas has lost his voice," he explained. "And he's deaf too. But we communicate." He crooked his forefinger and the cat came over to be lifted into the old gentleman's scant lap. Just then a shoot of sunshine through the butterflies on the lace curtains glorified the animal's fur and announced the storm's passing. It had been quick, leaving behind raindrop diamonds sparkling on the shrubbery, and a short, faint rainbow.

But jogging toward home, they found increasing evidence of violence. Debris of tree limbs and foliage was strewn everywhere. Wind and rain had wreaked havoc. The lane gate had become unhinged. Their ancient willow, uprooted, lay stretched across the yard. Low places were flooded. And there in the ditch water floated Jenny Hen's baby chicks, drowned, all but one.

★ ★ ★

Chapter IX

Uncle Joe never quite got over his disappointment that they failed to make the excursion to Ocean City. It troubled him on Jay's account. Hard times or not, the boy should have some happy memories. And after they got the Ford, he determined to try again.

He accepted the car in place of money so long owed him that he had chalked it off as a bad debt. Turning into the lane, he chuckled at the surprise of Jay and his mother.

"Step in," he invited them, "and we'll go for a little drive."

His sister demurred. "But, Joe, we look a fright."

"Never mind. We won't go far, and we'll keep to the back roads."

Without further thought, they climbed in just as they were: she in her old everyday work dress, her hair straggly, and Jay wearing a tattered shirt with his most disreputable scuff pants. Excited, feeling like millionaires, they chugged out the sparsely populated long point road, away from town, where they'd not likely meet anybody they knew. How exhilarating it was!

Then, deep in the country, the car stopped, giving everybody near heart-failure. They had run out of gas. Jay's mother was mortified that he had to trudge into town for a can of gasoline to roll them home.

"Well, that'll be a lesson to me," Uncle Joe said, disgusted with himself. "You can bet that I won't let it happen again."

For Jay the car was a great toy. He liked to go in the wagon shed and just sit in it—the seats were softer than those in the buggy—imagining himself out on the road with admiring friends.

The first opportunity, Uncle Joe announced that they would drive to Ocean City. Mrs. Malone just looked askance at him. Jay shouted, "Oh, boy!"

They left the house about daylight, covering familiar roads before sunup, then divided their time between admiring the pleasant landscape and making sure that Uncle Joe took the right turns. To Mrs. Malone the long trip was tiring. But Jay's excitement never waned until they pulled onto the edge of the sand beach and looked upon the breakers rolling in. Uncle Joe said, "Now that's a sight for sore eyes."

Parking at a spot where nobody else happened to be around, they fastened up the car curtains for privacy in quickly slipping into their bathing suits. The hours passed in joyous frolic, splashing in the surf, beachcombing for fancy shells, and Jay building an elaborate sand fort. They relished their picnic lunch spread out on a red checked table cloth. The day was perfect, except that Jay's camera somehow got left at home. So they dallied a little longer than they intended.

Ready to leave, they found the car stuck in the sand. With Uncle Joe behind the steering wheel, and Jay and his mother both pushing, still it was only after a helpful stranger lent his brawn that they finally got rolling.

A few miles out of town they had a flat tire.

By now the sun was well down toward the horizon. And Uncle Joe began to feel some qualms about driving into the night. He felt too inexperienced with a motor car to consider traveling strange roads after dark. As he said, you could never tell about an automobile. It hadn't the sense of a horse that would take you home in spite of yourself. Fortunately he'd had the foresight to engage Otis Tarbutton for the farm chores, just in case they were delayed. So they'd best play it safe, pulling into a grassy woods path along the road and sleeping in the car. They spent a miserable night. There was no way they could get comfortable. With the curtains up, the heat was oppressive; curtains open, they were eaten alive by mosquitoes.

At crack of dawn they pulled out. It had been a long night. Uncle Joe said ruefully, "I dunno. Seems like we're born losers."

His sister refused to complain. "But, Joe, let's remember the fun." She gave Jay a poke in the ribs. "Didn't we have a swell time?"

"Yeh," he answered with a little crooked grin.

Their joy in the Ford was short-lived. It happened the one Saturday night of the entire summer that they decided to take in a picture show. Coming out late, they turned briskly down the shadowy street, in laughing colloquy about the fun parts of the show. When they reached their parking, gaiety turned to shock. The car was gone! Two buggies stood at the hitching rack, but down towards the far end where they had left the machine there was only empty space. Stunned, they just stood there.

Charley Tarbutton, whistling and stepping along right lively as he returned from seeing his girl to her home a block away, recognized them and wondered why they were huddled in the street, since a rig besides his own was waiting at the rack.

"Good evening. Is there trouble of some kind?" And when they told him, he too stood dumbfounded, his glance absently searching about. "But who on earth could have taken it?"

"I've no idea," Uncle Joe said wearily.

Charley still pondered. "Maybe it was an emergency, and you'll hear from somebody."

"It's possible," Uncle Joe agreed. "But it does look mighty peculiar."

"Well," Charley said finally, "it's awful late to do anything. Let me drive you folks home. Then first thing in the morning maybe we can find out something."

They crowded into his buggy, Jay jackknifed into the back as was his usual lot. Jogging out the road, Charley kept puzzling over the mystery. "Now who in the world could have taken it?"

"I wish I knew," Uncle Joe said.

They soon found out. The thief, an escaped convict fleeing police, had been killed and the car demolished by a speeding train.

That ended it. And Uncle Joe bemoaned their loss until his sister finally said, "Oh, stop your fretting. It could have been worse. One of us might have been killed. We got along quite nicely without it before. And we will again."

As Uncle Joe had pointed out, Mrs. Tarbutton really could claim part ownership in the camera, since she had refused payment for her coupons. And in return for her generosity, Jay delighted the family with snapshots of everybody.

Two of the older boys had rescued from neglect and abuse a big old black horse. And when he was somewhat restored to health, they were eager for his picture. Choosing a mild Sunday afternoon with cloudless blue sky, Jay and his mother drove over to Tarbutton's. What was to have been a simple bit of business turned out to be a major production. Besides the horse, a dog and cat were added to the "sitters," and various others among the farm animals lent their unwelcome presence.

DRAMATIS PERSONAE

Charley Brown .... Horse, black, old.

Sport .... Dog, wheaten Terrier.

Lulu .... Cat, orange tabby.

Sweet William & Nanny .... Goats.

Connie .... Cow.

Priscilla .... Sow.

Buckwheat .... Burro.

Such a time they had with Charley Brown! He might be twenty-eight years old but feminine allure still stirred him and superhuman restraints could not hold him still. When Charley Tarbutton rode him over from his pasture, mares in a nearby field brought him pounding up the road bugling every step of the way. And he was determined to pay his respects to them. Charley and Jay struggled to keep him beside the stone wall of the barn lot. He whinnied and stomped about, dragging on his halter rope until Jay barked his knuckles on the rough mortar between the stones. To keep the big brute occupied, a bucket of grain was brought and doled out by the handful.

Meanwhile, little Billy boy wanted his wheat-colored Sport dog in the picture. Then Elly fetched out her orange cat. Jay decided that these two on top of the wall with Charley horse looking over would make a fine picture. It was not to be.

Sport had rolled happily in the barnyard and got his hair full of straw and stuff. Lulu cat, lugged out from her cool siesta in the house, wanted no part of the proceedings. Elly, hiding behind the wall, tried to hold her in place, but Lulu laid back her ears with a snarl, and scratched herself free of the grasping hands. So, they would concentrate on just two: Charley horse was bribed with little dabs of grain, and good-natured Sport tried to be patient. But the sun beat down and he began to pant. If not held in place he would jump down off the wall.

Meanwhile, the commotion attracted several other animals and they all fore-gathered to observe the goings-on. The goats, Sweet William and Nanny, crossed a wide field from its furthest corner, Connie the heifer came thundering around the barn and slid to a stop on her knees, an enormous white sow espied the grain bucket and had to get right in the middle of the melee. One and all they did their best to spoil the day's masterpiece.

Owner and horse having the same given name, it became necessary for Jay's directorial bellowing to distinguish whom he was addressing—Charley-man handling the grain bucket, or Charley-horse nibbling the goodies. So it was—

"Charley! Charley-man, hold the bucket away from the wall. (Git! to the goats crowding him.) Here Charley, Charley-horse. (Hey. Shoo, pig!)" He was down on his knees trying for the best high level shot. ("Beat it!" the goats back again.) And the sow sniffing around nearly knocked him over.

Everybody working like beavers, with flailing of arms and lifting of boot, they spent a heroic half hour without getting much to show, perhaps one decent picture. Charley Tarbutton's clothes were a mess. Charley-horse slobbered all over Jay's clean shirt, one of the goats sneezed and splattered his good suit with snot, and he stepped in dung with his second best shoes.

From the barn's cool shade came the voice of Buckwheat, the burro, "Haw ee, haw, haw, haw."

While the onlookers laughed, Jay could see nothing funny about it. And driving home, Mrs. Malone had trouble keeping a straight face.

For Uncle Joe the Ford had been a welcome addition to their stable of vehicles. Jay was fast growing up, and the buggy could not comfortably accommodate the three of them all at once. They needed something roomier. Now, once more faced with the problem, what they should have, he decided, was a surrey. One that could be bought cheap. And towards the beginning of winter, opportunity knocked. Attending a farm sale when the weather turned foul, so that the crowd was sparse, he picked up a bargain, so well kept that it shone like new. They gave it to themselves at Christmas. Now, there was not only ample room for family, but they could also enjoy a guest.

Their first adventure took them on a Sunday drive to look at a boat. This was a lifeboat said to have washed ashore, probably from the sinking of some ocean liner. It carried no identification, so the story went, and its origin was never discovered. Uncle Joe, liking the idea of something unsinkable, thought he might buy it.

"How about a picnic?" his sister suggested. "And invite Captain Roth. We'll go right by his place. And the boat should interest an old sea dog like him."

A capital idea! So she mailed a little note of invitation. And on Sunday next they packed a large hamper of crispy fried chicken with all kinds of goodies.

The Captain awaited them, seated on his porch and joined by several lazy cats taking their ease. In jaunty cap and dark blue coat with brass buttons, lively as a cricket, he skipped down his walk, gave them a quick little salute, and climbed up beside Uncle Joe.

"Very interesting,"' he commented, hearing about the boat. That it was now all over painted gray seemed to him very odd indeed. "I would suspect that the fellow who found it lost no time in covering all telltale signs."

"Well," Uncle Joe said, "that happened quite a while back. He's dead and gone now. And there have been at least two other owners."

A wizened farmer with eyes the color of a goonie and sandpaper whiskers led them along his pier. Uncle Joe, Jay and the Captain took the boat out for a try. They liked its smooth rowing over the water and its buoyancy. The taciturn farmer silently watched them, standing by the seat Mrs. Malone found for herself while she waited. He was surely not a man to waste words.

A deal being struck, and the farmer agreeing to deliver the purchase, picnic was next on their minds. But before they had found a suitable spot, they drove through a heavy shower that drenched the countryside. Not to be denied, they decided to picnic in the carriage. Dewey being fastened to a line fence beside the road, Mrs. Malone opened the hamper and began supplying each one's portion.

But Uncle Joe hardly got started. As he was about to bite into his big juicy drumstick, something, they never knew what, startled Dewey, and the carriage lurched as he strained against the fence. Uncle Joe wildly grabbed the reins to calm him, and lost his drumstick. What happened to it, they never knew. It appeared to be nowhere in the road, nor along the ditch beside the carriage. It seemed to have disappeared into thin air.

That was a picnic they never forgot. And the case of the vanishing drumstick always made Capt. Roth's pot belly shake.

★ ★ ★

Chapter X

At the beginning of his senior year in high school, Jay awakened to the bliss of romance. He was smitten by a charming new girl named Louise Johnson. She had "raven" curls, big dark eyes and a ravishing smile. After noticing her for a day or two, he realized that some of the fellows, who were better looking than he, had begun to take notice. So he sent her a little note up along the aisle in study hall.

"Hi, Girlie. I think you have some eyes. What do you say to ice cream after school? Jay Malone."

She turned her head over her shoulder and nodded, "Yes."

He tried to send her another tightly folded note, but the teacher intercepted it and waggled her finger at him. For half an hour he was uneasy that she might read it. But when the bell rang, she handed it back, clucking her disapproval.

After lunch, as they passed in the hall, Louise winked at him.

Jay learned that she lived three miles out of town and drove in each day. Persuading his friend Gus to let him leave his bike at the livery stable, he had a good excuse to walk over with her each day, carrying her books and treating occasionally to ice cream or elegant pink and green confections from the Greek candy store. Winsome Louise made a picture emerging from the stable in her little parasoled buggy drawn by the sleek black pony at a brisk trot. Jay knew that he was not Louise's only beau, but his camera was immensely popular.

When it happened that they were assigned to the same side of a debate, Jay was thrilled to find an excuse to call on Louise in her home. He rode Dewey over Sunday afternoon. Her parents were away, but the place was swarming with children. It was difficult to do much work, but still they were together for a little while.

He and Louise went steady, more or less, for the whole year. Especially was she devoted at Christmas time when with his meager hoarded savings he bought her the manicure set she hinted for.

Jay graduated from high school, valedictorian of his class. And Uncle Joe, who valued education (his own classroom attendance ended with the eighth grade), was so proud that he had to be restrained sometimes from bragging too much.

That milestone passed, now what? The question was nagging for all of them. Each wondered, but nobody brought up the subject.

Uncle Joe well knew how much he depended upon Jay. Yet he was ambitious for the boy. Farming offered no career for a smart young man. And farm work needed a person physically strong; whereas Jay was not at all robust. But until asked, the old gent was not of a mind to offer his advice.

Mrs. Malone shrank from painful thoughts, dreading that inevitable day when her son would leave home. For the time-being, she was content just to let matters take their own course.

Jay gave some thought to attending college. But getting married was also on his mind. And for that he needed a job. His mother, suspecting his inclination, prayed that he would not do some foolish thing.

Following graduation came the summertime and considerable distance separating them. Louise was nearly six miles away. And Jay, despite his ardent longing, found it difficult to call on her as often as he wanted. They did write. But letters hardly sufficed. Although he had told her that he was planning on a job in Baltimore, that had not come about. Uncle Joe, not so young anymore and troubled with rheumatism, seemed always to be needing him. So that whether from pure bone weariness or simply lack of time, Jay found it hard to very often go courting.

But bigger troubles lay ahead. A Tarbutton uncle died suddenly, leaving his huge acreage to the two brothers. So they had to give up farming on shares for Uncle Joe. The outlook was grim. Jay knew where his place was.

That year the weather prevented very much Fall plowing, which would mean a busier springtime. Still, they mended fences, replacing rotted posts and tacking on new wire. When it was too wet or too cold for anything else, they might oil and polish the sets of harness. Uncle Joe, like his sister, was a meticulous housekeeper. And repairs were needed on the old buildings, fixing this and that or some other thing.

Towards noontime of a blossomy day in the early spring, Jay, dreaming of his Louise, rode home from town after standing around all morning waiting his turn at the blacksmith's. He found his uncle astraddle the ridgepole of the barn repairing a leak in the roof. Dismounting he called up, "Need help?"

"Nope." Uncle Joe hammered in the last nail, "I'm just finishing." Shifting his position to step down the ladder, he suddenly disappeared on the opposite side of the building. Fearful thumping and bumping panicked Jay. Dropping the saddle just unbuckled, he raced around the barn to where his uncle lay on the ground. Grimacing, Uncle Joe whispered, "I'm afraid I can't get up."

Jay gasped, "I'll run fetch Mom."

Between them they managed to ease the stricken man onto a heavy horseblanket, then ever so carefully they carried him to the house. When finally he lay on the couch in the kitchen, Mrs. Malone began applying such remedies as she knew. Jay resaddled Dewey and galloped back to town for the doctor.

Uncle Joe had severely sprained his back and broken his right leg. "Well," Dr. Blades said, "it could have been worse." Meaning Uncle Joe could have broken his neck. Luckily he had pitched down the gently sloping roof on the side where it joined the hog pen by the wagon shed, and his fall to grassy earth was not more than four feet.

But Uncle Joe considered the damage bad enough. Never seriously ill a day in his life, he was a rebellious invalid. All during his convalescence he fretted and fumed over his uselessness, sitting there day after day, with all the work to be done and him unable to pitch in.

In the weeks following, Jay found out what he was made of. Together he and his mother undertook to handle the farmwork.

Every morning they rose shortly after five o'clock, going right out to the barn to feed the stock. While the cows were eating, they milked. Jay brought the milk up to cool in the half barrel filled with water at the pump, while his mother let the cows into the barnyard, watered them and started the herd out to pasture. While the milk was cooling, they ate breakfast.

By eight-thirty Jay was out in the field. He would plow until he saw the white rag on the post. Unhitching, he brought the horses up and watered them, standing by lest they drink too fast or too much. Then he fed them. After dinner, as soon as the team had finished eating, he would go out again and stay all afternoon. And he thought, "What the hell does a farmer need rest for? He's got from ten at night till five in the morning." Dragging his weary frame through the evening chores, he ate supper and fell asleep in his chair.

His mother fed the hogs twice a day, and the chickens. She tended the garden. Every Monday was wash day, each Thursday she baked bread. Wednesday night she got her yeast ready; next morning when Jay came down there would be a big old doughtray on a couple of chairs and she'd be putting warm irons into one end.

Their routine was monotonous as a treadmill. Forever work, rarely pleasure. And though it was the lovely season when a young man's fancy turns to thoughts of calling on his girl, Jay barely made it every two weeks. So he was rather relieved to get a note from Louise announcing that she was leaving on a trip to Philadelphia for a visit with her aunt. She did not say how long she planned to be gone. But by the time she returned, Jay imagined, Uncle Joe ought to be back in harness, and he could find more free time. Thoughts of the pleasures they would share sweetened his drudgery.

★ ★ ★

Chapter XI

Jay was probably the last person to learn the truth about Louise: that she had gone not to Philadelphia visiting her aunt but to Atlantic City on her honey-moon. One of her gabby little brothers spilled the beans. And right in the middle of Main Street! Jay despaired—always the loser.

On a Sunday afternoon, home alone for an hour or so, he lolled in a porch chair agonizing over his broken heart. Josh nearby offering his sympathy pricked up his ears and growled. Then recognizing their friend Flossy McGuire, he dashed out to meet her just entering the lane.

Flossy and her mother were regular visitors down from Baltimore to spend several weeks at Price's Inn on the opposite side of the point. Although she was a sophisticated city girl of twenty-three engaged to marry a navy man, Flossie looked scarcely older than a pretty teenager. Small and dark, her black hair nightly curled on rags, her smile dimpling both cheeks, she was a lively personality. The fleeting expressions of her pert countenance intrigued Jay. It troubled him not at all that her nimble mind could out-distance his. They were pretty good friends. And his mother had become immensely fond of her.

He met Flossy soon after Prices built their rustic pavilion overlooking the water. There by the light of lanterns, to music from a Victrola, young people gathered to dance—those staying at the inn mingling with couples out from town. Jay was not of their class. Not only were the fellows older and very smooth, but the girls acted stuck up, humbling him with their icy stares.

Still, he enjoyed watching them dance and listening to the music. On a gentle slope near the pavilion stood a solid old wooden two-seater swing that provided a front row seat comfortable for him and Josh.

Then one evening the imp that was Flossy tripped lightly down the path and paused beside him. "Hello," she said with her dimpled smile. "You're not dancing?"

It embarrassed him to confess that he didn't know how.

She ignored his diffidence. "Then it's time you learned. Come on, I'll guide you." She took him by the hand.

He hung back. "But I'm not dressed."

"Neither am I." She pulled him toward the pavilion.

"You wait here," he told Josh.

In a dim corner they began the lesson. Beyond a wave of her hand in greeting, Flossie paid no attention to the dancers. Jay's sense of rhythm helped him to catch on rather quickly. Soon he forgot his shyness. Generous with her praises, Flossy urged him to come over whenever he could. And after a few visits he felt at ease so that he dared invite Louise.

For that evening everything must be just right. He had even calculated on moonrise. He groomed Dewey and polished the buggy. For himself a barbershop haircut and his carefully pressed good suit turned out a nice young man whom his mother and Uncle Joe looked upon with fond pride.

Neatly dressed, with a light heart he was on his way. But starting down their steep stairs he slipped and skidded the whole way to the bottom. His descent raked the top off a big boil on his behind that he had been determined to ignore. And worse, he sprained his ankle.

Uncle Joe turned coward at the thought of Jay's bitter disappointment. He said, "I'll quick ride over to Johnson's so Louise won't be wondering." And the good man made his escape.

Flossy commiserated with Jay then, and she tried to console him now. She had walked over to let him know that she and her mother were down for three weeks, and to show him the present from her fiancé. It was a gold link bracelet secured by a heart-shaped lock with miniature key. It had belonged to his mother who died, which seemed to her so sweet.

Finding Jay downcast, she tried to coax a smile. "Well, what's ailin' you?"
"Nothin".

"Don't tell me that. I'll bet you and Louise have had a fallin' out."

"Guess again," Jay said somberly.

She gave him a sharp glance but didn't ask.

"She's married," he said dully, staring away.

Flossy fell back in her chair. "Oh, I'm sorry." she said sincerely. For a moment she was silent, stroking the top of Josh's head. She looked at his unhappy face. "But if it's over and done, Jay, moping won't help."

"I know," he said. "And I guess it's better this way, to break up now rather than after we'd be married."

"Right," Flossie agreed. "You'd not want an unhappy wife." She laid her hand on his arm. "Louise was bound to see that it wouldn't work out."

"Why?"

"Well, she must have realized that your mother wasn't keen about you getting married." Flossy looked very young but she had an old head, and she was close friends with Mrs. Malone.

"Mom never was rude to her."

"No. But there are other ways of letting your feelings be known."

"I see what you mean. My mother never let me know how she felt about Louise. But Louise knew."

"Exactly."

"She might have suggested that I bring her out to the farm. She never did though."

"How often did you call on Louise?"

"About every two weeks."

"When?"

"Sunday afternoon."

"What an ardent admirer!" Flossy laughed merrily. "Every two weeks on Sunday afternoon. How long did you stay? And what did you do?"

"I won't tell you. You're laughing at me now. Anyhow, it's private."

"But if you only called on her every two weeks, did you go right after dinner and stay till bedtime, or was it a short couple of hours?"

"I'm not going to tell you."

"My admirers come on Sundays at two-thirty and stay till Mama runs them home about ten-thirty."

"I'm not interested in the calling hours of your admirers."

"Yes," Flossie said reflectively. "I can perfectly understand Louise's viewpoint. Here was a farmer boy who called on her maybe—notice I said maybe—every other Sunday. She looked out to the farm and what she saw was dismal: a cool reception from the in-laws and a life of hard work. Pretty as she is, you can't blame her for accepting somebody else, Jay."

"She knew that I was thinking about a job in Baltimore," he offered.

"You told her, but had you made any definite plans?"

"No. Not yet."

"Then she probably thought you couldn't be serious."

"She probably thought if I could go away to Baltimore and certainly be gone more than one Sunday in two weeks, then I could come to see her oftener."

"Naturally. You can't blame her, Jay. It's just too bad for you. I'd say you're a victim of circumstances."

"That's been my lot since the day I was born," he said miserably.

"What did you do when you called on Sundays?"

"Took walks."

"Walks?" A smile hovered about Flossy's lips.

"Yes," he answered with dignity. "We went out walking."

"I suppose there was too much family for you to sit peacefully at home." Flossy drew with her long fingernail a neat part in the fur on Josh's head. "How many brothers and sisters does Louise have?"

"One, two, three—seven at first count. But I'm sure there are more. They all belong to her stepmother. One of her little brothers took a great fancy to me. She'd say to him, 'I think Daddy wants you in the yard.' He'd say, 'I'll be back in a minute.'"

"Then I suppose when his little back was turned you and Louise moved together on the sofa."

"There wasn't any sofa. Nothin' but straight chairs."

"What a handicap!"

"The first time I visited her, two of her brothers were playing Parcheesi on the same table where we were working on a debate."

"Oh, so a debate brought you together?"

"No. We met at school."

"Did you ever take her to see a movie?"

"No."

"You never did? Did you take her some candy?"

"Yes, But not every Sunday."

"Did you ever surprise her with a tiny bouquet in the wintertime?"

"No. But I took her an apple once."

"An apple!" Flossy was convulsed. "What a naive beau. An apple!"

"Some girls appreciate an apple," Jay said huffily.

"I can imagine." Flossy's lips twitched. "Really, Jay, I don't know why she put up with you as long as she did. If she was like the girls I know, she would have said to herself, 'Why should I sit at home and entertain him? If he can't take me out, I won't be bothered.' And she would have jilted you without any qualms."

"Well," Jay said mournfully, "that's exactly what she did."

48

Chapter XII

His love lost, Jay's melancholy seemed perpetual. His mother and Uncle Joe worried about his lack of interest in anything.

Then one Saturday driving home from town he mulled over a new idea. On the street he had run into a former classmate who was enthusiastic about his government job in Washington. Life in the city was a lark. The pay was good and regular. You could mail-order the study material to prepare for the civil service exam. This, Jay thought, was the push he had been needing. Now be felt freer to leave, since two of the younger Tarbutton boys had approached Uncle Joe about farming on shares.

When he opened the lane gate, no Josh came bounding to welcome him. Out with Uncle Joe probably. But Uncle Joe was at the house. Jay called and whistled. No response. By supper time he bad become genuinely alarmed. Josh never missed a meal. Jay searched the barn and the boathouse. And up late into the evening, by moonlight, he crisscrossed the fields, peering into thickets. A dog could get caught in broken fence. He called Josh's name and repeated his special whistle which usually brought the dog from anywhere in hearing.

Through the night, unable to sleep, he worried, several times going down, praying to find Josh on the porch. And Sunday morning he looked hopefully for the eager face and waving tail. After milking he gulped a cup of coffee, then went to search the woods. Their timber was posted, but some sneak might have set a trap. From side to side, forth and back, methodically he pushed through the underbrush, calling, whistling, peering right and left, pausing to listen for his pal's answering bark.

When for the third time he came out onto the old sawmill road, his heart stopped. There in a heap lay the beautiful golden brown body. Josh had been shot. And he must have tried to crawl home. With a moan Jay collapsed beside him, cradling the lifeless dog in his arms, his grief hysterical. One cheek pressed against the broad furry brow, he kept repeating, "No! No! No!" Suddenly he raised his head and glared, his face contorted with rage. Was somebody watching him? He'd kill the bastard!

But there was nobody. Only himself, alone there in the whispering stillness of the deep woods.

In misery he stumbled home. His mother was shocked to silence at the look of him. Without a word he climbed the stairs to his room and came down carrying a quilt from his bed. He went out, slamming the door, and took his little red wagon from the shed.

The sight of him returning wrung Mrs. Malone's heart. In the ancient family burying ground out back of the house, Jay dug a grave and gently lowered his beloved friend wrapped in the quilt. Runners of Grave Privet greened the spot.

Jay was grief-stricken. Wherever he looked, there was the vision of Josh. Open the door, he could see his eager pal waiting. But there was only emptiness. At the lane gate where he was always welcomed home; there at the end of the pier sharing secrets; on the old leather couch napping together. . . Memories made him cry inside, silently. Regrets—that he had not paused to savor more deeply their beautiful friendship. Guilt—remembering when Josh outside his closed bedroom door had given a little bark asking to come in, and he had been too busy to answer. Then he heard the dog go slowly down the stairs. Now, if only he could relive that moment. He tried not to remember. Only time could dim the visions that haunted him.

Miserable as he was, he knew that he had to get away.

His order for the civil service study material brought an early reply. And such was his careful preparation that he made an excellent passing grade.

In due time he received a job offer—Clerk in the War Department. The irony of it! After all his dreams of a military career, to perform his war service in the file trenches!

★ ★ ★

Chapter XIII

Jay arrived in Washington towards the middle of June. He had expected to stay at the Y, at least temporarily, but it was full. The desk clerk directed him to a private home. There the landlady had available only a third floor hall bedroom, very narrow with one small window, but Jay immediately rented it for fifteen dollars a month and dropped his worn valise beside the bureau. His budget would be darn tight to begin with.

How tight he learned next morning. Though he had come on an offer of $1200 per annum, what he got was $1140, "Right stingy of Uncle Sam," he mused. Nevertheless, this was his opportunity and he would do his best. His dependably good work—he kept at it, and no cheating just stuffing the files in any old place—in time brought a commendation from his supervisor and a piddling raise.

But he was so very lonely. The big city offered less excitement than he had imagined. He knew nobody; his former classmate had moved on. And Jay was not the sort who make friends easily. The people he met remained mere speaking acquaintances. He saw the sights, wandered for hours through the museums, hung around the Ellipse watching any ball games in progress. Evenings he read the newspaper, then went to bed. Sunday mornings he dropped in at the services of the Methodist Church around the corner. The congregation greeted him in friendly fashion, but there seemed to be few young members. Only very rarely did he allow himself the luxury of a movie. Living so close to George Washington University, he considered it criminal not to pursue his education. And for a class or two come Fall, he had to save.

His landlady's aged father, crippled by a stroke, was somebody to talk to. In fine weather Mr. Shaw sat on a bench in front of the house where his friends in the neighborhood stopped to chat with him. But during the winter months he must remain cooped up in his room with only his green parrot for company. Jay got into the habit of sitting with the old gentleman, sharing a pipe of fragrant tobacco and playing cards or checkers.

Because he saved carefully, Jay felt in the spring that he could afford to be a bit generous with himself. On Sundays, when the less expensive government cafeteria was closed, he might treat himself to dinner at Allies Inn. It was pleasant while enjoying the delicious food to watch the pretty hostesses in quaint dress as they served coffee. And to avoid the long lines early, he went towards mid-afternoon when the crowds thinned out.

That Sunday, though it was mid-afternoon, with weather cold and damp, an unusual crowd filled the place. Jay had a small table for two all to himself only briefly when he heard a gentle voice:

"Is this place reserved?"

He looked up into the dark eyes of a young woman in pea green jacket and peaked cap with a curled green feather, holding her loaded tray.

"No," he answered, rising to help her.

"You don't mind if I sit here?"

"I'd be delighted."

For a grown young woman, her face and hands were remarkably small and pale. She had black straight hair cut short with bangs. When she unbuttoned her jacket and dropped it over the back of her chair, there was nothing to her. Jay had never seen such a tiny-tiny person.

Clearing her tray, she handed it to a waiter and began on her soup. They ate in silence.

Across the aisle from them, two women sat at table. One was large and bulky, with a mannish haircut. She wore severely man-tailored clothes and a pince-nez. Her companion, small and shriveled, was clothed in miscellaneous garments of rusty black with an enormous plum color hat skewered by a monstrous "jeweled" hat pin. She had a goiter, and her ear was stuffed with cotton. She talked continuously out the corner of her puckered mouth, chewing at the same time. Mostly she mumbled, but suddenly her voice rose above the din of the diners—

"Sure I remember Joey. We all thought he was dead, you know, after the war. But the Germans had took him prisoner. They walked him two hundred miles and gave him one loaf of bread. So when he come home naturally he was crazy.

"One day he says to me, 'I'm gettin' married.'

"I says, 'You gettin' married. Who you gonna marry?'

"He says, 'She's a girl that was gonna marry a sailor. But he didn't come back. The weddin' day's set and he ain't here. So I'm gonna marry her.'

"I says, 'What you want to marry her for? You don't know her, do you?'

"He says, 'No, I don't know her very well. I only just met her day before yesterday.'"

Her cackling laugh turned heads across the room.

Jay and the girl exchanged twinkles of amusement. After a moment of silence, he ventured a pleasantry. "I see you have something that I missed. What's under all that whipped cream?"

"Chocolate pudding." With her spoon she scraped off a little of the cream so that he might see. "And it's very good. I'd already decided on it when I saw a lady take some of this gorgeous chocolate cake, and I had to have some too. My sweet tooth is positively sinful." Her smile charmed him.

He wanted to prolong their chitchat. "Don't you find chocolate and chocolate rather too much of a good thing?"

"Well, yes," she admitted. "I'm certainly a poor judge of my capacity." Obviously she accepted her shortcomings philosophically. Certainly she had no weight problem; you could practically span her waist with your two hands.

From time to time her glance had wandered over the lively dining room, and now she found what she had sought. "I must go," she said. "Thanks for sharing your table." Gathering up her jacket, she crossed through the tables to meet an older woman just coming down the stairs.

Jay lingered with the lively crowd as long as he dared take up table space. With nothing to do, and nobody for company, he reluctantly walked back to his dreary room. The four walls seemed to close in on him and his window framed a dismal view. He was in no mood to study or write his weekly letter home. Lying across his bed, he tried to fall asleep so the hours would pass quickly.

Ten days later he discovered that the girl was also a University student. He caught sight of her entering one of the classrooms. Then in the library he found a vacant seat near her desk and smiled at her when she glanced up. Another time, as she tried to reach a high volume, he was there to hand it down. And he began to consider it a good omen that their paths should cross so frequently.

One evening passing the gym and hearing a lot of noise, he stepped inside. The girls' basketball team was holding practice. At once he saw her. From the side-lines she exhorted the players, shouting and waving her arms. Amused, Jay thought, "She's little but she's loud." And he watched her, fascinated.

Shortly afterward, from a distance he saw her fall on the library steps. Two young men were immediately beside her. And Jay felt a twinge of jealousy that he was too far away to help her up.

When he came upon her sitting on a bench in the Yard, with her arm in a sling, he dropped down beside her. "Did this happen when you fell the other evening? I saw you but I was too far away to lend a helping hand."

"No," she answered pleasantly. "I fell and broke my arm when I was trying to pinch hit for a friend at basketball practice."

Jay chided her. "Surely you know that basketball is not the sport for petite and delicate young ladies."

"I should have remembered," she agreed ruefully. "I'll never learn my capacity."

They both laughed. And it seemed to Jay that he detected a thaw in her reserve. She glanced at her watch. "I must get to class."

Though her charming image dwelt in Jay's thoughts, he was at a loss just how to warm up the acquaintance. Something special was needed. And he immediately thought of her when he was given a pair of theater tickets. They were pushed under his door with a note from one of the men in the house: "Jay. Hope you can use these. A friend sent them to me, but now I have to be out of town. V. W." They were orchestra seats for "No, No, Nanette" on Saturday night. The idea of escorting her thrilled him.

His strategy was to be on hand at her usual library study time, inconspicuously waiting so that it might seem they met accidentally. As it happened, she was a day late, but on Thursday evening she finally came. Jay emerged from the shadows to climb the steps beside her. As he held open the door, he said, "My name is Jay Malone. Can I invite you to the theater Saturday night? To see 'No, No, Nanette'."

A moment's hesitation, then she replied, "Sounds interesting."

Elated he hurried on. "Pick you up about seven?"

She dropped her books on a handy desk, found a scrap of paper and scribbled: Joy Hansen, 615 21st Street.

He liked her name. Joy suited her. And for two days he thought of little else besides their joyful evening. Friday his mind wandered from his work. Saturday the hours dragged even more slowly than usual. He dressed with great care. Though he'd never had the money to dress well, he was neat in his best blue suit saved for just such an occasion as this.

Jauntily he climbed the steps of the tan brick house numbered 615. When he asked for Miss Hansen, the elderly landlady ushered him into the parlor and told him to have a seat. He watched her go and pull a cord that hung down the stairwell. A bell jangled on high, and the cheery answering voice gave him a thrill. He heard quick footsteps along the upper hall, then down the stairs.

As he rose to greet his date, a perfectly strange girl appeared in the archway. She was a blonde, attractive, but too tall for Jay. Smiling, she said, "Hello."

Jay stared at her. "You're Joy Hansen?"

"Yes, I am." Her expression was friendly.

So he had been stood up! "Excuse me," he managed to say in a choked voice. "I'm afraid there's been a mistake." She was a party to this; she knew who had tricked him. And he wanted only to withdraw as gracefully as possible. "I'm very sorry to have troubled you." With a little bow, he turned and walked out.

Furious, he was tempted to drop the tickets in the gutter. Then he thought, "Why should I let her spoil my evening? The little bitch." So he went on down to the National and enjoyed the program, sitting beside an empty seat.

By the time he returned to his room, his hurt and anger had eased. Well, you could hardly blame her. He was no ladies' man. Disgusted, he studied himself in the mirror. Little peanut head, thin sandy hair high off his forehead, and a brown mustache old-fashioned as Uncle Joe's. What woman would want a puny guy half blind and gimpy besides? Hardly the figure for romance. You couldn't blame her. He was no Prince Charming. Just a born loser. And as a permanent reminder of his defeat he left the spare ticket tucked into the frame of his mirror.

Once afterward he had the misfortune to meet her. Unexpectedly they found themselves approaching each other along the Yard's central walkway. Her face changed. Jay gave her a little crooked smile and turned away on one of the side paths.

★ ★ ★

~

Chapter XIV

The departure of two third-floor boarders gave Jay what he had long wanted: a chance to move out of his cramped quarters and into one of the large bedrooms with big bay windows overlooking the G. W. campus. And he was especially pleased to be rooming with a young law student named Will Dawson with whom he already enjoyed a pleasant friendship.

One dismal Saturday during the midwinter holidays, their only mail was a small shocking-pink envelope with blue forget-me-nots across its flap and addressed to Jay in a precise round hand. But other than the "M" impressed in a blob of gold sealing wax, there was no clue to the sender.

Just returned from lunch, he dropped into their worn leather armchair, found his penknife and slit the blue blossoms to draw out a single pink sheet that brought a smile. "It's from a girl named Marta Williams," he announced. "She and I were kids together over on the eastern shore." His gaze rested on the dreary prospect of wet campus roofs under leaden sky. "I've often wondered whatever became of Marta."

She had written a very short note. He read it aloud: "Dear Jay—How nice that you're in Washington! I live here now. Right close to Union Station. Can't you drop by? Love, Marta."

Finding his pipe, Jay tapped the bowl against his shoe sole, tamped in rich tobacco, and touched a light to it. "It'll be really interesting to see Marta again. She was a lively one and very pretty. We used to play man and wife, and I'd build houses for her. She was always wanting to comb my hair." He chuckled. "I never could understand why women like to get their hands in your hair."

"It's one of life's pleasanter mysteries," Will declared with a crooked grin, gathering up his books on his way to the Libe.

Alone with his reminiscence, Jay hardly noticed the gloom gathering around him and the squally rain lashing the big windows. His fancy played in the sunshine of those happy days, a smiling memory of Marta's big brown eyes that sparkled with mischief. What a tease she was! He tried to picture her now, the attractive young lady, larksome still no doubt. And remembrance fueled a desire to see her again.

It would be amusing to recall what they were up to this time seven years ago: business partners sharing the proceeds from sale of Christmas trees at twenty-five cents each. What a woeful pair they must have looked, poor patched country kids trudging door to door taking orders. And how rich they felt sharing Marta's purse full of coins! Then skating on the pond in the woods— their antics gave Josh fits.

Seven years ago! And he hadn't been on skates since.

Rather than write, he would just surprise her.

Recalling their many shared interests, he more sensibly appreciated Marta's happy disposition and unselfish comradeship. He visualized her as about his height, naturally blonde, with pale complexion, sparkling dark eyes, and a quick smile. With her instincts for quality and her kind heart, she must by now be a very charming person. And through the days following her note, his thoughts dwelt more and more on the pleasure of renewing their friendship . . .

Her address was toward the middle of a long brick row on Capitol Hill. Stepping into the vestibule, he pushed the button of a raucous buzzer. A smothered voice answered, "Coming!" And he felt again that proper awe of Mrs. Williams. The door was opened by a small aged woman leaning on a single crutch.

"Miss Marta Williams lives here?" He studied her curiously.

She responded with a toothless smile and a nod.

This agreeable person could hardly be Mrs. Williams. She must be Grandmama. "I'm an old friend of Marta's," he said. "I dropped by to see her."

"Well, come in." She stepped back to open the door wider.

He entered a narrow, dimly lit hallway and followed her through dark-paneled sliding doors into the parlor. "Oh," she exclaimed, "let me go turn off the stove. Have a seat here, will you? I'll be right back." And she hobbled off down the hall.

Accepting the chair she offered, Jay looked about him. The dark-hued room too was dim, its crowded mahogany smothering the gleam of one small lamp. But from the shadows loomed an immense oil portrait of a woman in red. She was not young. Her figure had spread, her chin sagged, and marcelled graying hair swept back from her temples. But she was vividly made up and lavishly jeweled. Her lips were shaped in scarlet, her eyebrows had been thinly penciled. A heavy strand of turquoise beads filled in the low neckline of her red silk dress. Bulky blue earrings, an ornate brooch of varicolored stones, and two huge turquoise rings—all this composed a prodigal display. Yet she had encircled her uplifted arm with a gold chain bracelet dangling weighty charms. Her gaze was haughty, her presence overwhelming.

The crone had stumped back down the hall. "I'm so forgetful," she said. "But I promised I'd be ever so careful. Don't want a fire." She settled into a chair opposite. "Now."

"I was admiring the portrait," he lied.

"That's my daughter, Mrs. Williams. She was a great singer, you know. Wonderful voice. A very beautiful woman in her day." She sighed. "But for a number of years now she hasn't been at all well. After Mr. Williams died, it seemed best that we all live together."

"I came to see Marta," he reminded her.

"Oh, yes. Well, Marta isn't home. She and her mother are having their dinner down at the Mason House. I'm too slow walking that distance; so they carry out mine. They should be back soon."

Jay was disappointed. He had hoped to catch Marta alone, but to wait here was out of the question. "Perhaps I could meet them at the restaurant," he suggested.

"You might. The food is really quite good," she said pleasantly. "And it's not far. Only three blocks down toward the Capitol. It's right on the corner. Marta and her mother always go early and sit at the table next to the cashier's desk. Anyway, you'll see Mrs. Williams's red feather hat." She giggled.

"Then I'll walk down and join them." Rising, he held out the package he had brought. "May I leave this?"

"Why yes. Just put it down anywhere."

He placed his gaily be-ribboned box of chocolates on the small table just under the lamp, which made it the brightest object in the room.

The old lady ushered him out the door. "Marta will be glad to see you," she called as he turned jauntily down the sidewalk.

Immediately upon entering the restaurant he spotted the bright feather hat. Mrs. Williams sat against the wall; Marta had her back to the crowded room. But when he had gone through the cafeteria line, Jay decided to take a vacant table nearby.

One glance at the pair in the corner left him in shock!

Instead of the charming, vivacious young woman he had confidently expected, he saw a big overgrown girl with pale skin. Of age she might be, but without adult graces. There was a dismaying immaturity about her— in her set expression and, oddly, the cling of her blond hair at the nape of her neck, which reminded him of a Tarbutton infant daughter. Her clothes were kiddish and unbecoming: a homely crocheted hat of white wool, black-braided blue serge coat tight across the shoulders, and flat-heeled strapped black shoes.

On the second finger of her right hand she wore a cheap gold ring with a "ruby" set. Jay had given her that ring. They were poking through the moldering ruins of an old house partially burned and abandoned after a gruesome murder happened there, when he turned over a half-rotted plank and uncovered the ring. It was too big for Marta then, but she wrapped it with string for a snug fit. What a happy day that was, when they found the ring! Marta in a teasing mood kept playing tricks on him. Full of silly giggles, they walked home hand in hand.

And now. . . This was Marta? To believe it would make you want to cry. What could have happened? Where was the vivacious and charming little girl he had known?

Mrs. Williams's face was gray and haggard, with a bright spot of rouge on each cheek. She talked continuously, her voice droning on and on. Marta said nothing. Even when her mother seemed to be addressing her, there was no response, not so much as a little smile. The girl had a disturbing, unnatural quiet. Her movements were slow and deliberate, seeming to require the utmost concentration, as if she were dim-witted. She sat very still, eating slowly, mechanically. Though her eyes might occasionally rest upon her mother, their gaze was blank. Nor did she show the slightest interest in people around her. Beyond the thoughtful attention she gave her own simplest acts, her apathy was complete. The meal finished, she drained her tall glass of milk, tilting it high. Then she looked down into it and raised it again, licking the rim with the tip of her tongue. That done, she sat waiting, indifferent, remote.

Mrs. Williams's voice grew louder. She pawed through her old purse. Marta's absent air quickened not the slightest. Still rambling on, Mrs. Williams rose and fussed with her wraps, fastening close to her throat a ratty fur with dangling tails.

Marta got up slowly, heavily, and began buttoning her skimpy coat. Painstaking, like a child just learning, she fitted the buttons, each the size of a silver dollar, into their corresponding buttonholes. Having gone from top to bottom, she went back over them, using two fingers and pressing each button with a slight rocking motion.

Mrs. Williams accepted the brown paper bag just brought to their table, handed exact change to the cashier, and led the way out.

Marta followed, eyes straight ahead.

Stunned, Jay sat on, staring at the doorway that had swallowed them. Remembering the sprite she was, he wondered—would this zombie come to life greeting him? Her letter had seemed as natural as old time. What could have happened to her since they waved good-bye? He kept seeing Marta's face framed in the bull's-eye window and her little hand waving.

The thought of entering that house with those three women terrified him.

Three days later he sent a little note: "Dear Marta: So sorry I missed you when I dropped by. My time was shorter than I realized. But I'll be in touch with you. Love, Jay."

★ ★ ★

~

Chapter XV

His third summer in Washington, Jay scraped together sixty-eight dollars and bought an old jalopy he called "Nellie." It was a horror to look at, but it took him where he wanted to go, which was out into the nearby countryside. Old Mr. Shaw enjoyed going for a drive. So the two of them took Nellie up and down the river and out toward the mountains, bringing back peaches or apples bought at the orchards. On sultry summer evenings they might take a little drive to cool off.

During the next winter Mr. Shaw died. Jay missed the quiet game and pipe. He tried to cheer up the poll parrot. All the other roomers as well talked to the bird, now removed to the parlor bay window so that the old gentleman's room could be rented out.

For some time Jay had been thinking about a little place of his own. Something to busy him in his leisure hours. A home where his mother might come to live, should anything happen to Uncle Joe. With the blossoming of springtime he began cruising the streets of Arlington. Living in Virginia would be convenient to his office, and real estate was rather more reasonable out there. He had to find something cheap.

What he unexpectedly came upon was just about his style. For dilapidation it matched "Nellie." A traffic tie-up detoured him through a side street, and half way along there it was!

A weathered "For Sale" sign hung askew at the edge of the yard grown up in tall rank weeds. Beyond it, in a smother of foliage, loomed an old gray house. Jay pulled to the curb and sat staring at it. Obviously this had once been somebody's nice home. The building, left to ruin, was roomy, with double porches. Fine old oaks shaded the land.

What a pity the once handsome old house had been so sadly neglected. It stood wide open to the elements and vandals. Tattered, yellowed shades hung at broken windows. All the doors were ajar. Birds' nests clogged the rusted gutters. A fire had charred the rear wall above the kitchen. In the cellar around a rusty ancient furnace and an old-fashioned laundry tub with hand wringer attached, lay a waist-high pile of debris. Relics of vanished dwellers rose out of the chaos: an old wooden rocker, a low bookcase, some white cups and saucers on a rickety table, and music rolls from a player piano scattered over the earthen floor. On the wall shelves still held paint cans in orderly rows. How long since the laundry had been done here, or the paint cans were taken down for a little freshen-up job?

The "For Sale" sign carried a telephone number that put Jay in touch with the real estate agent. She told him the owners were wild to sell the place and would accept a rock-bottom price. To discuss it, he arranged to meet her there Sunday afternoon.

She was an overweight, over-eager gabby female. And not too bright, Jay thought. She began by telling him quite cheerfully, "It's called the haunted house."

"Why?" he asked, gazing up at the dumb facade.

She shrugged, perhaps afraid that she had said too much. "Oh, probably just the noises of wind and weather."

"Well, that's quite possible," Jay assented, "open like it is."

"Or maybe the former owners, wherever they may be, aren't happy with the indifference of their heirs," she added, trying to be clever.

"In that case," Jay said, "we might reasonably expect them to feel kindly toward anyone who cherishes it."

"I've heard there's a romantic story in its past," she rattled on.

"Romance only adds to its charm for me," he told her.

Then and there he mortgaged his future, wedded to restoring a dwelling in its decline. He knew that he had his work cut out for him, enough to last through years and years to come.

Restoration proceeded slowly, as Jay's time and funds permitted. Hardly had he been able to patch the worst scars so that the building was weather-tight, when Uncle Joe died. This meant that his mother would now come to live with him. Her letters had told how her brother's health failed before her very eyes. Heavy colds plagued him, and dizzy spells made him fearful. They thought something like that happened when he went out in the Clarabelle and failed to return. Otis Tarbutton found the empty boat and alongside, the old man's body snagged oddly in the anchor line.

Jay and his mother inherited the farm. They made sale of all but family belongings. And it seemed right that the Tarbutton boys were able to buy the land and stock, after they had pretty well managed the place since Uncle Joe got past working.

Though the house was anything but homey when she arrived, Mrs. Malone settled down with great pride in Jay's place. Never before had they enjoyed a home of their own, having always to rent or live in with others. She delighted in lending a hand toward beautification. She could hang wallpaper and paint woodwork. While Jay labored with hammer and nails, she kept the sewing machine humming. Her handiwork draped the windows and dressed the bedrooms. And under her green thumb, the yard blossomed with colorful flower borders. Favorite of hers were the Heavenly Blue Morning Glories that each year vined exuberantly over fancy wirework screening with beauty their porches, up and down. Looking for furniture, they frequented the busy auction houses downtown, afterwards disputing in amiable fashion just the right spot in the house for their latest finds. Once again Jay could enjoy companionship at home. He had hardly realized how much he missed his mother's good cooking. Together they settled into a comfortable quiet life.

When "Nellie" developed terminal disability of the rear end, Jay picked up a secondhand Chevy coupe which he painted light gray ornamented with red stripes across each door panel. He had a habit of referring to it as "the coffee pot." Now they could take trips up to Pennsylvania. Besides visiting with the few home-folks left, they liked to attend the farm sales.

A special drive up was called for when they learned that a sale would be held of effects from a family named Malone. (No kin that they knew of; way, way back maybe, but no recent connection.) The sale was already underway when they arrived and there was a goodly crowd. But they examined the glassware and dishes, prowled through the sets of old-timey furniture standing out in the yard. Then they joined the folks watching and waiting.

A bearded Amisher walked up. "Where's Catrine?" he asked. "She ain't out."

"She don't want to see her things sold," a voice answered.

Five fat old women sat in a row along the house wall, comfortably settled in the shade where they could keep track of and bid on items of the miscellaneous assortment piled on tables across the porch. Nearby stood odd little Miss Eby whose house full of old things Jay and his mother had visited. Thin, bent out of shape, dressed in an assortment of cheap, faded garments that were not too clean, wearing no stockings, her legs grimy and scratched, her strubbly "cheese and applebutter" hair escaping from under a small, shapeless hat, she paid strict attention to the selling.

Squatted in front of the five women and sitting on a basket was the penny man. He had big feet and big false teeth that he constantly gritted, and a good-natured idiotic grin. There was so much downright junk—saucepans you could see daylight through, jugs without handles, pitchers with snouts broken—that discards rained in upon him, rapidly filling his baskets. The auctioneer kept prodding him with penny purchases that nobody wanted. One box was already filled with trash, and he seemed puzzled over what he'd got, poking about in the clutter. A severe-faced old gentleman sitting nearby reached across and hooked the crooked handle of his cane over the edge of the box. The penny man grinned at him but kept a firm hold.

A simple-looking lad with dirty teeth laughed foolishly at every little bit of horseplay, his mouth glazed with spit.

The property was to be included in the sale. The auctioneer insisted that Mr. Malone built the house himself, and "it's built the way you like it— it has got wapor heat." In truth the building was crumbling, gingerbread trim in disarray and paint peeling. Its only charm was the sturdy trumpet vine in bloom that supported one corner of the porch.

The auctioneer held up a glass pitcher. "What am I offered for this nice little milk pitcher? It's got only one little bitty chip off the base, no crack up top. Who'll start the biddin' at one dollar? One dollar?" His glance roamed over the crowd. "Who'll gimme seventy-five cents? Seventy-five? Seventy-five? Fifty cents anybody? Twenty-five cents? Twenty-five?" He pulled from his hip pocket a blue bandanna and wiped his forehead. "Who'll have it fer nothin'?"

"I will," Mrs. Malone spoke up. In answer to Jay's quizzical smile, she defended herself, "Well, it's a Malone pitcher."

Jay bought for twenty cents a stack of linen napkins ironed and folded, commenting aside, "Hell, nobody ever wears out a napkin." But he made the mistake of unfolding one or two, and was chagrined to find them very much worn out. You could see his face through the holes in their centers. His mother teased, "Hell, nobody ever wears out a napkin." And people round about enjoyed the joke. Disgusted, Jay tossed the bundle into the penny man's basket.

Slowly the auctioneer inched his way toward an old shelf clock, grubby and abused, that Jay insisted spoke to him. Miss Eby took a notion to bid, but a dollar was her limit; so Jay got the piece for one-fifty.

Driving home they sympathized with poor Catrine, hiding so's not to see her things sold. "Poor woman," Mrs. Malone said, "outside her furniture, and even it was not all that great, she had a sorry lot of belongings."

Jay wondered that they hadn't thrown out the trash beforehand. "What do you suppose will happen to her now she's got nothing?"

After supper they took a look at their Malone family treasures. The quaint pitcher, on the dining table between them, was a jewel. Scrubbed of the cloudiness left by hard soap and over-used dishwater, the glass sparkled. Its pattern nearly equaled the intricacy of cut glass. Large clear ovals in relief were edged with beading of tiny glitter diamond points. In between were deep crosshatchings in small geometric designs. A scalloped band encircled the top, and on the handle a tiny sunburst provided the thumb-rest.

Mrs. Malone turned it about in her small pretty hands. "I'd be afraid to use it," she said. "Suppose it got broken. Besides being beautiful, it is eloquent of mysterious Malones."

"You wonder," Jay mused, "who bought it and what she looked like. Perhaps we should have talked with poor Catrine."

His mother still studied their find. "It should be just a shelf piece," she decided. "Set in place by a right-handed person—not left-handed like you—the chip would be hidden on the back side."

Jay grinned at her. "And where do you propose to show it off?"

"Oh," she replied airily, "I'll have to look around for the perfect spot."

And there was the clock. A humble timepiece, it was small and plain, with a pointed top, its face circled by large, black roman numerals, a rectangle of mirror hiding its pendulum. Its worn paint blistered and strips of veneer missing, it was a relic of hard times, likely over many years in some poor farm kitchen near the cook-stove, kept on a shelf with an oil lamp and a flyspecked calendar.

Opening the door on its front, Jay read aloud a printed sticker pasted inside: "8 day and 30 hour Gothic clock, one of the marine-lever timepieces for ships, steamboats, locomotives, and dwellings, made by Ansonia Brass & Copper Company, Ansonia, Conn." It was disappointing to find no date.

The clock's rusty striking was harsh and frantic—bang! bang! bang! But it didn't want to run. Jay made sure that it was wound, then nudged the brass pendulum. Several times, after two or three wags, it stopped.

"Needs a good dose of coal oil, I'll bet," he said. "From the looks, it never had any care. You know, it's kinda pathetic."

He went to collect his tools.

Meanwhile, Mrs. Malone dealt herself a hand of cards for a little game of solitaire.

Jay removed five small screws and lifted off a thin wood panel that completely closed the back. On the inside he found a notation written with pencil: "To Bill Malone for a Pig."

That gave them pause. Mrs. Malone sat holding in midair the card she had intended to lay down. They looked at each other. The story intrigued them. As Jay remarked, "Those few words raised questions thick as dandelions in springtime." Why had somebody felt it necessary to record the transaction inside the tightly screwed up case? Was there mistrust? What was the value? Where did this happen, and when? What were the people like? If only they could look back upon that little swap! In the past neither Jay nor his mother had given much thought to Malones beyond their immediate family. But these chattels, perhaps of their distant kin, casually happened upon, piqued their curiosity.

Jay said, "I told you it spoke to me."

★ ★ ★

Chapter XVI

For Jay the supreme event of a decade was the 75th Anniversary of the Battle of Gettysburg, which would be observed at the battle field with a final reunion of the Grand Army of the Republic and the United Confederate Veterans. Grampa Malone had been gone now some years, but here was one last chance to see and speak with surviving old soldiers, and to relive his boyhood hero worship, when he could still dream of military service.

He drove up to Gettysburg on Sunday, July 3rd, leaving home towards seven in the morning and arriving before nine. The air was cool after rain in the night, and at that early hour traffic was light.

On this day seventy-five years ago Pickett made his famous charge. The morning paper had recounted that tragic event. But Jay already knew the whole story. In his long preoccupation with military affairs he had thoroughly studied the Civil War. Poring over the pages of his wonderfully graphic history Blue and Gray, he learned the complete rosters of both armies and thrilled to the stirring descriptions of the various campaigns and battles. Pen portraits of the brilliant, dashing leaders, and reminiscences preserved, gave him a feeling of actual participation. His hero was Sheriden, "the war's most brilliant general," "the perfect warrior," reckless of his personal safety as he led his men... and "the earth trembled beneath the furious tread of his invincible legions of war steeds." He was brilliant, dashing, chevalious. Jay had dreamed of being such a man.

As he drove along, that day's action seventy-five years ago was vivid in his mind...

All morning both sides were busy making preparations. Then at 1 PM began their terrific artillery duel. The rows of 115 Confederate and 100 Federal cannon burst on the silence with hideous fire and roar. And for one and a half hours the air was filled with the continuous, deafening thunder of the big guns "hurling their bursting bolts of death." The earth shook. Fences, trees, rocks were blown to bits. A pall of smoke darkened the sky.

Into this fearful storm of leaden hail, half an hour after the bombardment began, charged the Confederate infantry, 15,000 strong. Eyewitnesses described Pickett's charge as like a dress parade; never was there a more gallant sight. In formation the column of assault pressed forward under heavy fire across the mile-wide open plain, into the bloody angle, their faces gaunt, their bayonets fixed. Shot and shell from the federal batteries tore great gaps in the advancing line. Each time, they closed ranks and moved on, unflinching. More than four thousand men in gray and nearly three thousand in blue fell within a few minutes.

But the desperate courage and appalling sacrifice was to no avail. Lee's brave men were repulsed. And of the magnificent column that had been launched so proudly, only a broken fragment returned. Pickett's charge was considered the climax of the engagement at Gettysburg, itself called "one of history's greatest battles."

A reenactment of the charge had been considered for this anniversary. But the plan was opposed on grounds that it might engender bitterness.

Probably today the countryside looked very much as it appeared before the three-day battle began. On the one hand stretched young green corn, knee high just as when the fighting trampled it into the ground. On the other, there was wheat in shocks. Lilies and hollyhocks were blooming. And tenting now on the old camp ground at the edge of the battle field were several thousand veterans—men mostly in their nineties, but some past the century mark. Today crowds of people from near and far would fulfill their country's "eternal honor upon its sons who gave their best, both victor and vanquished, in that war of brothers and neighbors."

Parking just two blocks from the encampment, Jay strolled along the boardwalks of the tent city. As he passed, old soldiers sitting in the shade of their tents greeted him with a smile and a salute. Some of the old fellows moved about in a daze, but many others were remarkably spry and alert for all their advanced years. Visitors shouted questions at them and they responded with ready answers. One aged officer quaveringly tooted his flute, to the enjoyment of a small crowd gathered. Another, hearing band music, executed a little jig with his stiff old legs. The courtesy and friendliness of the visitors was heartwarming. Everyone admired the veterans, and they responded with quaint little mannerisms in individual ways to the sincere homage.

The first veteran Jay met in the Union camp happened to be a visiting Confederate. He was a bent little old man in soiled and wrinkled gray, his coat sagging open, his pants legs rolled up, his shoes rusty. That uniform badly needed loving hands at home. Ninety years old, he had fought with the 36th Georgia Battalion. He said little, absently wandering around with his son in tow.

But in fine form was a veteran from Iowa who had been a sailor. His long gray hair curled up under the brim of this black hat with gold cord and GAR encircled by gold leaves. His white vest and the medals on his blue coat were dressy. He invited Jay to have a chair and rest a bit.

Though 92, he felt wonderfully well, except that he was rheumatic in the lower limbs. "So many of the comrades have rheumatism," he said. With suppressed eagerness Jay asked questions. The veteran sailor had served under Porter south on the Mississippi from Cairo to the Gulf as bosun's mate; that is, he was the petty officer on the gun deck who gave the orders.

He told Jay that his father and four brothers fought for the Union; his four uncles and their families fought for the Confederacy. "After the war," he said, "I made friends with the males, but the women never would see me. They felt their losses more than the men did. They never forgave Lincoln."

When Jay asked what he considered his most memorable experience, he answered, "I couldn't tell you." And gazing absently away, he repeated, "I couldn't tell you."

Next Jay stopped to visit with a fellow Pennsylvanian who was a telegrapher and received the word that Fort Sumter had been fired upon. What had impressed the young man was the wave of patriotism that spread over the north. He had been at Gettysburg, he said, "high private in the rear rank."

Oldest of all those Jay happened upon was another Pennsylvanian, 100 years and 9 months old, who had served in the 140th Pennsylvania Infantry under General Hancock. The poor old gentleman was peevish with fatigue. When his attendant sought to turn him around, he fussed, "Let me alone. Don't pull me about. Quit pushing me. I'm hunting the carpenter shop to get me some wooden legs." He had faced Pickett's charge. They marched all night and went into battle without any breakfast. But he was not wounded until the Wilderness.

As Jay was about to cross over to the Confederate camp, he met on the boardwalk two smiling veterans, one plump, the other lean, resplendent in fresh gray uniforms. Ninety-two and ninety-three, they had served with the 19th Tennessee cavalry. Jay marveled at their vigor. He said to them, "Your uniforms held up wonderfully well."

They chuckled. The senior comrade replied, "We just had 'em made three weeks ago."

And now, entertaining a crowd, here was an ebullient showman from the Southland who had served with the 16th South Carolina Regiment under Ben Goodley. He was 96, but acted younger than many men half his age.

"Do you feel 96?" He was asked.

"No. Only about 18," he replied. "I have a good time wherever I go. I'm full of anecdotes. A good laugh is better than medicine."

Below the brim of this black hat his white hair curled to shoulder length. He said, "I let the girls feel of my hair and beard. But the men? Never!"

A young woman lifted a curl to test him. He was telling one of his anecdotes. "A lady I let feel of my beard one day said, 'That don't feel like hair.' I said, 'It ain't hair.' 'Well, then,' she says, 'what is it?' I says, 'It's whiskers. And if you'll look close, there's two to a hill.' She says, 'Yes, there's two in each hole all right.'"

His audience laughed; so he went on. "I ain't married, but I've been lookin' around." He let his glance wander over the crowd before him. They waited, half smiling, for his next disclosure. He said, "In my time I've made peach and apple brandy and ten thousand gallons of liquor—enough to swim a horse from here to yonder."

"Did you drink it all?" piped up a bright-eyed youngster.

"No!" he thundered. "But," he added sweetly, "a little nip makes the ladies look so pretty."

After the war, when he came up for a pension, they asked whether he had ever been wounded. "No," he told them. "I never was mortally wounded. But I've been mortally scared."

"What do you remember best?" an admirer asked.

He grinned. "The running I did mostly."

Charmed by the old soldiers, his camera full of pictures, Jay was surprised that almost four hours had slipped by. Now that the tremendous crowds made quiet visiting impossible, it was time to leave. Though only one o'clock, the throng was estimated at 150,000, and all the roads were clogged with arriving cars.

But leaving was easy. And as he drove along, Jay reflected that he had heard no more talk of combat exploits from these old soldiers than he had from Grampa Malone. Nobody reminisced about the actual carnage. As one ninety-five year old Confederate veteran put it:

"The man who talks most about a battle was a long ways back. A man right in the fightin' don't have time to look here and there. He only loads and shoots."

★ ★ ★

Chapter XVII

Three days after Pearl Harbor, tragedy overwhelmed Jay.

Arriving home from the office he called his usual cheery, "Yoo, hoo!" as he closed the street door. But tonight there was no warm response. Puzzled, he looked about. Everything appeared ready to just warm the food and sit down to supper, except, where was his mother? This was so unlike her. She never failed to be there. It was her pleasure, she said, always to welcome him home.

About to glance over the house, he suddenly remembered that she had spoken of a trip to Alexandria with her sewing circle friends. This must be the day. But she had expected to be home in good time. No doubt she'd come soon. As he sat down to wait, the telephone rang. It was the hospital calling. Would he please come? Mrs. Malone had been in an auto accident.

Jay hardly knew what he was doing, speeding to the hospital, in a panic. It was even worse than he had feared. His mother was dead. Killed instantly in a freak accident. A truck out of control had collided with the car in which the five ladies were riding. Impact occurred just where Mrs. Malone was sitting, and she received a sharp blow to the head. None of her friends was seriously injured.

Grief-stricken, numb, Jay went about the necessary arrangements. He made sure that she wore her favorite rose silk dress with the brooch of pearls he had given her. When he found fault with the way her hair was done, the undertaker suggested that he might like to dress it himself. Combing a little more fullness about her face and coiling her long black tresses in a neat bun on the top of her head, as she always wore it, made her pretty face more lifelike.

And he must take her home to Pennsylvania; she would want to be laid away amongst family. But his return to the old home town was a painful experience. Nothing turned out as he had hoped. So few older Malones were left. And the younger generation, growing up, had responded to the lure of big city jobs. Even the kindly minister, whom Jay remembered fondly, despite his youthful distaste for attending church, had answered the call of a distant, larger congregation. The manner of his successor, Rev. Frost, was less warm, and a great disappointment to Jay. And he was a stranger. Besides, the weather turned wintry; between dark skies and sere earth, the still air was raw, with the hint of snow. The brave little cluster of kindly souls who had come to the cemetery stood bundled up, with their shoulders hunched against the chill. The faded flags hung limp and listless over the veterans' graves. Against the dismal scene Jay saw again the flower-scented sunny day when the crowd of friends and family stood waiting, and he proudly marched like a soldier.

Nature's gloom on this particular day hurt him. His thoughts about summed it up: cold sky, cold earth, and a preacher named Frost!

Back home, life hardly seemed worth living. He dreaded the long winter evenings, hating to turn his key in the lock. The big house was so empty and still. His loneliness enveloped him, there was a cloud over his days. Only his little Gothic clock had any life. Why was he such a born loser?

For a little company at mealtime, he got into the habit of eating his suppers at a small restaurant just three short blocks from home. The place occupied a charming old house once owned by wealthy people, so that the rooms were spacious with high ceilings, tall windows and working fireplaces. The chairs were comfortable, the tables not too crowded, and service was provided by attractive, sociable waitresses. During the dark days of winter Jay found some comfort there. He sat at the same table every night, and was waited upon by a pert young woman named Millie whom he liked to jolly.

One gloomy Saturday in March, feeling more than ordinarily depressed, he dropped by for lunch. Though it was still early, two other diners, a young couple, were already there, sitting just in front of him.

Three minutes before the hour serving was to begin, Millie entered the dining room. In her hand she held her stiffly starched little white apron, and as she listened to gossip from another waitress she tied it on. But not like the others did she catch it around her waist. Quite the contrary. Very particularly she placed the apron on front to back, and over her stomach she tied a great stiff bow in the wide strings. Her glance flitting from the face of her friend to the work of her hands, she measured the strings and formed a perfect big standing bow. That done, she twisted the apron around and smoothed its small circle down over her full skirt of gay flowered cotton. Jay got such a kick out of watching her.

Outside the sky was stormy. More rain threatened. Against a high wall great mounds of boxwood stood somberly dark. The young couple occupied a table beside one of the tall windows that admitted cold gray light, but their small table lamp gave their faces a lovely glow. An atmosphere of warmth and happiness surrounded them. They conversed in low tones, with eyes only for each other. He regarded her with adoring attention; she caressed him with smiling glances.

A banjo clock just visible in the hall chimed eleven. Millie edged away from her chatty friend, placed two glasses of water on a tray, and came to take the couple's order.

Though the menu indicated ham, there was no ham, because of rationing. Eggs there were, yes, and perhaps some bacon. The waffles were very good though they might want butter. The young pair, having had nothing to eat earlier, decided to combine breakfast and lunch. They agreed upon waffles with maple syrup, bacon (if any), scrambled eggs and coffee. Millie, waiting with pencil poised above her order pad, listened, then wrote down these items after verifying each one, and noting very particularly how the eggs must be scrambled not too firm. She had scarcely turned her back before the young people, sipping from their glasses of water, became once more absorbed in each other.

Coming for Jay's order, she gave them a smiling sideways glance with a little shrug. Millie was attractive and saucy at times. Jay enjoyed chitchat with her. She had told him that she was an only child, her father died years ago, and her mother clerked in a downtown department store. He liked her immensely. But he had seen her after hours hanging onto the arm of a husky, handsome guy in uniform.

Usually Jay lingered as long as he dared. Then when the room began to fill up, he settled his bill and closed the door on the animated crowd. Today, as he reached the wet sidewalk, he found himself looking into the wistful dark eyes of a handsome German Shepherd. The dog seemed to be lost.

"Hello," Jay said. "Where do you live?"

There was a slight wag of the tail in response.

Wondering how far he dared count on friendliness, Jay extended his hand. The dog touched it with the tip of his nose, remaining perfectly quiet.

"Will you let me read your tag?" Jay asked. Out the corner of his eye he could see the next intersection where five streets converged heavy traffic that could be murder for an animal. He had to get this fine fellow safely home.

"Yes," answered the tip of the tail, and its owner stood still while Jay twisted the collar around to read his ID. The address was somewhere up back of his place, he thought, though he couldn't be sure. "Come on," he said. "Show me where you live."

Obediently the dog turned and led him in the direction of home. The Malone house backed against a wooded hill down which dipped a rutted road, long unused, and it was up this way that the dog took him. "Hey! Wait for me!" Jay called as he fell behind, stumbling across the washouts filled with loose stones. The dog kept looking back, pausing while his rescuer caught up, then moving slowly on. Over the brow of the hill they came to a dirty white house where the street number hung upside on on the door frame. As they approached, there emerged a big beefy man with close crew cut and a dangling toothpick between his teeth. He looked at them without speaking.

At sight of him the dog stopped in his tracks.

Jay said, "I've persuaded your pet to come home. I was afraid he'd be killed in traffic."

"You want a dog?" the man asked abruptly. "You can have him. He ain't liked stayin' around since my daughter left. And I'm too busy to go huntin' fer 'im."

Jay looked down into wistful dark eyes looking up.

"He's a good dog, I guess," the man continued. "Anyways, my daughter paid a-plenty fer 'im. Don't ask me why. He's a dumb damn mutt. But now she's went to New York fer a job where she's got no room fer 'im. And he ain't been the same since she left. I was thinkin' mebbe I'd take him out in the country some'eres and dump him alongside the road. I ain't got the time to be no dog nurse."

Red hot anger flashed through Jay. But he said quietly, "I'll be glad to have him. Thanks."

"Wait," the man said, "and I'll get you his things." He went back inside, slamming the door. Jay stroked the dog's head, smiling down at him. And the tip of the tail responded.

When the man returned with a brown bag and a stout leash, Jay went forward to accept them. The dog did not move.

"He's got papers some'eres," the man said, "But I've no idee what my daughter done with 'em."

"Oh, I don't need them," Jay replied as he and his new found friend turned away. He hooked on the leash because he had decided, rather than negotiate the abandoned road, to go around the block. But the dog needed no control. He went along willingly.

Unlocking his door, Jay said, "Come in." And his guest politely entered.

Two bowls; pulled from the brown bag were filthy. Jay quickly washed and scalded them, filling one with fresh water. The dog lapped thirstily. He probably was hungry too. A little bite would stay him till his regular supper time. Jay offered some canned food from an unopened tin among his friend's "things." Three gulps and it vanished.

Having a pipe in his easy chair by the dining room bay window, Jay pondered this unexpected turn of events. The dog at first sat close by, studying his face. But invited to do so, he hopped up and lay on the cushioned window-seat. Jay wondered how anyone, even the stupidest, could give up such a handsome animal. His coat was so lustrous, his expression so intelligent. You got the impression that he understood every spoken word.

The dog must have a name but Jay hadn't thought to ask about it. He'd have changed it anyway. Breeders usually favor such ridiculous monikers.

"Well, now he's a Malone," Jay thought, "and probably the only family I'll ever have. Maybe I should christen him J. J. IV. Jack for short." The dog was watching him. "Jack?" he said, "Do you like that?"

"Yes," answered the responsive tail.

His ID should be changed. Jay went to find the pliers, and Jack followed along. Then they got busy putting together a suitable bunk bed in a snug corner of the bedroom. When supper time came, rather than slip down to the restaurant where Jack would not be welcome, Jay cooked a meal for himself and concocted for his companion something tastier than the usual dog food.

They spent a blissful evening, just the two of them. Rain poured outside, but indoors they enjoyed cozy companionship. Jay could hardly believe his rare good fortune. It occurred to him that he had given the man no information about himself. For that he was glad. Fickle daughter might change her mind about her job, might have other ideas about her pet. And from here on, nothing could persuade him to part with his treasure.

★ ★ ★

Chapter XVIII

So began their devoted comradeship. From the beginning, neither wanted the other out of his sight. When their first weekend passed all too quickly, Jay took a short leave. Contentedly puttering about, catching up on chores he'd not had the heart for, he talked to Jack, always close by. And they took long walks together beside the quiet branch in the woods of the nearby park. This mini-vacation brought Jay comfort he had not known lately.

But a man must earn a living. Inevitably, Monday morning came again, and with it, parting. Jay took the big dog's head between his hands and told him, "You look after things till I get back," then forced himself to close the street door. At the turn of this key that evening, Jack was ecstatic. He tried his best to talk.

Theirs was a joyful springtime. While Jay worked at this gardening or sprucing up their dwelling, Jack lay on the lawn observing the activity in their street. He made friends with the passersby: grown-ups walking down from the bus stop, youngsters going to or from school. The dog loved people.

And the kids, especially, thought he was wonderful. Jack knew what time to expect them and he usually stood at the front gate watching. If they stopped in, he willingly romped with them, chasing a ball, or retrieving any stick they threw. He was one of them. When a little girl in pink sweater and hair ribbons stooped to smell a pretty posy, Jack trotted over to have a sniff too. They could do anything with him. Once Jay happened to glance out the window in time to see a very small boy slap Jack in the face, then stamp on his toes. The dog only yawned.

Jack's earliest conquest was a black-headed, robust lad called Butch. He came down the street gnawing on an apple and paused to peer into the gutter, twisting his neck to read a sheet of water-soaked funnies plastered down with the sodden brown leaves. Glancing up, he became aware that he was being watched. There stood Jack inside the gate left ajar. A moment of wariness, then the boy ventured a "Hi!" And Jack responded sociably. Jay, up painting a porch post, called, "Don't be afraid. He won't hurt you." Butch crossed the sidewalk. "He loves company," Jay added, stepping down the ladder. "He'd be delighted to have you come, if you can spare the time."

The charmer in pink sweater and hair ribbon was Butch's baby sister, with the lovely name Aurora. Her mother and she walked over one Sunday to meet this fascinating character named Jack. Jay coming around the house was surprised to find them standing on the shade-dappled front walk. "Your garden is perfectly beautiful," she said.

Jay smiled, with a little nod and glance around.

She was a young, attractive, lightly-freckled redhead, wearing glasses, and her dress was of some soft material in pale frosted green. "I'm Catherine Warren, Butch's mother."

Jay knew that she was a war widow, and his sympathies embraced her. Butch had said, "My Dad died in the war." And Jay answered, "So did mine, nearly twenty-five years ago." With a wave of his hand he indicated his rustic bench. "I'm very pleased to meet you. Won't you have a seat?"

"I'm afraid we can't stay but a moment," she said. "Working mothers have many weekend home duties impossible to shirk. But I wanted to meet your wonderful dog—he has a five-star reputation—and to make sure that Butch doesn't annoy you. He's a great admirer of yours."

Jay shook his head. "No, indeed. Believe me, I'm having a ball."

She reached out to Jack and he offered his paw. She laughed. "Now who could resist such a greeting?"

Aurora had let go of her mother's fingers and toddled over to the nearest flower bed. Jack cocked an eye in her direction, then followed, to share in the perfume of a pretty blossom. "Don't pick, Hon," Mrs. Warren called.

Jay said, "Oh, let's give her a little bouquet. And you, since you haven't time to visit, must accept some roses to enjoy at home." For Aurora he cut three dainty single roses, each no larger than a twenty-five cent piece, pearly pink and richly fragrant, and carefully peeled off their thorns. "My mother was the gardener. She had a remarkable green thumb. But one of her whims I never could understand. Somebody gave her an unusual white rose, a gorgeous creation, beautiful to look at, but it had no more perfume than a tallow candle." For Mrs. Warren he was clipping long-stemmed perfect buds, rich red with heavenly fragrance.

Jack's circle of acquaintances among the younger set had grown. Butch introduced his buddies, Bill and Phil, the twins, and from time to time brought other friends. The kids all lived in tight little homes with hardly any yards to speak of, so that Jay's woods hollow offered the perfect gathering place. They whooped through episodes of cowboys and Indians, staged elaborate battles.

After a while there was Hallie, a lonesome little hanger-on. Tow-headed and tacky, she reminded Jay of the youngest Willey he had tormented so unmercifully. (What a stinker he was to tease her so, poor kid.) He was kinder to Hallie. So pathetically homely, a skinny child with lank hair, pale eyes and crooked teeth, she was still too young to realize the curse of her ugliness. She was an eager tomboy, but the fellows, noisily engaged in their private games, tolerated her only after Jay described the war exploits of brave Molly Pitcher.

It seemed that even then they tolerated her only because they could impose on her their dirty work. But Hallie was idiotically happy.

One of her playthings was a short length of sashcord which she liked to twirl for Jack to jump at. If he caught the rope between his teeth, they had a tug-of-war. He growled fiercely, she chuckled and shouted with laughter. Hallie adored the dog. And it made no difference to him that she was ugly as a mud fence. When next Valentine's Day rolled around, she left in the mailbox an "original" Valentine addressed to Jack Malone.

The coupe replaced by a sedan, several times during the summer Jay took a car full to the amusement park. Catherine Warren with Aurora shared the front seat. And though it was a bit snug for three kids and a dog in the back, they happily managed. Everybody, including Jack, had a barrel of fun riding the merry-go-round.

That was a year of pure happiness for Jay. He and Jack were inseparable. And they gathered around themselves quite a nice little family of other people's lively youngsters.

In October, Jay accepted an invitation to Tarbutton's big family reunion. It was good to see the boys again, and Mrs. Tarbutton's flushed face beamed on him as fondly as on one of her own numerous brood. The food was delicious, the friendliness and gaiety heartwarming. And Jay's snapshots of nearly everybody would fill a nice fat album.

While there, he meant to revisit the old haunts. Driving out to Uncle Joe's place his recollections unfolded like scenes in a motion picture. That familiar road—the many miles he'd traveled over it would likely have taken him half way around the world, and back. Five miles a day, twenty-five a week, and hundred a month just to and from school, not to mention numerous trips—walking, riding, driving—on other necessary business. Just imagine! And how much had happened since that first night when they rolled along in the hearse through the stretch of black-dark woods where foxfire glowed weirdly!

His mother had been petrified coming home late with their neighbor-lady. They were in the buggy behind her poky old horse. Midway through the stygian tunnel in close-pressing trees, where you could hardly see your hand before your face. Mrs. Davis said, joking, "Did I ever tell you about the bride who was murdered on the lonely road?" Mrs. Malone said, "Shut up!" What a relief when they finally turned out under open sky. They laughed about it afterward.

Just here he slid down Dewey's roached mane when the big Collie suddenly stepped out of the woods. And now the roof was collapsed on the ruined log house. How he had worried over Santa's plight in case the old fellow had gotten stuck down the chimney! Arriving once more at the lane gate, Jay could see again his beloved Josh, so eager to escort them up to the tall, mustard-color farmhouse, dark and silent in the embrace of giant trees.

In town, too, Jay had a mind to relive the past. Nosing in among the parked cars at the old hitching rack, he and Jack walked along the quiet street between the Episcopal Church and the jailhouse where the littlest Willey had permanently disabled him. They arrived at the school just as a bell sounded for the end of recess. From noisy revelry the square suddenly became silent. Time had brought changes. The big privies out back were gone; indoor plumbing had put an end to time-honored customs. In Jay's time the kids of the primary school considered it "the thing" to burst out of doors and race down the path to the privies, yelling, "Save a hole for me!"

On the harbor, a man working over his boat mentioned that the Ferry family had sold their big farm, and the fine old mansion was now an inn. Aha!" Jay thought. "That's where I'll spend the night." Imagine! Him sleeping in one of those elegant rooms! Him, a poor country boy never in the same class with the moneyed Ferrys. Their boys were older, of course, but he had envied their gay yachting crowd. The nearest he ever got to any Ferry was casual friendship with the hired man's kids.

Back at the parking he had just slipped behind the wheel when a sleek blue sedan pulled up alongside. Out of it stepped a plumpish, pretty, well-dressed woman. And he recognized Louise! As she faced Jay, her eyes betrayed recognition, but there was no change in her expression. Slamming the door, she walked away.

With a shrug, but touched by poignant memory, he backed out and drove over to the Ferry Farm. With secret excitement he climbed the front steps and eagerly entered the wide hallway. Everything—the floors, the furniture—was so beautifully polished, such elegant rugs lay before him, and against one wall a handsome grandfather clock ticked solemnly.

To the pale young man behind the desk, Jay offered his apologies for the lack of a reservation, explaining that he only just learned of the inn a half hour ago. Fortunately they had a room. But before he could sign in, the clerk caught sight of Jack waiting in the car. "You have a dog? I'm sorry. Dogs are not allowed."

Jay had practiced guile before. "He's my seeing-eye dog for night blindness." he explained. "If my one good eye fails me, as it sometimes does, I must rely on him. He's widely traveled. I assure you he has elegant manners and won't cause the least problem."

"Well." the clerk was doubtful. "But understand, dogs are not permitted in the dining room."

"Of course. Only on his personal blanket in my room."

Jay dressed for dinner. He found the dining room most attractive and the food delicious. If only his mother could have shared it with him. What a treat for her! It would have been nice to invite Louise...

In the evening he and Jack walked down to sit on the pier while he smoked his pipe and watched the big full moon rise over the river. It reminded him of his careful planning and happy anticipation of escorting Louise to the dance by moonlight on Price's pavilion. And then wouldn't you know, he had to slide down their steep stairs on his boil. Bad luck was his lot in life.

Except when he found dear old Jack.

Now he realized that it was well Louise had taken their future into her own hands. They were not meant for each other, as he then fondly imagined. He would have had trouble with her. Still, the dream was sweet while it lasted.

All night long quiet enfolded the house. Sleep was dreamy. And he awakened to a cool morning perfectly still. The mirror surface of the river reflected a wooded point opposite with its old gray house and short pier. Two ducks paddled about. Soon the rose-gold ball of the sun lifted above the far horizon and shot a sparkling path toward Jay's feet. No one else was up to enjoy this lovely scene. And Jay wondered how often the Ferrys had paused to appreciate it. So many of life's pleasures crowded their days, had they ever taken the time to drink in this beauty at their very door?

His enjoyable trip roundabout brought Jay and Jack home again. The accumulation of mail, which Butch had daily emptied from the box out front and hidden in a wood chest on the back porch, was mostly junk.

Lighting his pipe, Jay leaned back, reliving his adventures. It had been an experience, his night at the Ferry Inn. But, even now that he could afford to pay for the hospitality, he was out of his class. Acceptance by such people no longer mattered to him. He was quite content with the ordinary homines about him. Such polish as made you hesitate to touch things, to walk across the floor even, required the vigilance of many servants or hours of personal elbow-grease, neither of which he was prepared to provide. Jay was a neat housekeeper, but not persnickety. His furniture wore the patina of grime from long, hard usage, which he had hardly noticed before. So, why disturb it? As good-natured Charley Tarbutton used to say when his overburdened wife lagged behind with her housework, "Be it ever so dirty, there's no place like home."

Their personal easy corner where he and Jack spent their leisure hours suited him perfectly. His comfortable brown wing chair, with a carpet-covered hassock, faced the padded window-seat where his pal relaxed. Beyond the triple windows a flourishing, richly green Magnolia refreshed the gaze, and in season offered gorgeous blooms. At his right elbow stood an end-table with double drawers, drop leaves and handsomely carved legs, a treasure in walnut picked up for a song at a farm sale. On it he kept his student lamp, electrified from oil, and framed photographs of all his family, not forgetting Josh and Jack. Inside its drawers he stored tobacco, extra eyeglasses, and a package of Jack's favorite sugar biscuits. On his left was a quaint trunk, vintage of Grampa Malone's youth, where among other things he treasured, Jay kept the old gentleman's big American flag and his service pistol. Above, on a wide shelf supported by ornate brackets, he kept his collection of books and the little country Gothic clock, object of barter by some unknown Malone long departed. Its busy tick-tock had the vigor of youth alongside the measured, dignified TICK-TOCK of the Ferry grandfather; and its hoarse, tinny striking sounded not unlike someone beating on a tin pan with a spoon, raucous compared with the mellow chimes of the stately aristocrat. In his cozy nook Jay was quite content. It felt good to be home.

In the early evening Jay rang Catherine Warren to let her and Butch know that he had returned. Their landlady's news chilled him. "Oh, Mr. Malone, I was waiting for your call. Mrs. Warren and the children had to leave for Iowa on a moment's notice because of a death in her family. An auto accident killed her father and left her mother hurt badly. Poor dear, she was so upset. An uncle of hers came in his car to take them and their things. She seemed to think it ain't likely she'll get back here. I have her address, if you want it. She said you'll be hearing from her. And Butch wanted me to tell you that he had arranged with the twins to care for your mail."

Jay was stunned. He could hardly speak. "How sorry I am to hear this," he managed to say. "Yes, I would like her address, thank you." He hung up and sat staring straight away. Jack watched him anxiously.

This was tragic! Having to give up her job where she was succeeding—she'd just recently had a raise. And to take Butch out of the school where he was doing so well... True, she had only a War Service appointment, just for the duration; yet the experience was good, and would undoubtedly prepare her for something better. In Iowa what had she to look forward to? Drudgery behind the counter of a country store left by her father, and the difficult care of her invalid mother.

As time passed during their brief acquaintance, Jay had observed her gradual recovery from the depression of early widowhood. Hers was a serene personality. A rare sunny smile and spoken responses that were soft, distinct and well-worded gave little hint of inner turmoil. Yet she must have suffered from doubts about raising her two fine children alone. Butch was an upstanding young lad and Aurora such a little doll. Why should the lot of this fine family be stagnation in some hick town miles from nowhere? Jay's anger flared. Yet he was powerless to change the course of events. She was gone. Her loss, and his, left him despairing. There was only Jack to console him.

Winter's blight kept them pretty much to themselves. The twins might drop by for help with their math homework or to join in a short stroll through the park. Hallie's only return was her gaudy Valentine addressed to dear Jack. Letters from Iowa were all too brief and infrequent. Catherine had her hands full. And Jay, living his monotonous routine, found little to write that might interest her.

Time passed uneventfully.

★ ★ ★

Chapter XIX

But there was a war on. And news items told of the great need for dogs in the service. Jay regularly did his bit contributing to the War Bond drives at his office, as well as diligently helping with the collection of scrap metal and rubber for the war effort. But more was needed. And as he read of the call for dogs, a horrible suspicion blighted his happiness.

Yet—No, he couldn't do it—send his spirited, intelligent, loving pal into the battlefield—he simply could not do it.

Not until he got a telephone call from one of Jack's sidewalk acquaintances who identified himself as John Hendry and asked if he might drop around for a moment. He was a clean-cut young man with a soft voice and gentle manner. Jack greeted him enthusiastically. Jay's heart sank. He knew what was coming. Their visitor was obviously uncomfortable, and Jay blessed him for that. He spoke of the desperate need for dogs. Those already in service had saved many lives. It was a matter of record that in the fifteen months since the war began, no patrols led by dogs had been fired on first or suffered casualties.

Jack would be trained as a messenger dog, with Hendry as one of his handlers. And when the war was over, he would receive an honorable discharge and be returned to Jay.

"Just think it over," Hendry said softly. "Here's my phone number."

Into the evening, while Jack dozed on the window seat, Jay agonized over his heartbreaking dilemma. How much easier to go himself. But he was no good. His best was pushing the War Bond drives. And there was no telling how many fine young men might live to come home if Jack was there. Then, when the war was over, the two of them would live happily ever after. He liked Hendry, and if it had to be, he could hardly ask for a kinder person.

Though he felt that it was sinful to postpone his decision, he knew that he must have a few more days with Jack before they were parted. A week's leave from the office gave him twenty-four hours a day to lavish on the dog all his loving attention, and to savor each moment, fixing it in his mind to sustain him later.

When he had verified Hendry's credentials, Jay thought he was ready. Twice he picked up the phone, twice he put it down. Finally he took himself in hand. It was arranged that Hendry should come for Jack on Monday morning, after Jay had left for the office. To personally hand him over would be torture he could not bear. And he needed the whole day, his mind occupied with urgent matters, before he could face his loss. But his thoughts kept shirking business, to imagine the sequence of events at home.

That Monday night was pure Hell. Pulling into his driveway he was overwhelmed by the big dark house. He couldn't go in. Delaying that awful moment, he walked over to the restaurant for his supper. A sour-faced biddy waited on him.

"Where's Millie?" he asked.

"Gone," was the laconic reply. "Quit to get married."

No pleasant chit-chat there to cheer him. Pretending to eat, he kept remembering the day he left the place and found Jack waiting outside.

Going home he dragged his feet. Reluctantly he unlocked his door and stepped inside the silent, empty house. There was no joyful welcome, nobody to care whether he came. The misery of it brought tears. Switching on his student lamp, he sank into his easy chair. Jack's presence was everywhere.

Doubts assailed Jay. Had he done the right thing? A little glimmer of hope crept in: perhaps Jack would fail his training. Then he could welcome him home in good conscience. Yet he knew the thought was unworthy. Jack was too intelligent to fail, and his nobility and courage would carry him through. Jay reminded himself that he had wanted to be a soldier. Now Jack, the better of the two of them, was fulfilling his dream. He should feel proud. But he was heartbroken. Wherever he looked, the vision of his wonderful pal haunted him. A dusting of sugar biscuit crumbs on the window seat choked him. Jack had such a sweet tooth. Only whisper "sugar biscuits," and he was all attention.

At last, emotionally drained, Jay went to bed… and had nightmares.

When the twins inquired for their canine friend, Jay struggled to keep his voice steady as he told them huskily that Jack had gone to be a soldier. "He'll be a messenger boy," he explained, "and carry letters for the men. Who knows, he may get a medal for bravery."

"Oh! How exciting!" they exclaimed in unison.

Jack's training lasted three months. Of course he passed. Brilliantly. There came a note from Hendry—they were so very proud of him.

Jay felt proud too. But his loneliness almost drove him to drink. Still, in public he put on his best face. Life must go on. The war couldn't last forever. Indeed, a Brookings authority had predicted that it would be short. Japan, the authority said, did not have the resources for a long war, so would make a desperate effort for a quick victory. Jay prayed that he was right. Whimsically he cut from the back of Hallie's Valentine a blue service star to hang in his window like those in the homes where men were overseas. It proclaimed his sacrifice, reminding him each evening when he came home to emptiness that he had one day less to wait for the war's end. He lived for that day.

In the market on Saturday, a dried-up old man ahead of Jay in line at the butcher's stall ordered half a pound of good liver. While it was being wrapped, he carefully detached precious stamps from his ration book and found in his pocket a moldy greenback.

The butcher, handing over his package, said pleasantly, "Eatin' this, you'll sure get your vitamines."

The old man shook his head. "Not me. This here's fer my cat." His face lit up. "I've got the liveliest little black beast you ever saw. She jest claws the bag to pieces when I fetch her the liver. I give it to her fer a special treat. When she's got her belly full, she curls up to sleep in my lap. She's comp'ny fer me. After I buried my wife I nearly went batty with jest four walls. I figger it's better to be meat hungry than love hungry."

And Jay, returning to his four walls, thought, "It's Hell to be love hungry."

All his hopes and prayers centered on a cease fire. Soon. SOON. He thought of little else. Jack's bed was ready with his neatly folded blanket, his food dishes remained as he had left them, the window seat nightly held Jay's vision of him.

The newspapers reported how the war was being waged with increasing ferocity overseas, and how "the exceptionally brave who lived to return were acclaimed as heroes by a nation eager to do homage to its gallant sons." But some "paid the price which glory ever exacts." And gold stars symbolizing a life lost in battle replaced the blue service stars in the windows. Coming from the store one evening, Jay passed such a house. Two elderly ladies stood conversing at the end of the walk. He caught a fragment of their conversation. "Yes," said one, "he gave his all. I say a man can't be any braver."

Hendry kept his promise to write, but not often, and always briefly. Yet his hasty jottings were reassuring—Jack and his handlers had so far safely fulfilled their missions. The dog had taken his war service in stride, Hendry wrote. He was unfazed by battle noises. Not once had he failed to accomplish his missions. And the work of the messenger dogs was desperately needed, since the walkie-talkies so often failed in foul weather. Jack and the men lived together, slept together, and if needed shared a bath in some handy stream. At one point Hendry wrote that Jack had made seven emergency messenger runs under fire when the regular lines of communication were out.

Through the pages of his atlas Jay kept track of their journeys further and further away from him, away on the other side of the world. Port Moresby, Nazdab, Kaiapit, Finshafen and other God-forsaken hellholes—places he had never even heard of before.

While a year and a half passed, and Jay suffered, Jack and his handlers accomplished wonders.

★ ★ ★

Chapter XX

In September 1944, Jay slipped from a ladder and sprained his back. Housebound for several days, he could do nothing but brood. To divert his thoughts, he went out to sit on the porch. From his old wicker rocking chair behind the screen of Heavenly Blue Morning Glories, he could observe people in the street going about their affairs.

At the moment nobody happened to be passing. Idly he watched construction progressing on the unwanted high-rise down the way. A monstrous hole had replaced the peaceful green woods, ruthlessly destroyed, where he and Jack used to take walks along the little stream. A sky-high yellow crane swung its long cable forth and back placing iron pieces beside beckoning workmen. Toilers in the deep excavation looked like ants.

A young woman, dressed in dark green from her hat down to her spike heels, clattered down the block. Small, with black hair, she recalled for Jay the girl he had met in Allies. Eons ago that seemed.

He watched two men move along the opposite sidewalk in single file, two steps apart. Other than the shabbiness of their clothing, they were exact opposites: the one ahead was big and burly, the one behind spare and stooped. The big fellow was full of life, loud-talking, gesticulating. His companion said nothing, shuffling along taking short steps, his chin tucked in, his eyes under the bill of his little gray cap bent on the ground. Suddenly he was brought up short by his gabby friend turning about and shouting, "Gimme sixty cents!" Obediently the old gent withdrew one hand from his coat and plunged it deep into his pants pocket. Talking, talking, the big man picked change from his friend's outstretched palm. Then single file they proceeded on their way and soon disappeared.

Sight of them left Jay depressed, thinking as he watched the old codger tagging along behind, "There but for a few years go I." Growing feeble and witless, he could count on probably none other than Jack's blind devotion.

Towards five o'clock—delivery was late that day—the postman appeared, stuffing mailboxes along the sidewalk. Not expecting much, but hoping for one of Hendry's terse reports, Jay strolled down and opened his box. Inside lay a single letter. It came from ARMY SERVICE FORCES, Office of the Quartermaster General. Sudden fear paralyzed him. A live bomb would have terrified him no more than that innocent-looking white envelope. But then he reminded himself, it could be good news. Jack was coming home!

Up the walk briskly he regained the privacy of his porch. With trembling hands he slit the envelope and drew out a letter two pages long:

"Dear Mr. Malone:

"It is with regret that I write to inform you of the death of JACK, the German Shepherd dog so generously donated by you for service with the armed forces."

Jay collapsed. His tears blurred the page. Furiously he crushed the cursed letter in his hands. Hope was lost; despair overwhelmed him. His wonderful Jack was gone forever.

Abruptly, fearful that his agony might be observed by some nosy neighbor, he got up and went indoors. Dropping into his easy chair, he sat staring straight away, his absent gaze fixed on the only bright spot in the room: a splash of sunshine lay on the dark carpet where shadows shifted as a breeze stirred the hemlock branches. Outside the bay window a gathering of little sparrows chirped excitedly, and nearby his Gothic clock ticked. He was unaware. Trying to collect his thoughts, he felt only his awful misery. He closed his eyes; yet he could not shut out the image of Jack there by his side.

The cursed letter waited. At last, switching on his reading lamp, he smoothed the crumpled pages across his knee and read on:

"Jack died in the Southwest Pacific Theatre after a career of outstanding achievement. He was a member of the first War Dog Tactical Unit operating in that theatre. The Unit was assembled at the War Dog Reception and Training Center, Beltsville, Md., in March 1943. It arrived at Port Moresby in July and went to a staging area for training and conditioning after several weeks aboard ship. In the latter part of August, the unit was first assigned to a Battalion of an Australian Division then operating near Nazdab, New Guinea.

"Traveling by plane, the Unit flew to Kaiapit, an airstrip near the front lines where a brigade was making ready for the advance up the Ramu Valley in the action to drive the Japanese back to Medang. As the brigade moved up the valley, the scout dogs worked with the reconnaissance patrols while the Command Post kept contact with the near elements by messenger dog. During this advance, the dogs worked out satisfactorily.

"In October, the War Dog Unit was reassigned to a Marine Raider Regiment of the Sixth Army. Again traveling by plane, the dogs and their handlers went to another staging area. In December, the Raiders moved to Finschafen to take part in the Cape Gloucester operations. The entire Dog Detachment went ashore with the first wave and figured prominently in the operation.

"Until March, the dogs were used continuously for patrol and messenger work. Lines were gradually extended to make contact with the Army Forces near Gilnit. In these weeks, there was not a single instance in which any of the dogs failed to accomplish a mission, nor was there an instance when a patrol led by a War Dog was fired upon first or suffered casualties; in contrast, dogless patrols suffered casualties, usually as a result of ambush or surprise attacks.

"During this period, the patrols led by dogs were officially credited with 180 Japanese casualties and 20 prisoners. Messenger dogs were especially useful, since the use of walkie-talkies was often impractical, due to terrific downpours and other unfavorable weather conditions.

"Jack, trained as a messenger dog, was unafraid of battle noises from the first. Throughout the period of the Cape Gloucester campaign, he distinguished himself on many occasions. His two handlers, Technicians 4th Grade William A. Matthews and John C. Hendry, reported enthusiastically on his consistently fine performance. His outstanding act of heroism was carried out during the advance on the airstrip. Near Turzi Point, the advance units were held up by Japanese pillboxes and fortifications and the aid of artillery could not be sought by the walkie-talkies, which were temporarily out of commission. A message was dispatched by Matthews back to Battalion Command Post through JACK. Although the dog had not seen Hendry since the night before, and although Hendry had changed his position and was then in a new location, JACK unerringly found his way to Hendry's foxhole. JACK had to travel through the tall Kunai grass, swim a river, and for part of the distance make his way beneath a curtain of mortar and tank fire; he finally had to jump a barbed wire fence that protected Hendry. As a result of this message, artillery fire was directed on the Japanese defenses, pulverizing them and permitting the American forward units to resume their advance."

An agony of grief convulsed Jay. As he read "curtain of mortar and tank fire," horror seared him. All shot to pieces, that's what! Goddam! Bitterly he reproached himself for deserting poor Jack. Yet even in his torment he knew that he was duty-bound. Cruelly duty-bound.

An hour of despair passed before he could bring himself to finish reading the cursed letter:

"This office has been working on a plan for the official recognition of outstanding heroism on the part of War Dogs. It is our pleasure to inform you that a citation will shortly be sent to you, awarded posthumously to JACK.

"I hope that the knowledge of JACK's remarkable record will compensate in a measure to you for his loss, and I trust that you will feel that your patriotic sacrifice has not been in vain; for there are many American boys today who owe their lives directly to the heroism of JACK, the War Dog, and indirectly to you who gave him up to serve your country."

Tears stung Jay's eyes. Try as he might, he could not console himself with pride in Jack's heroism and the many lives saved. He could only suffer. Slumped in his chair, his face stony, his thoughts filled with visions—Jack, his beloved companion, so adoring and faithful, there now in spirit only. Jack, the brave soldier, who fulfilled with unswerving devotion to duty his perilous missions through hell on earth. Over and over and over again.

Rainy dusk settled deep gloom through the house—so like their first evening together. And he could think of nothing but his tragic loss. Everything else was forgotten—dinner time, the liniment rub for his ailing back. A newspaper thudding against the front door was ignored.

As the evening wore on, the silence of his big empty house, broken only by the tick-tock of his little clock, grew ever more keenly intolerable. Memories tortured him. He closed his eyes, the pictures remained. With Jack's death died his dream of their happy reunion that had sustained him. Now he had nothing to live for. Looking ahead, he shrank from the prospect of his bleak future, the years of loneliness to come. He felt drained of strength, weak of will for the struggle. And he wondered, "Why bother?"

When the clock struck ten, he bestirred himself and laid aside the letter. In the kitchen he looked upon food with distaste. But brewing a cup of coffee, he nibbled a crust of bread and some sharp cheese. Then he swallowed a sleeping pill and fell into bed.

Next morning he rose at his usual time. Darkly overcast sky promised continued falling weather. Resolutely avoiding a glance in the direction of Jack's neat bed over in the corner, he went to the kitchen and fixed his usual breakfast of scrambled eggs, toast with marmalade, and coffee. When he had finished his usual tidying up, he showered and shaved, and dressed for the office, wearing his showiest tie and a neatly folded handkerchief peeping from his breast pocket.

Then he phoned his lawyer, Will Dawson, the roommate of his University days who had remained his good friend ever since.

"Hi, Will. How's things?"

"First rate, Jay. What's up?"

"Why, I need you to handle a little matter for me. I'm out of the office for a few days. I sprained my back. But it's about well. I wonder if you can drop by on your way home this evening?

"Sorry. Not tonight, Jay. I'm staying downtown for a meeting. But I'll be coming out around lunch time and can stop then. Say about eleven-thirty? Will that do just as well?"

"Even better. My doorbell is temporarily out of order. And since I may not hear you knock, come around the house to the bay window. It will be open and I'll be sitting just inside."

Remembering yesterday's newspaper, he tossed it into the trash. Then he disconnected the doorbell. A quick look around assured him that the house was nicely in order.

In the drawer of his little end-table he found his pen and writing paper. A glimpse of Jack's box of sugar biscuits gave him a pang. "Being of sound mind," he wrote, with a sardonic chuckle. And he wondered—Now how does the rest of it go? Oh, well, just get said what's important. "I herewith leave all my worldly possessions to Mrs. Catherine Warren and her children. This is my last will and testament, superseding any previous document on record. Signed—John Jay Malone III." To this he clipped his card with her Iowa address. And on top he left a quick note: "Sorry, Will. I have no one else to call on but you. There's room for me beside my mother up home. And you know where the money is."

From the top of his antique trunk he swept a clutter of books and papers. Raising the lid he lifted out Grampa Malone's big American flag and the old soldier's service six-shooter. With great care he draped the flag across the window seat. Against the wall he arranged treasured photographs of John Jay Malone I and John Jay II, with III and IV side by side, taken together. Underneath he placed the Quartermaster General's letter.

Settled back in his easy chair, sadly smiling at the loved ones, smoke curling upward from his pipe, he remained lost in remembrance of Jack, so unique in all his lovableness. What a wonderful character he was! So obliging in games with the rowdy kids, such a dignified companion on their quiet walks together, so incredibly intelligent and brave in performing his soldierly responsibilities. Jack's, he thought, was a shining example of an exemplary life.

In the silence of his big empty house, the Malone family clock, on its small shelf above Jay's head, loudly ticked off the minutes. There was a rasping displacement of its works, a clearing of its throat so to speak, and it began eleven resounding strokes that were like the heavy beat of a drum.

Calmly Jay lifted Grampa Malone's little Colt to his temple and put an end to his misery.

His dreams of war service had been fulfilled.

★ ★ ★

Eilleen Gardner Galer
Author/Photographer

∼

Eilleen Galer was born in Charlotte, North Carolina in 1906. She is a freelance writer and has been a photographer for over 70 years, specializing in the preservation of animals and vanishing scenes and lifestyles. She was an officer for 20 years in the National Photographic Society in Washington, DC, and received the NPS Shaw Memorial Trophy for outstanding service in 1961. Her work is in the permanent collection of the National Photographic Society of America. Ms. Galer developed and presented a humane education outreach program for the Arlington Animal Welfare League, which included a photo essay designed to promote kindness to animals. This program has been viewed by more than 10,000 people of all ages.

Eilleen Galer recently authored a biography titled *Eugen Weisz, Painter–Teacher*, and a photographic book *God Barking in Church: And Further Glimpses of Animal Welfare*, both currently in bookstores. She also has contributed to two editions of the photographic book series *American Photographers at the Turn of the Century*, also available in bookstores. She has contributed to *Cats* magazine, *Cat Fancy*, *Advocate* (American Humane Association) and the *Journal of the Photographic Society of America*. She has been a *National Finalist* in the *Washington Star* animal category, *First* for farm animals by the American Humane Association, and won the *First Place Cup* for monochrome prints and color slides and *Print of the Year* by the National Photographic Society, Washington, DC.

Eilleen Galer's sparkling wit and charming style enliven her stories enabling future generations to know, appreciate, and cherish past lifestyles and events.

Additional titles showcasing the work of Eilleen Gardner Galer:

Eugen Weisz: Painter—Teacher

God Barking in Church
And further Glimpses of Animal Welfare

The Art of the Human Form

American Photographers at the Turn of the Century
Nature & Landscapes

American Photographers at the Turn of the Century
Travel & Trekking

Just Folks - Here and There

Available from Five Corners Publications